The Ministry of Louis Farrakhan in the Nation of Islam

Islam of the Global West

Series editors: Kambiz GhaneaBassiri and Frank Peter

Islam of the Global West is a pioneering series that examines Islamic beliefs, practices, discourses, communities, and institutions that have emerged from "the Global West." The geographical and intellectual framing of the Global West reflects both the role played by the interactions between people from diverse religions and cultures in the development of Western ideals and institutions in the modern era, and the globalization of these very ideals and institutions.

In creating an intellectual space where works of scholarship on European and North American Muslims enter into conversation with one another, the series promotes the publication of theoretically informed and empirically grounded research in these areas. By bringing the rapidly growing research on Muslims in European and North American societies, ranging from the United States and France to Portugal and Albania, into conversation with the conceptual framing of the Global West, this ambitious series aims to reimagine the modern world and develop new analytical categories and historical narratives that highlight the complex relationships and rivalries that have shaped the multicultural, poly-religious character of Europe and North America, as evidenced, by way of example, in such economically and culturally dynamic urban centers as Los Angeles, New York, Paris, Madrid, Toronto, Sarajevo, London, Berlin, and Amsterdam where there is a significant Muslim presence.

American and Muslim Worlds Before 1900
Edited by John Ghazvinian & Arthur Mitchell Fraas

Anarchist, Artist, Sufi
Mark Sedgwick

Amplifying Islam in the European Soundscape: Religious Pluralism and Secularism in the Netherlands
Pooyan Tamimi Arab

The British Muslim Convert Lord Headley, 1855–1935
Jamie Gilham

Interrogating Muslims
Schirin Amir-Moazami

Islam and Muslims in Victorian Britain: New Perspectives
Edited by Jamie Gilham

Islam and Nationhood in Bosnia-Herzegovina: Surviving Empires
Xavier Bougarel

Islam and the Governing of Muslims in France
Frank Peter

Islam as Critique: Sayyid Ahmad Khan and the Challenge of Modernity
Khurram Hussain

Muslims Making British Media
Carl Morris

Sacred Spaces and Transnational Networks in American Sufism
Merin Shobhana Xavier

The Ministry of Louis Farrakhan in the Nation of Islam

Dawn-Marie Gibson

BLOOMSBURY ACADEMIC
LONDON • NEW YORK • OXFORD • NEW DELHI • SYDNEY

BLOOMSBURY ACADEMIC

Bloomsbury Publishing Plc, 50 Bedford Square, London, WC1B 3DP, UK
Bloomsbury Publishing Inc, 1385 Broadway, New York, NY 10018, USA
Bloomsbury Publishing Ireland, 29 Earlsfort Terrace, Dublin 2, D02 AY28, Ireland

BLOOMSBURY, BLOOMSBURY ACADEMIC and the Diana logo are trademarks of
Bloomsbury Publishing Plc

First published in Great Britain 2024
Paperback edition published 2025

Copyright © Dawn-Marie Gibson, 2024

Dawn-Marie Gibson has asserted her right under the Copyright, Designs and Patents Act, 1988, to be identified as Author of this work.

For legal purposes the Acknowledgments on p. x constitute an extension
of this copyright page.

Series design by Dani Leigh
Cover image © Brian Stablyk / gettyimages.co.uk

All rights reserved. No part of this publication may be: i) reproduced or transmitted in any form, electronic or mechanical, including photocopying, recording or by means of any information storage or retrieval system without prior permission in writing from the publishers; or ii) used or reproduced in any way for the training, development or operation of artificial intelligence (AI) technologies, including generative AI technologies. The rights holders expressly reserve this publication from the text and data mining exception as per Article 4(3) of the Digital Single Market Directive (EU) 2019/790.

Bloomsbury Publishing Plc does not have any control over, or responsibility for, any third-party websites referred to or in this book. All internet addresses given in this book were correct at the time of going to press. The author and publisher regret any inconvenience caused if addresses have changed or sites have ceased to exist, but can accept no responsibility for any such changes.

A catalogue record for this book is available from the British Library.

A catalog record for this book is available from the Library of Congress.

ISBN: HB: 978-1-3500-6850-6
PB: 978-1-3504-2633-7
ePDF: 978-1-3500-6851-3
eBook: 978-1-3500-6852-0

Series: Islam of the Global West

Typeset by Newgen KnowledgeWorks Pvt. Ltd., Chennai, India

For product safety related questions contact productsafety@bloomsbury.com.

To find out more about our authors and books visit www.bloomsbury.com
and sign up for our newsletters.

For Gabriel and Faith

Contents

Acknowledgments	x
Introduction	1
1. The Garveyite Child	29
2. The Rise of Minister Louis Farrakhan	53
3. Atonement	85
4. Aftermath	117
Conclusion	163
Bibliography	169
Index	183

Acknowledgments

I owe a debt of gratitude to several colleagues for providing assistance with this book. I thank Patrick Bowen for sharing early copies of Minister Farrakhan's writings in the *Chicago Defender* with me. I also thank Imaobong Umoren and Dianne Kirby for providing helpful feedback on an earlier chapter from the book. The book has benefitted immensely from interviews with representatives from the Nation of Islam, the Deen Intensive Academy, and the Council on American-Islamic Relations in Chicago. I am also particularly grateful to Maurice Klapwald at the New York Public Library for assisting with early copies of *The Final Call* newspaper. The completion of the book has been delayed several times due to health problems. I thank Lily McMahon and Lalle Pursglove for their understanding and for extending my deadline for completion. I thank my husband for taking on extra childcare duties in the months leading up to completion of the book. The book would not have been completed without his unfailing encouragement. I also thank my family and my in-laws for their continual support and kindness. The book is dedicated to my children, Gabriel and Faith. *Ndinokudai nemoyo wangu wese.*

Introduction

In his national address to his followers, supporters, and critics on February 17, 2019, at the United Center in Chicago, Minister Louis Farrakhan set out what he considers to be a series of damaging accusations regarding his character. In his keynote address he remarked: "I've been called divisive … they even went as far as to call me in the Jewish paper this week, the new Hitler, a hater, a Klan lover, a conman, a bigot … Calling me these names is designed to undercut any support that you might want to give me."[1] The 2019 address was neither the first nor the last occasion on which Minister Farrakhan has addressed popular slurs that surround him and his faith community. He has long proven cognizant of and willing to vigorously defend himself against such smears. The 2019 address, however, is significant in that it came just weeks prior to the minister's ban from the social media platform, Facebook. His comments at the 2019 Saviours' Day convention thus suggest that he either anticipated or sensed that the campaign to silence and isolate him was somehow gaining momentum. Indeed, Minister Farrakhan's student minister Nuri Muhammad remarked in an interview with the *Breakfast Club* that his faith community knew the ban would come "at some point."[2] Minister Farrakhan and his followers construed the ban as an attempt to "silence the voice of the Nation of Islam" by "certain Jewish groups."[3] Moreover, the executive council of the Nation of Islam (NOI) referred to the ban as "completely unjustified."[4] The national response to Minister Farrakhan's ban in 2019 was largely muted. It appears that, with the exception of his longtime friend Father Michael Pfleger, few allies rushed to his defense. At the time Pfleger noted that he construed the ban as an attack on free speech.[5] In early May 2019 Minister Farrakhan accepted an invitation from Pfelger to address the ban from the pulpit at the Faith Community of Saint Sabina in Chicago. The event, while well attended, did not constitute a mass protest. In his speech from the church, Minister Farrakhan reiterated that he did not "hate Jewish people" and that his only crime was knowing the truth and standing "on God's word."[6] The muted response to Minister Farrakhan's ban in 2019 was rather telling. It appeared to suggest that his influence had waned significantly since the height of his popularity in pockets of the United States in the 1990s. *Chicago Tribune* journalist Dahleen Glanton rightly observed: "If Facebook had been around in the 1990s … the company could never have gotten away with banning Farrakhan. African Americans would not have stood for it … Twenty years ago, a call to stand with Farrakhan would have immediately gained traction among athletes, entertainers, activists and others … He no longer has that kind of pull."[7] Minister Farrakhan reached the pinnacle of his career when he led the Million Man March (MMM) in Washington, DC, in October 1995. The event witnessed the largest gathering of African American men in US history and testified to Farrakhan's emergence as a national figure in his own right. The number of men who in fact attended the march is disputed. Members of Farrakhan's own faith community claim that two million men showed up.[8] Attendance at the march should not necessarily be construed as an embrace of Farrakhan or his ideology. Indeed, as historian Manning Marable noted, the regressive racial climate of the time led many to conclude that they had "little alternative but to turn inward."[9] For members of Minister Farrakhan's own faith community the MMM was and remains "the greatest day of gathering and assembly in human history."[10] Minister Farrakhan's reputation as a dangerous antisemite and unorthodox Islamic leader has gained greater traction in recent years. The Anti-Defamation League (ADL)'s assessment of Farrakhan as the "pied-piper of hate" clearly holds significant weight with many political figures.[11] Indeed, former NOI member turned politician Keith Ellison has struggled to explain his earlier association with Farrakhan.[12] In an interview in 2021, for example, Ellison remarked: "Farrakhan's organization is tiny … They don't have any influence. Nobody listens to them. They don't have any answers for anyone. Nobody's paying any attention to them … I mean, give me credit for leading my life. Farrakhan is irrelevant to any politics."[13] Ellison's efforts to convince his allies within the Democratic Party of Farrakhan's irrelevance have been disingenuous at best. As noted, Farrakhan no longer has the kind of support that he once did. Islamic studies scholar Edward Curtis even suggests that the NOI has no more than 10,000 members.[14] However, Farrakhan is not a "fringe figure."[15] He retains something of a unique appeal. For his defenders, he is an uncompromising voice who represents the grievances, concerns, and aspirations of the poor, marginalized and African Americans in particular. His body of student ministers within the NOI consider him a "big brother" whom they are "blessed" to defend.[16] For his critics, he is a dangerous and divisive figure who misrepresents the Islamic faith. Minister Farrakhan's perception of himself as an "honorable" and "courageous" man is very much at odds with how his critics view him.[17] His assessment of his own record as a religious leader is informed by his unique and deeply personal understanding and representation of his spiritual father's teachings. Minister Farrakhan's faith community is, however, a very different community from the one that Elijah Muhammad led. Moreover, Louis Farrakhan is not the master of his own faith community. He is beholden to the NOI's executive council and the faith community's members. In short, he is both leader and captive of the NOI.

Minister Farrakhan rose to prominence as a minister in the Boston Temple of Elijah Muhammad's NOI in the late 1950s. The small faith community was formed in Detroit in 1930 by a mysterious peddler turned prophet, W. D. Fard Muhammad. Fard Muhammad remains a largely unknown figure in the history of African American Islam. His theology borrowed from the teachings of Marcus Garvey's Black Nationalist, Universal Negro Improvement Association (UNIA) and Noble Drew Ali's Moorish Science Temple of America (MSTA). Fard's teachings were, however, more radical than either Garvey's or Ali's. According to sociologist Erdman Beynon, Fard taught his followers that whites were "devils," created by a scientist known as Yakub and that African Americans were the chosen people of God. Beynon observed that such teachings led Fard's followers to gain "a new conception of themselves and regard themselves as superior, rather than inferior, to other people."[18] Fard's theology appears to have had a number of influences beyond Garveyism. Historian Patrick Bowen, for example, observes that Fard also borrowed from the teachings of the Jehovah Witnesses and Freemasonry. Indeed, Fard actively encouraged his followers to acquaint themselves with the works of Judge Rutherford. Bowen concludes that despite a detailed examination of Fard's possible sources of influence, we are not "significantly closer" to offering answers about his background.[19]

Fard's followers were composed exclusively of African American migrants to Detroit. Such individuals were part of the mass exodus from the South during the interwar years. The desire to leave the South was driven primarily by the realities of "economic disadvantage and discrimination."[20] Their collective and individual hopes of securing prosperity and escaping racial apartheid in the US South were dashed entirely when the economic depression of 1930 hit. The impoverished state that characterized their existence led many to seek solace in storefront churches and ghetto messiahs. Fard exploited the aspirations, frustrations, and wider context his audience found themselves in. His followers were drawn to what he referred to as their "natural" religion: Islam. It is important to note that Fard's early followers had no knowledge of Islam as practiced by other Muslim communities in the United States. They thus accepted his teachings as an authentic presentation of Islam.

The Muslim presence in the United States dates back to the 1500s. The arrival of enslaved West African Muslims during the transatlantic slave trade added to America's Muslim population. Islamic studies scholar Herbert Berg notes that 15 percent of enslaved Africans were Muslim.[21] The constraints that slavery placed on its victims drastically curtailed the practice of Islam among enslaved people. Moreover, forced conversion to Christianity in the mid-nineteenth century as a form of control restricted the religious practices of enslaved people.[22] Immigration from Muslim majority countries in the early twentieth century enriched and diversified the existing presence of Islam in the United States. However, early immigrants displayed little interest in proselytizing among African Americans. The failure of Muslim missionaries and communities in the United States to reach African Americans enabled Fard's theology to take root.[23] The failure of immigrant Muslims to share their faith with their African American counterparts is often a reference point in discussions regarding tensions between these communities. In his critique of early Muslim missionaries, for example, Minister Farrakhan noted that they had "no methodology to reach the black man … rather than teach us Islam, they just forgot about us."[24] Evidence of early proselytization among African Americans appears to be limited to a small number of groups. Islamic studies scholar Aminah McCloud, for example, notes that the Indian Ahmadis established a number of mosques in the United States and produced the first English Qur'an "for general use in America in 1917."[25] Moreover, the Ahmadis appear to have been the exception in their willingness to understand the Black Nationalist rhetoric of the UNIA and link such messages with the Qur'an.[26] It is estimated that the Ahmadis converted just over 1,000 African Americans to Islam between 1921 and 1925.[27] While their effort was commendable, it was not enough to prevent individuals like Fard Muhammad presenting themselves to unsuspecting migrants as legitimate Islamic leaders.

Fard appealed to his followers on the basis of what appears to have been a rather intimate understanding of their collective history and experience of domestic terrorism. His teachings, according to his successor Elijah Muhammad, were designed to emancipate African Americans and educate them about their history prior to enslavement in the United States. Elijah Muhammad noted:

> He used to teach us six hours. In fact the basic part of his teachings was the history of our people, their freedom, superiority and their civilization before they have been enslaved by the devil. The purpose of his teachings was to free us. For all of this I pray to Allah because I was so blind, deaf, and dumb before his coming.[28]

The NOI grew exponentially between 1930 and 1933. Political scientist E. U. Essien-Udom suggested that the community had amassed 8,000 members by 1933.[29] The accuracy of Essien-Udom's estimate is difficult to verify as the community has never kept records of or revealed their total membership. Fard's followers, according to Beynon, embraced an ascetic lifestyle and experienced a significant improvement in their finances as a result. In his pioneering study of the community, he remarked: "At the time of their first contact with the prophet, practically all the members of the cult were recipients of public welfare … At the present time there is no known case of unemployment among these people … They … rent homes in some of the best economic areas in which Negroes have settled."[30] Fard instituted segregated classes for male and female members of his community. The Muslim Girls Training and General Civilization Class (MGT–GCC) instructed women in all things related to the domestic sphere. It operated as a space where Fard's conservative gender norms could be enforced and where women could form kinship networks. The Fruit of Islam (FOI) by contrast instructed men in self-defense. Fard built up a devoted ministerial team including several supreme ministers. Such structures enabled Fard to take a back seat in his own faith community. According to Elijah Muhammad, Fard personally selected him as a supreme minister.[31] Elijah Muhammad (nee Poole) was introduced to Fard by his wife Clara. Clara and her husband experienced intense hardship in Detroit prior to embracing Islam as taught by Fard. Both had migrated from Georgia in the hope of securing a better life. However, Elijah found himself unable to secure steady employment in Detroit. His inability to provide for his family forced the burden of provision on to Clara and drove him to seek solace in alcohol.[32] However, Elijah flourished in Fard's community. Fard's message of moral reform, uplift, and redemption was well received by Elijah. Indeed, he was so struck by Fard that he immediately identified him as God incarnate.[33] According to Elijah, Fard promoted himself neither as a Prophet nor God incarnate.[34] Yet, it is also true that he did little to discourage the adulation of his followers.

Fard's work in Detroit was arguably a rather lucrative enterprise. Beynon, for example, remarks that Fard charged his followers for what he described as original Islamic names. Such names were awarded for a fee of $10.00. Early NOI members considered such names their "greatest treasure."[35] Prior to the awarding of an original name, NOI members replaced their surname with an X. The X represented their unknown ancestral surname and served as a marker of their new identity.[36] Original names and the use of the X to replace members' legal surnames made Fard's followers quickly and easily identifiable as NOI members. In embracing what Fard described as an original name, NOI members set themselves further apart from their surrounding communities. NOI members found a new self-respect and esteem in their religious setting. Fard's teachings, while alien to established Muslim communities, were embraced as a liberating tool and as a means to securing freedom from the terror that white supremacy visited upon his followers.

Fard's mysterious exit from Detroit came in the wake of allegations that his followers were engaging in acts of human sacrifice.[37] The Detroit Police Department's growing awareness of and interest in Fard's community appears to have quickened his departure. Fard's exit, whether announced or unannounced, caused his followers significant distress and quickly depleted the community's membership. Elijah's claims to have been groomed by Fard for succession were both vigorously and violently contested. As a result, he spent much of the remaining decade escaping attempts on his life. Fard's departure and the threats that followed did little to quell Elijah's determination to keep the community alive. Indeed, he established NOI temples in Milwaukee and Washington, DC, during this time. His efforts, however, came to an end in May 1942 when he was arrested for violation of the Selective Service Act and subsequently incarcerated. NOI members eschewed the draft on the basis of Fard's teachings. Elijah's incarceration further extended his absence from his wife and children and left him estranged from his youngest sons Akbar and Wallace. Clara played an instrumental role in keeping the NOI alive during her husband's incarceration. Little has been documented about Clara's life and leadership during this period.[38] Yet, it is undeniable that her role as an intermediary between her husband and the NOI's few hundred followers kept the faith community alive and that without her efforts the community could have withered away entirely.

Elijah's release from the Milan Michigan Federal Correctional Institution in August 1946 was a turning point for the NOI. Elijah left prison with a fresh determination to rebuild the NOI's membership, market its theology more effectively, build the community's resources and assets, and recruit dedicated ministers. The establishment of the NOI's public relations team and launch of several successful businesses in the 1950s transformed the community's image and focus. Elijah's Nation grew exponentially at a time when the emerging Civil Rights Movement was gaining momentum. Indeed, by 1955 Dr. Martin Luther King Jr. was recognized nationally and internationally as the face of the movement to end racial apartheid in the United States. NOI converts and their ministers construed the integrationist aims of the movement and their leaders to be misguided. Integration, for NOI members, was a less ideal alternative to complete racial separation and economic independence. Elijah's critique of race relations in the United States and advocacy among African Americans was aided enormously by the African American press, national media, and the talents of NOI ministers.

Elijah's ministerial team was composed largely, although not exclusively, of close male family members. Few from outside the family made it into the upper echelons of the NOI's national leadership. Malcolm Little (X) and Louis Walcott (Farrakhan) were, however, exceptions. Malcolm's life story and relationship with the NOI is generally well-known. Indeed, many assume that Malcolm made the NOI what it was in the 1960s. Such a view celebrates

Malcolm's contributions to the community, but it nonetheless evidences an impoverished understanding of the NOI's history, membership, and the context in which it operated. The NOI's collective success was down to the hard work and endless sacrifices of its membership. Individuals who embraced the NOI refused second-class citizenship and insisted on reclaiming their respect and dignity in a society that denied them of their humanity.

Malcolm was introduced to the teachings of the NOI via his brothers Philbert and Reginald while incarcerated. Malcolm was born into a Garveyite family. His father was a dedicated UNIA organizer and a freelance Baptist preacher while his mother Louise contributed to the UNIA's paper *The Negro World*.[39] Malcolm's family life disintegrated following the death of his father. His mother was subsequently institutionalized, and her children were separated and sent to various foster homes. Malcolm was an excellent student in school. However, his aspirations to be a lawyer were thwarted when a teacher crudely advised that such as a goal was unrealistic.[40] Thereafter Malcolm drifted into a life of petty crime in Harlem. Malcolm's foray into crime and pimping led him to prison. Malcolm was "barely literate" and suffering from addiction when he first heard of the NOI. Indeed, historian Claude Clegg notes that the teachings of Elijah Muhammad reached Malcolm at "his most desperate hour."[41] Elijah Muhammad's teachings transformed Malcolm's life. He began to read widely and devoted himself entirely to propagating the NOI's teachings on his release from prison in 1952.

Malcolm was a dedicated and talented organizer for the NOI. His work as a minister in the Detroit temple impressed Muhammad and his ministerial counterparts. Malcolm was thereafter appointed as a Minister in Temple Number 7 in Harlem in 1957 and promoted to first national minister in 1960. Malcolm had become the public face of the NOI by 1959 when WNTA-TV aired *The Hate that Hate Produced*. The five-part series exposed the NOI's theology, critiques, and membership to national scrutiny. Historian Garrett Felber notes that the documentary "sensationally situated the NOI as a 'hate group' similar to the Ku Klux Klan by referring to Black Nationalists as 'Black racists' and 'Black supremacists.' It was singularly responsible for launching the NOI into national discussions of race."[42] Malcolm relished the attention that the NOI received in the national media. He, perhaps more than Muhammad, understood the power of the press. In 1960, Malcolm founded the NOI's national newspaper, *Muhammad Speaks*. The paper set out the NOI's beliefs and effectively served as a window into Muhammad's otherwise rather secretive faith community. The paper, as historian Jeffrey Ogbar notes, became "the largest Black newspaper in circulation during the black freedom movement."[43]

Malcolm championed the work of Elijah Muhammad in multiple interviews, speeches, lectures, and articles. However, he fell out of favor with Muhammad when he made unauthorized comments concerning the assassination of President Kennedy. Muhammad subsequently punished Malcolm with a 90-day silencing. Malcolm's relationship with Muhammad appears to have faltered prior to 1963, however. Knowledge of Elijah Muhammad's extramarital relationships with several women who worked for him as personal secretaries reached Malcolm via Muhammad's seventh son Wallace. It is important to note that Malcolm first heard "rumors" about these relationships as early as 1955 and chose to dismiss them.[44] Malcolm discussed Muhammad's relationships with a number of NOI ministers including Louis Farrakhan. Louis subsequently informed Malcolm that he would relay the content of their discussion to Muhammad.[45] Malcolm announced his departure from the NOI in 1964. In his telegram to Muhammad announcing his exit, Malcolm placed the blame for his departure on internal power struggles and national officials in the community. His telegram did not mention Muhammad's infidelity or the suspension as factoring into his decision to leave.[46]

The campaign to discredit Malcolm gained even greater traction once he left the community. His decision to inform the national media about Muhammad's private life infuriated officials and ministers. Indeed, the paper that Malcolm founded in 1960 became the primary means by which his reputation was destroyed in the NOI. Farrakhan aided and abetted the campaign to destroy Malcolm. He was not, however, the primary architect of or responsible for the events leading to Malcolm's assassination in 1965. Malcolm's activities both in the United States and beyond during his final year were monitored closely by intelligence agencies. The Federal Bureau of Investigation (FBI) had long proven determined to destroy the NOI, its leadership, and its relatively good standing in African American communities. Their tactics, as discussed later, were both aggressive and, at times, highly effective. They placed the community's leaders under intense surveillance and placed informants in Muhammad's inner circle.

Muhammad was, of course, acutely aware of the presence of informants in the NOI, as were other ministers.[47] The full extent of the FBI's role in Malcolm's assassination in February 1965 remains the subject of ongoing and contentious debate. There can be no doubt, however, that the bureau was vicariously responsible for Malcolm's death. They knew his life was in danger and failed to act in a manner that would have afforded him any protection or deterred his assassins. Farrakhan has long maintained that he had no involvement in or prior knowledge of plans to assassinate Malcolm. Blame for Malcolm's death, according to Farrakhan, lies not with the NOI but with the bureau. Questions surrounding the extent of the bureau's involvement in Malcolm's death remain unanswered. The recent exoneration of two of Malcolm's alleged assassins, Muhammad Aziz and Khalil Islam, in 2021 have, if anything, added credibility to Farrakhan's charges of government culpability. The *New York Times* reported in November 2021, for example, that the FBI and the New York Police Department had "withheld key evidence" in the trials of the two men and that the exonerations represented "a remarkable acknowledgement of grave errors made in a case of towering importance."[48] The NOI responded to news of the exonerations in their official newspaper noting:

> We are not fooled. We want justice for Muhammad Aziz and the late Khalil Islam who were intentionally, fully, maliciously and purposely wrongly imprisoned for the killing of Brother Malcolm. These innocent men, the Shabazz family, the Nation of Islam and Black people deserve much, much more. We must demand the full truth, a full accounting and the release of all files, federal, state and local regarding what happened before, during and after that fateful day February 21, 1965, when Brother Malcolm was killed in the Audubon Ballroom.[49]

Malcolm's death in February 1965 did little to diminish the NOI's expansion. Indeed, the community continued to develop its businesses and expand its membership into the early 1970s. In 1972, for example, it was regarded as the "richest Black group" in the United States with estimated holdings at $75 million.[50] The plethora of business enterprises that the NOI operated was testimony not so much to Muhammad and his ministers but to the collective sacrifices of ordinary rank-and-file members of the faith community.

Malcolm's departure from the NOI opened opportunities for other talented ministers, none more so than Louis Farrakhan. Muhammad personally appointed Farrakhan to a number of roles once held by Malcolm including minister of Temple Number 7 in Harlem and national minister. These apparent promotions, however, were less than smooth sailing. Farrakhan was relocated to Harlem with his young family at a time when the NOI was widely blamed for Malcolm's death. Rebuilding the trust of Harlemites in the NOI was no small feat. Louis' dedication and persistence in Harlem paid off. He rebuilt the Harlem temple's membership and was described by 1975 as "the most influential black man in New York."[51]

Louis enjoyed a father–son relationship with Elijah Muhammad. Indeed, so close was their relationship that many assumed that he would succeed Muhammad. Elijah Muhammad refused to publicly appoint or name potential successors. His death in February 1975 thus left a leadership vacuum that his immediate family were left to fill. Muhammad's children quickly appointed Wallace as his successor, much to the dismay of other ministers.

Wallace's succession in February 1975 was publicly celebrated and championed in the NOI. Privately, however, many knew that Wallace would effectively transform the organization and its theology. Wallace moved quickly to introduce Sunni Islam and discredit his father's earlier teachings. He disbanded the FOI and the MGT and strategically relocated ministers and former captains who could potentially prove troublesome or stage a coup. Farrakhan was subsequently demoted and relocated. Wallace's succession ended Farrakhan's career in the NOI. Unhappy with the swift reforms, he decided to leave the community in 1977. Farrakhan left the NOI with little in the way of financial security. Indeed, he noted that when the community "fell" in 1975 his "cupboard was bare."[52] Farrakhan initially sought to restart his former career as a musician. His ventures proved unsuccessful and in 1979 he decided to rebuild the NOI.

Minister Farrakhan's resurrected NOI grew slowly in the early 1980s. So scarce were the community's finances that Minister Farrakhan struggled to publish the group's newspaper, *The Final Call*, on a regular basis. Farrakhan's early teachings mirrored closely in content and tone those of his spiritual father. It is nonetheless important to note that Farrakhan subjected Muhammad's teachings to some reinterpretation in the 1980s, as discussed in Chapter 3. Farrakhan's small faith community was unveiled to the nation in 1984 when he publicly announced his support for Jesse Jackson's presidential campaign. Indeed, 1984 marked the first time that Farrakhan had exercised his democratic right to vote. Farrakhan's foray into national politics was endorsed by the NOI's elders.[53] Such an approval indicates that the individuals who made up the NOI council at the time were not former members of Muhammad's original community. Farrakhan's support for Jackson became apparent for all when he vigorously defended Jackson against charges of antisemitism. Such charges emerged after *Washington Post* journalist Milton Coleman published off-the-record remarks in which Jackson referred to New York as "Hymie" town and to Jews as "Hymies." Jackson initially denied making the remarks and thus Farrakhan's early defense was based on an assumption of Jackson's innocence.[54] Farrakhan's vigorous defense of Jackson initiated what would become a long and damaging war of words between the NOI and the ADL. The events of 1984 exposed antisemitic undercurrents and sentiments within the NOI. However, Farrakhan had publicly criticized Jewish Americans before 1984. In his articles for the *Chicago Defender* in the late 1970s, for example, he set out his assessment of the "rift between Blacks and Jews" and his critique of their involvement in African American organizations.[55]

The publicity that the rift between Minister Farrakhan and American Jewish communities generated provided the NOI with significant exposure at a national and international level. Minister Farrakhan's NOI continued to grow steadily throughout the later 1980s and reached the height of its notoriety in the early 1990s. The regressive racial climate of the 1980s and early 1990s helped propel the community's growth. Moreover, the publicity generated by Spike Lee's biopic *Malcolm X* provided Minister Farrakhan with an ever-greater platform. Such forces brought the NOI and Farrakhan to a new plateau.

The late 1980s and early 1990s provided Minister Farrakhan with fertile ground in which to root the NOI's message. The Second Reconstruction in the United States radically reformed race relations and opened windows of opportunity previously denied to African Americans. As a result, the African American middle class grew considerably during the Reagan years. At the same time, however, the "bridge" between the poor and the affluent grew. Community studies scholar Luke Tripp, for example, notes:

> Reaganism … did not bode well for life in the African American community. Virtually all of the major indicators of being of the African American community showed that it was in a state of crisis. The social fabric of the

community, which had been weakened in the 1970s by some conservative trends, was torn further apart in the 1980s by long-term unemployment and underemployment, low wage jobs, reduced real income, smaller college participation rates, increased deterioration in the quality of elementary and secondary education, increased impoverishment of the youth, reduction of health and social services, a drop in the accessibility of decent housing and a general increase of anxiety and insecurity.[56]

The factors that Tripp sets out above made Minister Farrakhan's message of self-help, uplift, and reform particularly appealing for those who felt alienated from the political process and trapped by poverty. It would be wrong, however, to assume that Minister Farrakhan's NOI was exclusively a working-class community. Farrakhan's NOI attracted a sizeable number of college students and professionals in the late 1980s and 1990s.[57] Such individuals have been promoted to highly visible roles in the community and have helped with the recruitment of college students.

Farrakhan's faith community worked tirelessly throughout the early 1990s to promote his message of uplift and moral reform. Their reputation as agents of social change gained momentum in the wake of the FOI's successful security operations for neighborhoods considered problem areas. The formation of the NOI's Dope Busters program, for example, manifested the outgrowth of the community's efforts to transform the lives of African Americans and rid poor areas of drugs. The daily efforts of Minister Farrakhan's recruits won the NOI the respect of African American communities across the United States.

Minister Farrakhan's reputation as an agent of moral reform was initially threatened by the resurfacing of questions regarding his possible role in Malcolm X's exodus from the NOI and subsequent assassination. Such questions came to the fore as a result of the success of Spike Lee's biopic, *Malcolm X*. Farrakhan took part in a series of interviews, lectures, and media appearances prior to and after the release of Lee's film in order to clarify the nature of his role in Malcolm's demise. Such efforts were part of his campaign to limit the reputational damage that the film would inflict. Farrakhan's efforts proved sufficient. Yet the belief that the NOI bears responsibility for Malcolm's death continues to linger. So much so that NOI minister Demetric Muhammad released a book seeking to clarify the matter in 2020. The book is based on

Muhammad's earlier lectures and sets out to defend the community and effectively clear its name. In the introduction to his book, Muhammad notes:

> The most popular myth in the Black community is arguably the myth that the Nation of Islam killed Malcolm X. Everywhere I go as a representative of the Nation of Islam and the Honorable Minister Louis Farrakhan, I run into this controversial myth … The myth has become a psychological deterrent that keeps many among the suffering masses of Black youth from embracing the teachings of the Most Honorable Elijah Muhammad and the Nation of Islam.[58]

Despite the commercialization of Malcolm's image in the early 1990s and lingering concerns about the NOI's involvement, Farrakhan's community continued to grow and develop networks of support. Farrakhan reached the zenith of his career in 1995. However, it is difficult to determine tangible achievements that resulted from the MMM. The march itself was supported and aided by dozens of civil rights organizations and Christian clergy. Indeed, if anything the event highlighted Farrakhan's positive standing with Black clergy and civil rights activists.

In the aftermath of the march, Farrakhan embarked on a series of international tours that effectively exacerbated his reputation as a demagogue in pockets of the United States. Farrakhan's forays abroad held little benefit for the NOI. However, his prolonged absences did allow for several of his subordinates to gain greater experience in managing and leading the community, none more so than Ishmael Muhammad.[59] Ishmael is the biological son of Elijah Muhammad and his former secretary, Tynetta Muhammad. He has long enjoyed a close relationship with Farrakhan and refers to him both publicly and privately as a father figure. Ishmael is widely regarded as Minister Farrakhan's heir apparent. As Farrakhan's national assistant he is responsible for overseeing the administration of the NOI and its ministries.

Farrakhan's prolonged absences from the NOI combined with his health problems in the aftermath of the MMM effectively forced him to restructure the NOI's chains of command. Moreover, his battle with prostate cancer in the late 1990s led him to reconsider the NOI's relationship with the broader American Muslim community. As a result, Farrakhan organized a public reconciliation with Imam W. D. Mohammed at the 2000 Saviours' Day convention. The events leading up to the convention and Farrakhan's address at the convention itself revealed his then personal and private gravitation to Sunni Islam.[60] Minister Farrakhan's public embrace of more traditional Islamic teachings proved short-lived. As noted in Chapter 3, for example, he reverted to propagating the NOI's foundational theology in 2001. Farrakhan's failure to effectively lead his followers to Sunni Islam evidences his limitations as a leader. Moreover, it highlights that alterations to the core beliefs of the community lie with the believers themselves and not Farrakhan.

Farrakhan's public relationship with Imam Mohammed and his followers remained largely positive in the immediate aftermath of the 9/11 attacks. Farrakhan condemned the atrocities publicly and sought to protect his followers from the rampant Islamophobia that ensued.[61] Farrakhan's personal and private application of Sunni Islam is something that has largely gone unexamined in the aftermath of the MMM. Publicly, Minister Farrakhan has remained steadfast in his insistence that Allah appeared in the person of Master Fard Muhammad in 1930. Such pronouncements can be heard on a yearly basis at the NOI's annual Saviours' Day conventions. Such declarations, however, limit possibilities for NOI members to engage with other Muslim communities. Indeed, Minister Farrakhan's community has grown and evolved largely outside and beyond the influence of other prominent African American Muslim communities. African American converts to Islam compose one-fifth of America's total Muslim population.[62] Moreover, African American mosques account for 13 percent of America's 2,769 mosques.[63] NOI mosques are not counted toward or included in surveys of Muslim America. Indeed, many Islamic organizations and Imams reject identification with the NOI. Minister Farrakhan and his followers are thus somewhat isolated from debates and discussions that relate to Muslim America. Minister Farrakhan has made a number of overtures to America's Sunni Muslim community. In 2012, for example, he appointed Imam Sultan Muhammad as a resident Imam at the NOI's headquarters at Mosque Maryam.[64] Sultan's connections to the NOI and Chicago's Muslim communities run deep. He is the great-grandson of Elijah Muhammad and is well connected to Sunni Muslim communities and organizations. Prior to taking up his post at Mosque Maryam, for example, he worked as the outreach coordinator at the Chicago chapter of the Council on American-Islamic Relations (CAIR). Moreover, he has also previously worked alongside the Inner-City Muslim Action Network (IMAN) in Chicago.[65] Sultan has been responsible for introducing Jummah prayer services in the NOI and serves publicly as the "orthodox" face of the community. He has also played an important role in facilitating dialogue with well-known African American imams in Chicago. Such dialogue has in recent years led to the formation of the Deen Intensive Academy (DIA). The DIA is officially led by Imam Jalil Muhammad who is deeply connected to the NOI via his marriage to NOI member and staff writer, Nisa Islam Muhammad. Imam Muhammad has never been a member of the NOI. However, Minister Farrakhan is the "reason" he "accepted Islam" at the age of nineteen. Muhammad has known Minister Farrakhan for over forty years. The DIA host a series of seminars that cover a range of topics including prayer, the life and legacy of Prophet Muhammad, the unity of Islam, and the divinity of Allah. The DIA provides a forum where NOI members and other Muslims can come together in a "safe space" to learn more about Islam without fear of being "ridiculed." The DIA perceive their work as rewarding and remark that it is regrettable that other Muslim organizations and leaders have not reached out to the NOI in the same manner. The failure of other Muslim groups to reach out to NOI members is perceived by the DIA to be a result of "flat out racism."[66] It is important to note that Minister Farrakhan's community remains a predominantly African American faith community. It rarely engages with immigrant Muslims and it is entirely unclear whether such engagement is welcomed by members.

The DIA is composed of a number of well-known NOI ministers and African American imams. Together, these individuals work to help NOI members better understand the teachings and practices of Sunni Muslims. Minister Farrakhan's public embrace of the work of the DIA alongside the mixed messages he has provided about the NOI's beliefs in recent years has led to some confusion regarding the faith community's theology. Indeed, such confusion was evident on March 3, 2021, when Student Minister Ishmael Muhammad hosted a believers' meeting in which he corrected a small number of errors he personally made when delivering the 2021 Saviours' Day address. One such error, as identified by Minister Farrakhan, was Ishmael's comment to Imam Siraj Wahhaj, leader of the Al-Taqwa Mosque in New York, that Elijah Muhammad never told his followers to pray to Fard Muhammad. In his comments he remarked: "We do pray to Master Fard Muhammad … he is Allah … Master Fard Muhammad … the supreme being is alive."⁶⁷ The fact that Minister Farrakhan's national assistant is unsure about whether the community prays to Allah or Fard Muhammad speaks volumes about the theological confusion that exists in the community.

Sunni Islam is not, however, the only theology or belief system that influences the fluidity of the NOI's faith and competes for the hearts and minds of its members. NOI members and ministers have been encouraged by Minister Farrakhan to engage with and apply the teachings of the Church of Scientology (COS) since 2011. Dianetics Auditing is now common practice in the NOI and is compulsory for all NOI ministers. Moreover, the faith community now have a national Auditing co-ordinator, A'ishah Muhammad. According to A'ishah, Dianetics Auditing is a "tool" that NOI members can employ to "help deal with" trauma or traumatic experiences.⁶⁸ Minister Farrakhan has publicly refuted allegations that he was paid by the COS to introduce his followers to Dianetics Auditing. In defense of the practice, he has noted that Auditing has the potential to be particularly "valuable" for African Americans.⁶⁹ According to historian Jacob King, Farrakhan's relationship with the COS was first exposed in 2006 when he was honored at the Ebony Awakening Awards. His first introduction to Auditing, however, occurred much earlier in the 1990s via his interactions with singer Isaac Hayes and Baptist minister Alfreddie Johnson. King notes that it is important to observe that it is Auditing and not Scientology itself that Farrakhan has embraced.⁷⁰

Minister Farrakhan appears to personally embrace a number of theological influences, perhaps none more so than Christianity. He has promoted his unique teachings as having "no label" and being devoid of denomination for decades.⁷¹ Indeed, his student minister Nuri Muhammad remarks that the minister is the "perfect representative of God in the way a human being should be. He thinks so big and he's never isolated to denomination or religion. He sees God in everything and pulls the God out of everyone."⁷² Such pronouncements evidence how far both he and his community have strayed from Elijah Muhammad's teachings. Moreover, they rather tellingly indicate that Minister Farrakhan has proven unable or unwilling to fully divorce his followers from the Church or guide them toward Sunni Islam.

The Ministry of Louis Farrakhan in the Nation of Islam is neither an attempt to exonerate, justify nor condemn Minister Farrakhan's leadership. Rather, it is an effort to contextualize and explore Farrakhan's religious life, leadership, and the ongoing work of his faith community. The book explores Minister Farrakhan's early life, membership, and ministry in Elijah Muhammad's NOI and career as the leader of the Resurrected NOI (RNOI) and the trajectory of his faith and faith community in the aftermath of the MMM. The book examines Minister Farrakhan's relationships with other religious actors and explores the pressures and challenges he faces from purists in the organization. The book concludes with an assessment of Minister Farrakhan's student ministers and the implications of revised theological teachings within his small faith community.

Minister Farrakhan and his faith community have received considerable attention from scholars and journalists. In the aftermath of the MMM, several significant books and scholarly articles were published and added to the excellent body of early scholarship on the NOI.[73] Moreover, in 1996 HarperCollins published journalist Arthur Magida's biography of Minister Farrakhan. Magida's *Prophet of Rage: A Life of Louis Farrakhan and his Nation* remains the only published biography of Minister Farrakhan.[74] The book was based on interviews with Minister Farrakhan and some archival sources. Yet it lacks rigor. Indeed, the book falls short in its lack of archival depth. Moreover, it fails to provide enough breadth to place Farrakhan, his rise, and appeal in historical context. Mattias Gardell's book, *Countdown to Armageddon* (1996), provides something of a biographical account of Minister Farrakhan. Indeed, the book is richly researched throughout but stops short of assessing the NOI in the post-1995 period.[75]

The Ministry of Louis Farrakhan in the Nation of Islam makes several interventions in the existing scholarship. It examines in considerable depth Farrakhan's early life and the influence and role of his mother in inadvertently leading him to Elijah Muhammad's NOI. Moreover, the work focuses heavily on Minister Farrakhan's career as a religious leader in the post-1975 period and considers his evolution as a religious leader in the aftermath of the MMM. Minister Farrakhan's work and theology, as noted, have expanded greatly since the publication of Magida's book. This book thus explores Farrakhan's maturation as a leader in the aftermath of the MMM. It examines the NOI's relationship with other Muslims and in doing so unveils the complexities and sensitivities surrounding interactions between Minister Farrakhan, his followers, and their counterparts in Muslim America.

The Ministry of Louis Farrakhan in the Nation of Islam draws on several archives including those compiled by the NOI and their detractors. The book employs the use of NOI newspapers including *Muhammad Speaks, Bilalian News,* and *The Final Call. Muhammad Speaks* was founded in 1960 by the NOI's first national minister, Malcolm X. The paper outlined the NOI's program, theology, and activities and included testimonies from its followers. The paper was an important arsenal in the NOI's efforts to defend itself from the rather unflattering manner in which the mainstream media depicted it. Indeed, the paper was regarded by Elijah Muhammad as an extension of his ministerial team.[76] Elijah Muhammad took a keen interest in the content of the paper and the work of its writers. Former newspaper editor, Askia Muhammad, for example, recently remarked in an interview concerning his work at the paper that prior to assuming the position of editor, Muhammad had instructed him to "See what's good. See what's bad ... and look out for the interests of the Nation" at the printing plant.[77] Askia was initially asked to work as a copyeditor at the plant under the tutelage of the paper's then editor Leon Forrest. Forrest's departure from the newspaper came after he accepted an invitation to take up a teaching position at Northwestern University. His departure opened a vacancy which Muhammad awarded to Askia. *Muhammad Speaks* undoubtedly provided outsiders with a rare and fascinating glimpse into Elijah Muhammad's community. The *Muhammad Speaks* newspaper presented an image of the NOI as a place of brotherhood, harmony, and mutual uplift and as an escape from the domestic terrorism and oppression that haunted African American communities throughout the United States. The reality of the NOI as a faith community was, however, much more complex. Indeed, as noted in Chapter 2, abuse of members within the NOI was problematic. *Muhammad Speaks* was undoubtedly a tool for propagation of NOI teachings. However, it is nonetheless an important source in that it provides unique insights into the community and the daily work of its ministerial team.

Bilalian News replaced *Muhammad Speaks* as the NOI's official newspaper following the death of Elijah Muhammad in 1975. The newspaper evidenced the faith community's gravitation to Sunni Islam and embrace of their identity as US citizens. *Bilalian News* is an invaluable archive in that it provides a fascinating insight into how former NOI members understood and navigated Sunni Islam under the tutelage of Muhammad's seventh son and successor,

Imam W. D. Mohammed. Imam Mohammed's conversion to Sunni Islam occurred long before 1975. The speed at which he transformed his father's community caused significant pain to those NOI members who held fast to the founding theology of the community. For those members, Minister Farrakhan's RNOI offered a path back to normality.

Minister Farrakhan launched *The Final Call* newspaper in 1979. The entire first issue of the paper was written and paid for by Minister Farrakhan. The paper was initially sold for 50 cents and was intended to be published monthly. The cost of producing the paper, however, ensured that it increased in cost and was published irregularly until the RNOI had become more firmly established and financially secure. *The Final Call* newspaper archives are housed at a number of research libraries in the United States. However, no complete collection appears to exist. The paper was published on an irregular basis until 1996 when it started to appear on a weekly basis.[78] *The Final Call* is now available as both a hardcopy and digital edition. The newspaper archives evidence the evolution of the RNOI as a faith community and offer rare glimpses into the concerns, grievances, aspirations, and work of NOI members both within and beyond the walls of their faith community. They also provide a record of Minister Farrakhan's activities, interfaith initiatives, and outreach efforts.

The RNOI have built up a rich archive of Minister Farrakhan's and his student ministers' lectures since the early 1980s. The archives include lectures, talks, and interviews. Importantly, the archive also includes talks that were intended for a NOI audience alone. These archives evidence the tensions and theological changes that have occurred within Minister Farrakhan's faith community. Importantly, they also reveal the maturation of the NOI's student ministers and their own understanding of the NOI's theology. Minister Farrakhan's recorded lectures and addresses are invaluable in that they evidence his own development and the maturation of his theology. Importantly, they also reveal how and why he has departed so far from the faith community's original theology.

Elijah Muhammad's faith community was hounded by the FBI. The bureau proved determined to destroy the community, its leaders, and its reputation. The bureau's campaign to destroy the community is generally well-known among its members and ministers. Indeed, Minister Farrakhan's national assistant Ishmael Muhammad has referred to the community's survival as a "miracle." In his comments at the community's 2018 Saviours' Day address, for example, he noted: "The Nation of Islam is a miracle. The Nation of Islam has survived the evil and wicked plans of the enemy."[79] The NOI was considered to be a dangerous and ultimately anti-American entity by the United States and its intelligence agencies. The full extent of their efforts to annihilate the faith community and create disunity among its ministers was unveiled via the extension of the Freedom of Information Act. The bureau's online vault contains several extensive, and heavily redacted, files relating to the NOI and its leaders. The files contain a vast wealth of original material. They reveal, however, more about the bureau than the reality of the NOI itself. Minister Farrakhan has often encouraged his followers to consult the files particularly as he believes their contents vindicate him and his colleagues from any suggestion of involvement in the assassination of Malcolm X.[80] Minister Farrakhan and his ministers firmly believe that their activities remain under the watchful eye of the FBI. Indeed, at the 2018 Saviours' Day convention, Farrakhan noted: "Since the Million Man March, the FBI has worked to destroy the mosque from within. Do you think that everybody in the mosque that says As Salaam Alaykum is a Muslim? Hell No, these are agents, some of them."[81]

The Ministry of Louis Farrakhan in the Nation of Islam consists of four chapters. Chapter 1, "The Garveyite Child," examines the formative influences that shaped Louis Farrakhan's religious life and his understanding of race relations in the United States. The chapter sets out the nature of Farrakhan's relationship with his single-mother Sarah Mae Manning. Manning had a profound impact on her son's early life. Indeed, as the chapter argues, it was Manning who inadvertently led her son on his journey to the NOI in 1955. Manning arrived in New York from Barbados in 1919. Her new life in New York was impacted directly by the US racial hierarchy and the politics of reactionary Black Nationalist movements. Manning was a Garveyite but her commitment to Garvey's teachings, as noted in Chapter 1, is questionable. She neither shielded her children from the reality of race relations in the United States nor encouraged them to view the country of their birth as a place where they would receive justice. Indeed, Farrakhan has often noted that his mother discussed the reality of racial apartheid in the United States openly in her home. During his annual address at the 2020 Saviours' Day convention, for example, he noted that he has never said the pledge of allegiance and that his mother instructed him to replace "justice for all" with "justice for white" when repeating the pledge.[82] Manning was a strict disciplinarian and neither of her children escaped physical punishments. Manning told Farrakhan little about his biological father beyond the fact that he was a Garveyite, Jamaican, and a womanizer. Farrakhan's early life was shaped by the absence of his father and father figures. He was instructed in Christianity at the Episcopalian church where the majority of members where immigrants from Barbados. Chapter 1 sets out the nationalistic influences Farrakhan encountered in the church. Moreover, it examines the impact of Farrakhan's early education on his later life. The chapter outlines Farrakhan's introduction to the NOI in 1955 via a friend. It details his initial hesitancy regarding the NOI and his rather unflattering first impression of its spiritual leader Elijah Muhammad. The chapter closes with a discussion of Manning's response to her son's decision to embrace Islam, as taught by Elijah Muhammad.

Chapter 2, "The Rise of Minister Louis Farrakhan," outlines Farrakhan's early embrace and understanding of Elijah Muhammad's teachings at Temple Number 11 in Boston. It considers his efforts to translate and promote NOI teachings via his most well-known plays, *The Trial* and *Orgena*. The chapter argues that the success of both plays within the NOI accelerated Farrakhan's career as a NOI minister and quickened the development of his relationship with Elijah Muhammad. The chapter examines the NOI's exponential growth during the height of the Civil Rights Movement and outlines the small faith community's efforts to contest media-driven narratives about them and their leaders via the establishment of their own newspaper, *Muhammad Speaks*. The chapter assesses the FBI's efforts to disrupt the NOI and manufacture power struggles within the group. The chapter outlines Farrakhan's relationship with the NOI's first national minister, Malcolm X, and examines his role in Malcolm's demise within the community. The chapter considers the impact of Malcolm's assassination on the NOI's reputation and Farrakhan's efforts to rebuild the Harlem temple in 1965 when he replaced Malcolm as both the minister of Temple Number 7 and national minister. The chapter examines Farrakhan's efforts to promote the faith community in the 1965–75 period. Elijah Muhammad's death in February 1975 devastated his many thousands of followers throughout the United States and his devoted team of ministers. Farrakhan felt the loss of Muhammad acutely.

Indeed, he appears to be the only minister to have cried publicly following Muhammad's death. The succession of Muhammad's seventh son, Wallace Muhammad, in February 1975 brought to an end Farrakhan's prospects and promotion within the faith community. Wallace introduced Sunni Islam at a speed that alarmed Muhammad's ministers and many followers. The structural reforms that followed, including the collapse of the FOI and the MGT, caused many members further distress. Wallace successfully thwarted potential coups by strategically scattering ministers, including Farrakhan. The chapter considers the impact of Wallace's reforms on Farrakhan and closes with an assessment of his decision to leave Wallace's community.

Chapter 3, "Atonement," sets out Farrakhan's work to rebuild the NOI and revise Elijah Muhammad's teachings. The outset of the chapter considers the revised theological teachings that Minister Farrakhan infused into his writings and public speeches and lectures. In particular, the chapter explores Minister Farrakhan's efforts to find favor with and work alongside Christian clergy. The chapter considers Minister Farrakhan's 1985 vision in Mexico and the implications for the NOI. The chapter sets out the origins of Minister Farrakhan's war of words with American Jewish groups and assesses the impact of ongoing tensions on the NOI. Minister Farrakhan engaged in a number of high-profile interviews in the 1980s and 1990s. Such engagements provided him with a national and international platform and ultimately created further opportunities for the NOI. Minister Farrakhan's profile was further raised in the early 1990s when well-known and commercially successful artists began to refer to him in their artistic output. The early 1990s, however, also proved challenging for the NOI and Farrakhan. The resurfacing of questions regarding his role, if any, in Malcolm's death via the release of Spike Lee's successful biopic *Malcolm X* had the potential to create enough reputational damage to hamper the NOI's growth. Farrakhan managed to navigate and quell the storm of questions regarding his relationship with Malcolm X. Indeed, if anything, the publicity that the biopic generated helped Farrakhan appeal even further to younger generations of African Americans for support. The MMM in October 1995 evidenced Farrakhan's and the NOI's rise in the United States. As noted, the event witnessed the largest gathering of African American men in US history. The chapter closes with a consideration of the significance of the march.

Chapter 4, "Aftermath," sheds light on one of the most neglected periods in the NOI's history and Farrakhan's career: the post-1995 period. The MMM brought Farrakhan to the pinnacle of his career, but its aftermath proved his limitations and contradictions as a leader. The chapter examines Farrakhan's efforts to internationalize the NOI via a succession of deeply unpopular tours post-1995. It thereafter explores the impact of Farrakhan's personal health problems on the NOI's leadership and theology. Moreover, it examines the impact of Minister Farrakhan's public reconciliation with Imam W. D. Mohammed in 2000 and his efforts to align the NOI more closely with Sunni communities in the aftermath of the September 11 terrorist attacks. The chapter considers how Farrakhan's absence from the NOI in 2006 impacted the NOI's theology and leadership. The chapter examines in-depth the workings of the NOI council of thirteen and rise of Ishmael Muhammad in the faith community. The chapter considers the impact that Dianetics Auditing and influences from Muslim organizations have had on the NOI and Farrakhan. The chapter argues that Farrakhan's assessment and critique of race relations in the United States have been largely consistent.

The conclusion summarizes the book's arguments and briefly considers Farrakhan's legacy as a religious leader.

Notes

1 Louis Farrakhan, "A Saviour Is Born for the Whole of Humanity: No One Need Perish." Speech delivered at the United Center, Chicago, February 17, 2019.
2 "Brother Nuri Muhammad Speaks on Malcolm X, Valuable Relationships, Economic Empowerment + More." YouTube (accessed November 3, 2021).
3 https://www.finalcall.com/artman/publish/Perspectives_1/Facebook-s-Ban-on-Farrakhan.shtml (accessed June 12, 2019).
4 Javonte Anderson, "Minister Farrakhan Invited to St. Sabina after Facebook Ban," *Chicago Tribune*, May 7, 2019.
5 Ibid.
6 Louis Farrakhan, "We Are Farrakhan: Community Rally in Support of the Honorable Minister Louis Farrakhan." Speech delivered at the Faith Community of Saint Sabina, Chicago, May 9, 2019.
7 Dahleen Glanton, "Some African Americans Look Past Farrakhan's Bigoted Words and Hear a Message of Love," *Chicago Tribune*, May 6, 2019, 2.

8 Student Minister Abdul Sharrieff Muhammad, "Bearing Witness to Divinity: A Testimony from the Founder of Rise Magazine," *Rise Magazine*, September 2020, 7.
9 Manning Marable, "Black Fundamentalism: Louis Farrakhan and the Politics of Conservative Black Nationalism," *Dissent*, Spring 1998, 69.
10 Ishmael Muhammad, "Holy Day of Atonement and Million Man March 26th Anniversary." Speech delivered at Mosque Maryam, Chicago, October 17, 2021.
11 "Louis Farrakhan … Again | Anti-Defamation League" (adl.org) (accessed October 18, 2021).
12 According to Minister Farrakhan, Ellison was previously a NOI member and assisted the community by selling copies of their national newspaper, *The Final Call*. See comments made by Minister Farrakhan at the 2018 Saviours' Day address delivered at the Wintrust Arena in Chicago on February 25, 2018. Moreover, in 2016, the community also published a photograph of Ellison selling the community paper: see http://www.finalcall.com/artman/publish/editorials/article_103405.shtml (accessed October 21, 2021).
13 "Keith Ellison Pans Louis Farrakhan's Nation of Islam: 'Nobody Listens to Them,'" *Washington Examiner* (https://www.washingtonexaminer.com/news/congress/keith-ellison-pans-louis-farrakhans-nation-of-islam-nobody-listens-to-them) (accessed October 18, 2021).
14 https://www.nytimes.com/2018/03/09/us/louis-farrakhan-facts-history.html (accessed August 13, 2018).
15 "Louis Farrakhan … Again | Anti-Defamation League."
16 Demetric Muhammad, "The Plot to Outlaw the Nation of Islam." Speech delivered at Mosque Maryam, Chicago, June 24, 2018.
17 Farrakhan, "A Saviour Is Born for the Whole of Humanity."
18 Erdmann D. Beynon, "The Voodoo Cult among Negro Migrants in Detroit," *American Journal of Sociology*, vol. 43, no. 6 (May 1938): 894.
19 Patrick Bowen, *A History of Conversion to Islam in the United States, Volume 2: The African American Islamic Renaissance, 1920–1975* (Leiden and Boston: Brill, 2017), 275.
20 Stewart E. Tonlay, "The African American 'Great Migration' and Beyond," *Annual Review of Sociology*, vol. 29 (August 2003): 214
21 Herbert Berg, *Elijah Muhammad and Islam* (New York: New York University Press), 10.
22 Michael Gomez, *Black Crescent: The Experience and Legacy of African Muslims in the Americas* (New York: Cambridge University Press, 2005), 160.
23 Berg, *Elijah Muhammad and Islam*, 13.
24 Louis Farrakhan, "The Sentence of Death on America—The Reality of Genocide." Speech delivered at the University of Wisconsin, February 1, 1980.

25 Aminah Beverly McCloud McCloud, *African American Islam* (New York and London: Routledge, 1995), 19.
26 Edward Curtis, "The Black Muslim Scare in the Twentieth Century: The History of State Islamophobia and Its Post 9/11 Variations," in *Islamophobia in America*, ed. Carl W. Ernst (New York: Palgrave Macmillan, 2013), 86.
27 Ibid.
28 Hatim A. Sahib, "The Nation of Islam," *Contributions in Black Studies*, vol. 13/14 (1995/1996): 27.
29 Essien U. Essien-Udom, *Black Nationalism: A Search for an Identity in America* (Chicago: University of Chicago Press, 1962), 4.
30 Beynon, "The Voodoo Cult among Negro Migrants," 905.
31 Dawn-Marie Gibson, *A History of the Nation of Islam: Race, Islam and the Quest for Freedom* (Santa Barbara: Praeger, 2012), 28.
32 Gibson and Karim, *Women of the Nation*, 8.
33 Nasir Makr Hakim, *The True History of Elijah Muhammad: Messenger of Allah* (Atlanta: M.E.M.P.S., 1997), 39.
34 Sahib, "The Nation of Islam," 70–1.
35 Beynon, "The Voodoo Cult among Negro Migrants," 902.
36 Gibson, *A History of the Nation of Islam*, 18.
37 Editor, "Intended Voodoo Victims' Number Still Mounting," *Detroit Free Press*, November 23, 1932.
38 Ajile Rahman, "She Stood by His Side and at Times in His Stead: The Life and Legacy of Sister Clara Muhammad: First Lady of the Nation of Islam." (Doctoral Dissertation: Clark Atlanta University, 2000).
39 Ted Vincent, "The Garveyite Parents of Malcolm X," *The Black Scholar*, vol. 20, no. 2 (March/April 1989): 10.
40 Malcolm X, *The Autobiography of Malcolm X* (New York: Penguin: 1965), 118.
41 Claude A. Clegg, "Rebuilding the Nation: The Life and Work of Elijah Muhammad, 1946–1954," *The Black Scholar*, vol. 26, no. 3/4 (Fall/Winter 1996): 55.
42 Garrett Felber, *Those Who Know Don't Say: The Nation of Islam, the Black Freedom Movement, and the Carceral State* (Chapel Hill: University of North Carolina Press, 2020), 18.
43 Jeffrey Ogbar, *Black Power: Radical Politics and African American Identity* (Baltimore: Johns Hopkins University Press, 2019), x.
44 Malcolm X, *The Autobiography of Malcolm X*, 404.
45 Louis Farrakhan, "The Murder of Malcolm X: The Effect on Black America." Speech delivered at Malcolm X college, Chicago, February 21, 1990.
46 James Booker, "Why I Quit and What I Plan Next," *New York Amsterdam News*, March 14, 1964, 51.

47 Gibson, *A History of the Nation of Islam*, 61.
48 "2 Men Convicted of Killing Malcolm X Will Be Exonerated," *New York Times* (nytimes.com) (accessed March 22, 2022).
49 Naba'a Muhammad, "A Step toward Justice, But Much More Is Required," *The Final Call*, November 30, 2021, 16.
50 William Reel, "Call Muslims the Richest Black Group," *Daily News*, April 16, 1972, 60.
51 Paul Delaney, "Shift of Malcolm X's Successor Stirs Black Muslim Speculation," *New York Times*, June 12, 1975, 20.
52 Louis Farrakhan, "Closing Remarks at the 2021 Saviours' Day Address." Delivered at Mosque Maryam, Chicago, February 2021.
53 Farrakhan, "A Saviour Is Born for the Whole of Humanity."
54 Dawn-Marie Gibson, *The Nation of Islam, Louis Farrakhan and the Men Who Follow Him* (New York: Palgrave, 2016), 40.
55 Louis Farrakhan, "Final Call," *Chicago Defender*, September 29, 1979, 6.
56 Luke Tripp, "The Political Views of Black Students during the Reagan Era," *The Black Scholar*, vol. 22, no. 3 (Summer 1992): 45–6.
57 Gibson, *The Nation of Islam, Louis Farrakhan*, 42.
58 Demetric Muhammad, *"But, Didn't You Kill Malcolm?" Myth-Busting the Propaganda against the Nation of Islam* (Chicago: Nation of Islam, 2020), 10.
59 Gibson, *A History of the Nation of Islam*, 141.
60 Sheikh Shaker Elsayed, "After Twenty-Five Years Rift, Farrakhan Joins Warith Deen Muhammad," *American Muslim*, vol. 1, no. 2 (April 2000): 24.
61 http://www.finalcall.com/artman/publish/National_News_2/article_7947.shtml (accessed June 13, 2013).
62 "Black Muslims Account for a Fifth of All U.S. Muslims." Pew Research Center (https://www.pewresearch.org/short-reads/2019/01/17/black-muslims-account-for-a-fifth-of-all-u-s-muslims-and-about-half-are-converts-to-islam/) (accessed November 15, 2021).
63 "American Mosque Survey 2020 Report 1." ISPU (https://www.ispu.org/public-policy/mosque-survey/) (accessed November 15, 2021).
64 "A New Imam and a New Day of Unity, Cooperation" (finalcall.com) (accessed November 15, 2021).
65 "Chicago Muslim Oral History Project: Muhammad, Sultan—Oral History Collection (Chicago History Museum)—CARLI Digital Collections" (illinois.edu) (accessed November 15, 2021).
66 Author Interview with DIA Representative, November 18, 2021.
67 Ishmael Muhammad, "Believers' Meeting." Speech delivered at Mosque Maryam, Chicago, March 3, 2021.

68 Anisha Muhammad, "The Mission Comes First: Faith, Hope and Healing as Black Families Search for Missing Loved Ones," *The Final Call*, November 9, 2021, 4.

69 Louis Farrakhan, "Preparation of the Mind and the Qualifications to Act for Christ," *The Final Call*, March 15, 2011, 21.

70 Jacob King, "Clearing the Planet: Dianetics Auditing and the Eschatology of the Nation of Islam," in *New Perspectives on the Nation of Islam*, ed. Herbert Berg and Dawn-Marie Gibson (New York: Routledge, 2017), 219.

71 Farrakhan, "The Sentence of Death on America."

72 "Nuri Muhammad Breakfast Club Interview, December 18, 2019: Brother Nuri Muhammad Speaks on Malcolm X, Valuable Relationships, Economic Empowerment + More." YouTube (accessed November 3, 2021).

73 Edward Curtis, *Islam in Black America: Identity, Liberation and Difference in African-American Religious Thought* (New York: State University of New York Press, 2002); Arthur Magida, *Prophet of Rage: A Life of Louis Farrakhan and His Nation* (New York: HarperCollins, 1996); Mattias Gardell, *Countdown to Armageddon: Louis Farrakhan and the Nation of Islam* (Durham, NC: Duke University Press, 1996); Manning Marable, "Black Fundamentalism: Farrakhan and Conservative Black Nationalism," *Race and Class*, vol. 39, no. 4 (1998): 1–22; Robert Singh, *The Farrakhan Phenomenon: Race, Reaction, and the Paranoid Style in American Politics* (Washington, DC: Georgetown University Press, 1997).

74 Magida, *Prophet of Rage*, 1996.

75 Gardell, *Countdown to Armageddon*.

76 Gibson, *The Nation of Islam, Louis Farrakhan*, 44.

77 Askia Muhammad, "Memories of the Honorable Elijah Muhammad," *The Final Call*, October 19, 2021, 17.

78 "The Final Call Is Now Weekly," Advertisement in *The Final Call* newspaper, June 4, 1996, 29.

79 Ishmael Muhammad opening remarks at the 2018 keynote address for the annual Saviours' Day convention at the Chicago Wintrust Arena on February 25, 2018.

80 See, for example, Richard Muhammad and Donald Muhammad, "A Step toward Healing," *The Final Call*, May 24, 1995, 3.

81 Louis Farrakhan, "Saviours' Day Keynote Address."

82 Louis Farrakhan, "The Unravelling of a Great Nation." Speech delivered at the 2020 Saviours' Day convention at the TCF Center, Detroit, February 23, 2020.

1

The Garveyite Child

Sarah Mae Manning arrived in New York City in 1919 from Barbados where she had lived since the age of twelve with her mother and brother. Sarah was born in St. Kitts in the Caribbean in 1900. Little is known about Sarah's early life or her parentage. According to her youngest son Alvan, she fled Barbados at the age of nineteen following the death of her first husband from a flu epidemic.[1] Sarah was among the thousands of West Indian immigrants who sought to make a new life in the United States. New York was a hub for West Indian immigrants like Sarah.[2] In New York, Sarah found steady work as a domestic in the homes of local whites, despite being a qualified seamstress. Though her work life as a young widow was undoubtedly hard, Sarah found new love in her host city when she met Percival Clarke, a light-skinned Jamaican man. Clarke was a supporter of Marcus Garvey's UNIA.[3] Sarah loved Clarke dearly, but she also knew that he was a "philanderer" and subsequently threw him out of their marital home.[4] Clarke's unfaithfulness and frequent absences led Sarah into the arms of another man Louis Walcott, who fathered her first child, Alvan, in 1932. Sarah thereafter briefly rekindled her relationship with Clarke and fell pregnant with his child. The pregnancy left Sarah "frightened and worried" that Walcott would leave her when he found out that the child was not his.[5] Sarah subsequently tried to abort the child no less than three times using a "metal hanger." After her third failed attempt she decided to continue with the pregnancy but nonetheless prayed earnestly that the child would be a girl with dark skin, like herself and Walcott.[6] Sarah carried the child to full term but was certainly disappointed when she was delivered of a light-skinned boy in May 1933. She named the child Louis Walcott, after her lover. Walcott knew that the light-skinned baby boy with curly auburn hair was not his biological son and subsequently left Sarah. Sarah raised Alvin and Louis alone in Boston,

Massachusetts, as a single parent. Louis keenly felt the absence of a father and a father figure throughout his young life. Indeed, he notes that his maternal uncle, Samuel, "was the only man in my life as a youngster."[7] Sarah raised her children as devout Christians and attended St. Cyprian's Episcopal Church where Louis was a choirboy. Christianity, however, was not the only influence shaping the minds of her young children and Louis in particular. According to Louis, his mother was on the "periphery" of the UNIA.[8] Louis comments that it was his uncle Samuel and not his mother who first taught him about Garvey. He remarks that it was during a visit to Samuel's home that he encountered a "big picture of a black man on his wall." Louis was intrigued by the picture. Samuel subsequently told Louis that the man in the picture was Marcus Garvey, a man who "had come to unite our people." Louis asked if it was possible to "go and meet him." Samuel advised his young nephew that Garvey was dead. News of Garvey's death brought Louis to tears: "I wept, because I thought I had come so close to the man I was looking for only to find out that he was gone. My search continued until I heard that God had raised a Messenger for us."[9] Samuel's home struck Louis as very different from his maternal home. According to Louis, his mother's home had many images of whites including King George and Queen Elizabeth.[10] Such comments suggest that Sarah did not fully subscribe to Garvey's critiques of "idolism" of whites.[11] The young Louis cannot have been anything but moved by his uncle's stories of Garvey's heroism. Such stories led Louis in search of a man he considered to be of equal stature to Garvey. He was to find such a man at the age of twenty-two in the person of Elijah Muhammad in Chicago. His introduction to Muhammad's Black separatist NOI forever changed the trajectory of his life.[12] Muhammad undoubtedly shaped Louis's early career as a Muslim minister. Muhammad's influence on Louis remains discernible today. Yet, it was Sarah who had the most profound impact on the development of Louis's sense of racial identity and racial politics in the United States. She instilled in her children an appreciation for learning, diligence, and self-help along with a realization of how the racial hierarchy operated to exploit and oppress them. Such lessons were reaffirmed for Louis in his church setting under the tutelage of Reverend Nathan Wright. Louis's journey into the fold of the NOI began not in Chicago in 1955 but in his maternal home. Indeed, Sarah became a registered member of the NOI herself in 1957 and received her "original" name, Sumayyah, shortly thereafter.[13]

Sarah entered the United States at a time when the oppression and exploitation of minoritized communities, and African Americans in particular, was sanctioned and condoned by wide sections of society and championed by their elected officials. The subjugation of African Americans in the United States was solidified in law in 1896 when the Supreme Court passed *Plessy v. Ferguson*. The case legalized a preexisting system of "separate but equal" spheres for whites and their African American counterparts. In practice, "separate but equal" meant that African Americans existed as second-class citizens in the United States. The *Plessy* ruling, according to legal scholar Michael Klarman, "reflected … the regressive racial climate of the time."[14] The aftermath of the Civil War and the ensuing Reconstruction amendments more broadly certainly enabled a form of social mobility and political participation for some. In short, it offered a brief window of opportunity for those able to take advantage of it. Repressive Black codes, racial etiquette, the threat of extralegal violence, and the economics of the sharecropping system disenfranchised formerly enslaved people and limited opportunities for social mobility. The onset of the First World War, however, provided a rare opportunity to escape the multiple oppressions they endured in the South.

The Great Migration of 1.5 million African Americans from the South to the North and Midwest during the interwar years was according to historian Stephen Tuck a "form of protest" and a "rejection of the oppressive terms of the plantation system."[15] The economic opportunities created by the First World War lured African Americans from the rural South and away from the sharecropping system. The northern Black press championed the mass exodus of African Americans from the South as "a much needed response to racial oppression."[16] The National Association for the Advancement of Colored People (NAACP)'s magazine, *The Crisis*, and the *Chicago Defender* led the way in endorsing the migration as a crusade for racial uplift. Migrants left the sharecropping system behind but the exploitation that underpinned it was present in Northern cities in different forms. The influx of Southern migrants to industrial cities exacerbated existing racial tensions and intensified competition for jobs and economic opportunity. Wages in Northern industries paid significantly better than agricultural work in the South. In some cases, for example, a worker could earn $4 more per day in industrial work than in agriculture.[17] Yet, African Americans experienced frequent periods of underemployment and intense discrimination in employment practices.[18] They were, in many cases, the "last hired and the first fired." Racial strife manifested itself in extrajudicial killings, violent attacks, and race riots. Extralegal violence in the form of lynching served to reinforce the color line and evidenced an abysmal failure and unwillingness to protect Black life. The fact that lynch mobs frequently evaded justice sanctioned horrific attacks on African Americans. In 1917, for example, thirty-eight African Americans were lynched and in 1919, seventy were lynched. Moreover, from May to September 1919, race riots erupted across the United States.[19] The Red Summer of 1919, as it became known, witnessed an unprecedented level of violence directed toward African American communities. Indeed, the riots of 1919 were "less organized" than lynchings and unlike lynchings involved both women and teenagers as opposed to adult white males alone.[20] The riots of 1919, according to historian D'Weston Haywood, illustrated that "racism and racial violence were not a regional phenomenon, but national in character."[21]

It is difficult to determine how much Sarah knew of existing racial tensions in the United States or to what extent she was prepared for life in New York. Her journey to New York as a nineteen-year-old widow must have been simultaneously terrifying and perhaps equally exhilarating. Her migration was surely prompted by the death of her husband and her desire to escape the "limited opportunities" that islands such as St. Kitts offered. Migration, as sociologist Phillip Kasinitz notes, was a "survival strategy" for people in the Caribbean.[22] Sarah was part of the "enormous influx of West Indians" to the United States in the early 1900s.[23] Immigration from the West Indies averaged between 5,000 and 8,000 per year between 1908 and 1924 when immigration restrictions ended the influx.[24] Sarah's host city soon offered her an education in race relations in the United States and her place in its racial hierarchy. Sarah found a tight-knit community of West Indian immigrants in Roxbury where she created a home for herself. Roxbury's West Indian community was "singularly cohesive" with a "strong sense … of place, of identity."[25] Sarah quickly found work in the homes of local whites as a domestic. Opportunities for Black women to pursue alternatives to domestic work were rare. Though the industry was certainly not exclusive to Black women, it is true that as the twentieth century progressed, they dominated the profession. By 1940, for example, Black women accounted for 60 percent of such workers in the United

States.[26] Domestic work, though hard, insecure, and potentially dangerous, enabled Sarah to provide for herself and exercise economic independence—something she construed as an important source of pride. The few details that exist about Sarah's life in St. Kitts suggest that she operated her own business as a seamstress and that she was a keen entrepreneur. Sarah surely found that New York lacked the kind of opportunities that would have enabled her to relaunch her business on US soil. Moreover, her domestic work reaffirmed on a daily basis her status in the United States as a Black woman. Sarah was to find companionship and love in Roxbury when she met a light-skinned Jamaican man, Percival Clarke, whom she later married. It was via Clarke that Sarah appears to have first encountered Marcus Garvey's UNIA.

Marcus Garvey established the Black Nationalist UNIA in 1914 in Jamaica, but its headquarters was situated in New York. Garvey offered damning critiques of the racism and brutality that African Americans and his West Indian counterparts endured in America. Garvey's movement grew quickly and by the mid-1920s the UNIA had 800 chapters in the United States.[27] The UNIA's overwhelming success owed much to the domestic context that his followers found themselves in. Historian John Henrik Clarke, for example, notes: "The appearance of the Garvey Movement was perfectly timed" and that the "broken promises of the postwar period produced widespread cynicism in the black population."[28] Such cynicism provided Garvey with thousands of followers who had lost faith in the promises of America. Percival and Sarah were in many ways quite typical of UNIA followers in that they were both West Indian, recent immigrants, and both occupied the bottom rung of socioeconomic groups in the United States. Garvey's Black Nationalist movement certainly gained traction among African Americans, but it was his West Indian followers that the UNIA's message spoke most to. Historian Nicholas Patsides, for example, notes:

> Garvey ideology reflected the cultural background of Jamaican society in a number of ways. In general terms, his doctrine of race nationalism had special meaning to Caribbean immigrants, because it served to support their economic ambitions abroad and aid their social and psychological adjustment in the United States. Despite the incorporation of a New York branch of the UNIA in May 1917, Garvey continued to speak predominantly to the people of the Caribbean at home and abroad, because he shared their

colonial mentality and pursuit of social mobility through material wealth. Most immigrants hoped to translate their sojourn abroad into economic and social progress back home, and Garvey believed that this predisposition to return home made them the natural harbingers of democratic reform in colonial society.[29]

Sarah's interest in the Garvey movement may well have been rooted in an appreciation for both its politics of Black protest and its gender norms, given her experience as a domestic worker in New York. Such norms emphasized the performance of traditional gender roles and the protection of Black women. This conservative message was greeted by UNIA women not as repressive but as a "welcome alternative" to their vulnerable position at the hands of white employers and particularly when employed in white homes.[30] Garvey's critiques of American racism extended to churches and Black churches in particular. In an address in New York in 1924, for example, Garvey chided Black Americans for "worshipping a false God" and called for his followers to establish a "new religion." In one of his many addresses in New York in 1924 he proclaimed: "God tells us to workshop a God in our own image … we are Black and to be in our image God must be Black … We must create a god of our own and give this new religion to the Negroes of the world."[31] Despite such critiques, Garvey refused to introduce a "new religion" to the UNIA. Garvey's speeches and writings borrowed heavily from the Bible, and he often used religious imagery rather extensively. Historian Randall Burkett, for example, remarks that every address that Garvey gave was a "call to commitment, determination, and sacrifice, with a not infrequent note of apocalypticism creeping in."[32] Garvey's agitation in the United States caused significant concern among civil rights activists such as W. E. B. Dubois and the Bureau of Investigation. Dubois considered Garvey to be a "foreigner" and thus ill-equipped to understand the complexities of African American suffering in the United States.[33] Under the watchful eye of J. Edgar Hoover, the Bureau of Investigation launched an investigation into Garvey's "aggressive tactics." He was subsequently charged with mail fraud in 1925 and deported in 1927. Hoover had dreamed of deporting Garvey from as early as 1919 when he wrote that "Unfortunately, [Garvey] has not yet violated any federal law whereby he could be proceeded against on the grounds of being an undesirable alien, from the point of view of deportation."[34] Garvey's removal from the United States devastated his followers and left a vacuum that was filled by successive Black Nationalist movements, perhaps none more so than the NOI.

Sarah and Clarke may both have felt some devotion to the UNIA. It is evident, however, that it was Clarke and not Sarah who was staunchly committed to the movement. Louis's comments regarding images of whites in his mother's home indicate that her devotion to Garveyism was questionable at best and that his first lesson about Garvey came from his uncle Samuel at the age of eleven during a rare visit to his home in New York. Clarke thus appears to have been responsible for and the driving force behind Sarah's apparent interest in the UNIA.

Sarah endured a tumultuous but short-lived marriage. Clarke's philandering and extended absences led her to seek solace in the arms of Louis Walcott—an immigrant from Barbados who made a steady income from his work as a taxi driver. Walcott fathered Sarah's first child, Alvan, who was dark-skinned like herself and Walcott. However, shortly after Alvan's birth, Sarah briefly rekindled her relationship with Clarke and fell pregnant with Louis. Her second pregnancy caused significant anguish. Louis's comments relating to his mother's attempt to abort him imply that she was determined to destroy the evidence of her brief liaison with Clarke in order to save her relationship with Walcott. Scant details exist regarding Sarah's early years in New York or her marriage to Clarke. Indeed, it is unclear when exactly they married or divorced. In successive interviews concerning his father, Louis has repeatedly stated that "my father was not known to me."[35] Louis knows, or is willing to convey, very few facts about his father: that he was a Garveyite, a philanderer, and hailed from the parish of Trelawney in Jamaica. Why he appears to know so little of his father is in itself interesting. It suggests that Sarah spoke rarely about Clarke and in doing so intentionally limited how much she relayed to Louis about his father. Her possible motives for restricting details about Clarke also raise questions. Did she limit what she professed to know of Clarke to dissuade Louis from searching for a man she believed would only disappoint him? Did she resent Clarke for ruining her relationship with Walcott and how in turn did this inform her relationship with Louis? Certainly, it is possible that all the above scenarios are viable. The little that Louis knows about his father indicates that he was a man who put his desire for women above the love and care of his wife. Whether Sarah ever told Clarke that she was pregnant with his child is also unclear. Sarah's relationship with Walcott, according to Louis, was a happy and secure one at a time when the onset of the economic depression was wreaking havoc on the lives of US citizens. Sarah's work as a domestic and Walcott's earnings as a taxi driver provided the couple with a source of relative economic security. The loss of such security via Walcott's departure and the burden of providing for an additional child alone surely weighed heavily on Sarah and drove her to unsuccessfully, and continually, attempt to end the pregnancy. Louis has spoken publicly about his mother's efforts to end his life in the womb multiple times. How young he was when she first told him of her attempts to abort him and what motivated her to relay such information to him is unknown. In his book, *Torchlight for America*, he notes:

> My mother tried to abort me three times. Although she eventually decided to have me, the effect of her thinking is on me. However, God has used that effect for His purposes ... As my mother lay dying on her bed, she told me while cradling her womb, "son, I thank God for what he allowed my womb to produce." She prayed that God would forgive her for even trying to kill such a precious child.[36]

The fact that Sarah was unable to end the pregnancy appears to have fueled Louis's sense of himself, certainly later in life, as "special" or created for a unique purpose. In his writings, for example, he states: "I love the unborn Black child ... I believe I was born into the world to live and die for the liberation of our people."[37] It is entirely possible that Louis interpreted his survival in this way after joining the NOI or after leading the NOI himself. What is not clear is whether Sarah told him of her attempts to abort him during his younger life and what impact this may have had on him and his relationship with her. On at least one occasion Louis has noted that he "suffered" for much of life thinking that his mother did not "love" him.[38] Louis's comments about his early life are largely consistent and portray an image of a child who was raised by a busy, strict single mother in a family that lacked any significant male influence or presence. The only man in Louis's young life was his uncle whom he encountered on a few occasions. He credits his uncle with first introducing him to Garvey when he was eleven years old. This event appears to have affected him profoundly and evidences an early interest in Black Nationalism, race relations, and liberation and a desire for "unity" among Black people.

Sarah's life as a single parent in Boston was undoubtedly hard. African American migrants and West Indian immigrants such as Sarah found the onset of the Great Depression in 1930 particularly difficult. The Depression caused whites significant hardship, but it was undoubtedly tougher for Blacks given the frequent exclusion they faced from relief agencies. Sarah's domestic work kept her family financially afloat, but it left her little time to lavish her children with either affection or attention. Sarah's love for her children manifested itself in her sacrifices and provision for them. She was, according to Louis, a "wonderful mother" but she was not given to emotionalism in the form of "hugging" or "squeezing" her sons.[39] Sarah's apparent lack of affection for Alvan and Louis may be due to a host of factors. The circumstances surrounding Sarah's work certainly impacted her mothering. Sarah worked in an industry that required long hours and grueling labor. Her days belonged not to herself but to the whims of her respective employers. As a result, she likely returned home to her children exhausted from an industry that exploited her labor and vulnerability. Sarah fulfilled the role of both nurturer and provider for her children and while Louis struggled to understand his mother's lack of affection as a child, he has since reasoned that she demonstrated her love for her children through her provision.[40]

Sarah's industriousness and work ethic were not lost on her children. She taught Louis the value of hard work and financial independence—lessons that were reinforced in his local church and later in weekly orientation and Fruit of Islam (FOI) classes in Elijah Muhammad's NOI. Sarah was a staunch disciplinarian and did not shy away from physically disciplining her children. Louis's comments below, for example, highlight both Sarah's seriousness and resilience as a parent but also her determination to correct and manage the behavior of her sons:

> My mother was not a foolish woman; I never saw my mother engaged in foolishness. I never got out of bed before my mother did. And, when she put me to bed, she was still working. My mother didn't care if the men in her life did not support her children. She said she would do it herself. And when my mother would beat me, she always did so for a principle. One of the things that she would beat me for, more than anything that I did, was when I lied about what I did. Because I couldn't fool her, she would trap me in my lie, beat me for what I did, and then, beat the hell out of me for the lie! … She

was making me into a man that would not be afraid of the consequences of telling the truth.[41]

Sarah's interest in the UNIA and her need for a support network likely informed her decision to join St. Cyprian's Episcopalian Church in Boston. According to historian Abdul-Tawwab, the church "nurtured a strong Garveyite tradition."[42] The church was formed by West Indian Episcopalians and "established itself as a racially proud, progressive institution, dedicated to a program of self-help."[43] The church's current representative notes that the church was born out of a need for West Indians in Boston to have their own place of worship. West Indians in Boston initially worshipped in "white churches" and were subsequently "politely" told they would be "better off" if they had their own building. St. Cyprian's has historically been dominated by immigrants from Barbados although it has also had African American members.[44] The church's emphasis on self-help encouraged its members to form their own businesses and indeed, many Black businesses in Boston belonged to members of St. Cyprian's.[45] Louis was a choirboy at the church and describes it as his "second home." He notes:

> I had a wonderful Christian upbringing. My church was my second home ... It was the West Indian church mostly. We weren't accepted by the real American Black people so in that church I found joy and peace ... the people who nursed me the most were from the tiny island of Barbados. It was Barbados that really raised me.[46]

Louis's comments relating to his church life are telling. They suggest that as a child he felt that his "blackness" was challenged and rejected by African Americans and that unlike his contemporaries in the NOI, his church life was not a source of oppression. This sense of rejection may well have impacted Louis rather significantly and sheds light on why at the age of eleven he desired to see "unity" among Blacks. The church representative notes that tensions between African American Christians and their West Indian counterparts in the community have existed historically and that "that tension is still there now." He observes that this tension results from the fact that the West Indian church has "never been militantly black" and that unlike African Americans, West Indians "were never a minority people."[47]

St. Cyprian's was led by Reverend Nathan Wright from 1950—a "prominent and early advocate of Black Power."[48] Rev. Wright called for the creation of

Black universities and buy Black campaigns and an investigation into how viable the division of the United States into two countries—one Black and one white—would be. In 1959, for example, his church received a $3,683 check for their joint *Ebony Subscription* drive.[49] Wright's penchant for Black Nationalist activism was outlined in his books *Black Power and Urban Unrest* and *Ready to Riot*. The former book outlined the need for economic empowerment, upliftment, and self-help. In one section of the book, for example, Wright observes:

> There is, on the part of the Negro, a manifest need for self-development. Yet, of recent years, we as black people have assumed that a slave mentality of dependence upon others, as we had in former years, was appropriate for the twentieth-century destiny to which we are called. This crippling dependence upon others has hung like an albatross on our necks. It has led us to a state of stagnation and bewildered consternation which we find, with few notable exceptions, pervading the life of the black people of America today. The experience of all rising ethnic groups in this our beloved land has been that each rising group in American life must do for self itself that which no other group may do for it.[50]

Wright's books provide some sense of the ideas and sympathies that likely informed his sermons at St. Cyprian's. The above extract, for example, suggests that he held dear Garveyite notions of upliftment, self-help, and self-reliance tempered perhaps by an apparent affection for the "beloved land" of the United States. Wright was critical of the emerging Civil Rights Movement and, like Elijah Muhammad, thought the call for integration an "insult." He grew up in Cincinnati and was first exposed to Garveyism as an "altar boy in St. Andrew's Church in Cincinnati—where the second general chaplain of the UNIA, George McGuire, had served as a rector. Wright's father had served as the president of the Cincinnati branch of the NAACP and it appears that Wright construed their work positively. Indeed, St. Cyprian's became the first church in Boston to subscribe to a lifetime membership of the NAACP.[51]

Church members, including the young Louis, were already cognizant of the NAACP's work prior to the church subscription in 1956. Louis notes that his mother sought to educate both Alvan and himself about the realities of racial oppression. She gave her children copies of *The Crisis* at home and encouraged them to read about civil rights campaigns. Racism in America was something that Sarah and her friends also discussed at home and Louis frequently overheard these discussions.[52] According to his longtime associate, Larry Muhammad (now known as Akbar Muhammad), Louis would "cry himself to sleep after hearing his mother and her friends talking about the plight of Black people" and would "lay on the floor looking up at the blue sky asking God why he would send help to other people and not to the Black people of America?."[53] Louis developed a sensitivity to the sufferings and humiliations that African Americans endured in the United States. Reading copies of *The Crisis* during his childhood, and perhaps even his teenage years, can but only have encouraged that sensitivity and opened his eyes to the very real horrors of America's race record. *The Crisis* certainly enlightened Louis about the brave men who defended his freedom abroad during the Second World War. Equally, however, articles and editorials made clear to readers that the war was being fought to defeat both Hitler and the pseudoscientific racist theories that resulted in a denial of democracy in Germany and the United States. An editorial from 1942, for example, noted:

> With our country at war for little more than a month, *The Crisis* would emphasize with all its strength that now is the time *not* to be silent about the breaches of democracy here in our own land. Now is the time to speak out, not in disloyalty, but in the truest patriotism, the patriotism with an eye, now that the die is cast—single to the peace which must be won. Of course, between the declaration of war and the making of a just peace there lies the grim necessity of winning the conflict. To this task the Negro American quickly pledged his fullest support. Be it said once more that black Americans are loyal Americans; but let there be no mistake about that loyalty. It is loyalty to the democratic ideal as enunciated by America and by our British ally; it is not loyalty to many of the practices which have been—and are still—in vogue here and in the British Empire. The highest expressions of patriotism in these war years will come in the critical analysis of our objectives, in the refusal to ignore, now or later, those evils among us which are blood brothers of the evils against which we are warring ... It must be that we declare the life blood of our fighters and the sweat of our workers to be a sacrifice for a new world which will contain a Hitler, but not Hitlerism. And to thirteen millions of American Negroes that means a fight for a world in which lynching, brutality, terror, humiliation, and degradation

through segregation and discrimination, shall have no place- either *here* or *there*. (emphasis in original)[54]

Editorials such as this were part and parcel of the publications to emerge during the Double-Victory campaign. The Double-Victory campaign was fought by African Americans to defeat Hitlerism in Europe and second-class citizenship at home and demanded "Democracy in Our Time." The campaign and the war's effect aided the mass politicization of African Americans. Indeed, during the war years, membership of the NAACP grew exponentially. Historian Simon Topping notes that the NAACP "became more mass-based during the Second World War: in 1940 it had 50,000 members in 355 branches; by 1946 it had 450,000 members in 1,073 branches." Moreover, membership became "more representative" of the broader African American population.[55] The NAACP's growth in the war years is but one indicator of the war's effect. The significant increase in the circulation of leading African American newspapers further attests to the impact of the war. The 1940 commerce report, for example, illustrated that circulation of African American newspapers had increased from 600,000 in 1933 to 1.27 million in 1940.[56] The war accelerated demands for civil rights at home and injected renewed vigor into organized protests for significant and meaningful change. Increased demands for rights at home was read by many whites during the war years as an indication of disloyalty on the part of African Americans. A heightened determination to enforce and maintain the color line was evidenced by the level of violence directed toward African Americans. The "boiling racial cauldron" of the war years exploded in 1943. In that year alone, Fisk University recorded 242 clashes in thirty-seven cities.[57]

The pervasive nature of racism in the United States was something that Sarah discussed with frankness with Alvan and Louis. She neither sought to shield them from it nor disillusion them about how likely they were to encounter injustice and discrimination because of their color. Such discussions appear to have heightened Louis's interest in race relations in the United States. Sarah's efforts to prepare her children for the discrimination they would later encounter appears to have also informed Louis's decision to study in the South.

Louis excelled academically at his "integrated" school, English High in Boston. He notes that he had friends from various ethnic groups and that they all appeared to get along rather well.[58] His first love, however, was music, and the violin, in particular. Louis began receiving violin lessons at home at the age of five. His mother initially oversaw his study of the violin and insisted that his schoolwork take precedence over his love of the violin. Louis was by all accounts an excellent student, but his love of music dominated his time. He comments that "once I gained the love of my violin, my mother no longer had to require me to practice. Every free moment I had I would practice my craft. Sometimes I would practice four hours, five hours, and six hours at a time."[59] Louis firmly desired to seek out a career in music but Sarah insisted that he attend college. His choice to study in the South and in North Carolina was driven by a desire to "sense and feel what my brothers and sisters in the South were feeling."[60] Louis's biographer, Arthur Magida, notes that as a young student Louis was disinterested in his studies and relied heavily on his high school learning to get through the first two years of college. Louis confirmed this view in subsequent interviews with Jabril Muhammad when he reflected:

> My high school education was so superior that when I went to college, I never bought a book. I never was mentally challenged by anything that was being offered as a course of study. I went there because my mother desired that I have a fall back position, in case music failed.[61]

Louis did suffer some degree of racism. He noted, for example, in an interview with Henry Louis Gates that while traveling through Washington he was denied access to a movie theater and was told that "We don't sell tickets to Negroes." This encounter led Louis to pen a calypso entitled "Why America Is No Democracy!"[62]

Louis's studies and time in the South came to something of an abrupt end in 1955 when his high school sweetheart, Betsy Ross, discovered that she was pregnant. The pregnancy was unplanned and presented Louis with the dreadful prospect of telling Sarah that she was soon to be a grandmother. Louis has discussed this moment on few occasions noting that his mother did not think Betsy was "good enough"[63] for him and that it was "one of the worst days of my life."[64] The reasons for Sarah's objection to Betsy are unknown. Louis has never elaborated on his comments concerning his mother's objection. Louis, by his own admission, dropped out of college so that he could "make a living to feed my wife and my child."[65] The young couple were married by Rev. Nathan

Wright at Louis's childhood church and subsequently settled in Boston where Louis embarked on a career as a calypso singer.

Music had long been Louis's first love. In his early career he performed under the stage name, *The Charmer*. Louis decided on the name after being told by a group of people he had been entertaining during a performance in Canada that his performance "was so charming."[66] Louis's music career brought him into contact with numerous individuals including the NOI's charismatic minister Malcolm X. Louis's encounter with Malcolm occurred at a "famous hangout" known as the "Chicken Lane."[67] Despite the brief introduction, Louis was dismissive of the NOI and less than impressed by the NOI's message, which he initially understood to be about "hate." He notes:

> I came back home, I would sing in the nightclubs in Boston. Malcolm was preaching at that time, and I heard that he was preaching this hate against white people. I know white people that done us pretty bad, but I didn't want to be a part of any hate. One night I went to a very famous hangout which was called "The Chicken Lane." [Laughs.] Malcolm was standing in front of the door, I had to go right past him. I was introduced to this imposing man with his brown tan, brown coat, and brown gloves, and I really was a little afraid because of all the negative things I had heard. I shook his hand, immediately dismissed myself, and got into the ticket line. Then a friend of mine tried to get me to go to the temple. He said, "You know, Gene, the white man is the devil." I looked at him and I said, "If I go home tonight and my wife is in bed with a black man, she has committed adultery. If I pick up a gun and kill them, I have committed murder. Where is the devil in that?" He couldn't give me an answer. So I went on about my business. I wasn't about to join the Muslims.[68]

That Louis would conclude the group were "preaching hate" is entirely unsurprising. Media coverage of the Nation, even within the African American press, was notably unfavorable. Certainly, many construed the group to be harmful to the demand for rights at home.

Louis, like so many NOI converts, knew nothing of "orthodox" or traditional Islam. Indeed, so pervasive was ignorance of Islam in African American communities that many of Elijah Muhammad's converts considered NOI teachings as a legitimate representation of the faith.

Islam and Islamophobia both have a long history in the United States. As numerous Islamic studies scholars note, Muslims can trace their history in the

United States back to 1527. The number of Muslims living in the United States increased steadily with the arrival of West African slaves during the transatlantic slave trade. Estimates suggest that just under 10 percent of such enslaved people were practicing Muslims. Slave owners vastly restricted the ability of enslaved Muslims to practice and fulfill the obligations of their faith. Enslaved people were forcibly converted to Christianity though Baptism did not change their legal status. Enslaved Muslims left a number of lucid accounts of their experience of slavery in the United States.[69] These resources provide rich material and invaluable insights into their experiences. The constraints that slavery placed upon its victims coupled with the cultural genocide it created ensured that Islam was all but a distant memory among African Americans by the outset of the twentieth century. Moreover, immigrant Muslims in the early twentieth century did little to familiarize African Americans with traditional Islam.

Immigration from majority Muslim countries to the United States emerged in distinct waves with the first lasting from 1875 to 1912. Islamic studies scholar Herbert Berg notes that these immigrants "quickly assimilated" and that "none of these immigrants engaged in any significant or organized missionary activity with African Americans."[70] America's Muslim community totaled around 60,000 by the mid-1920s.[71] However, their collective priority was by no means proselytization among racial minorities. Kambiz GhaneaBassiri, for example, notes that many of these Muslims argued that "they should be considered white …" and that "ethnicity played a greater role than did Islam in shaping their sense of national belonging and their representation of themselves on the national stage."[72] Thus, efforts to convert African Americans to Islam were few and far between. Yet, the Ahmaddiyya movement did provide an English copy of the Qur'an and converted 700 Americans to Islam by 1923.[73]

Noble Drew Ali's Moorish Science Temple of America was one of the earliest movements in the twentieth century to actively appeal to and cater for African Americans. Historian Jacob Dorman's 2020 book, *The Princess and the Prophet*, revealed that Drew Ali was in fact a "veteran performer" earlier known as John Walter Bristor. Dorman notes:

> The tale of Walter Brister's metamorphosis into Noble Drew Ali has never been told because historians have been looking for the wrong person in the wrong places. A skilled magician who was adept at making people appear

to disappear, Brister faked his own death prior to his emergence as Noble Drew Ali.[74]

Ali founded the MSTA in 1913 and taught his thousands of followers that African Americans are "Asiatics" and "Moors" who could trace their ancestry back to the Canaanites.[75] He argued that Christianity "belonged to Europeans" and he firmly "rejected integration."[76] The MSTA suffered numerous divisions from within and ongoing power struggles blighted the community. Drew Ali's arrest and subsequent death in 1929 ensured that the MSTA fragmented shortly thereafter. The MSTA, though numerically small, played an important role in familiarizing African Americans with a variant of Islam. Indeed, as noted earlier, Fard Muhammad borrowed heavily from the MSTA's teachings and model of entrepreneurship.

Fard Muhammad's NOI emerged in Detroit in 1930. The small and unorthodox community borrowed their teachings from earlier separatist and nationalist movements. Their uniqueness lay in their beliefs regarding the innate goodness of Blacks and the inherent evil of Yakub's children. Fard amassed thousands of followers in Detroit by 1933. Prior to his disappearance in May 1933, he had effectively handed over the running of the group to Elijah Karriem (Muhammad) who he had personally appointed as a student minister.[77] The NOI fell into disarray following Fard's disappearance. Elijah's succession claims and subsequent incarceration on charges of draft evasion in 1942 fragmented the group. Elijah's wife, Clara, ensured the NOI's survival during her husband's incarceration. The NOI's membership fell drastically following his release from prison in Michigan. Marable suggests that the community had no more than 400 members by the time Muhammad was released.[78] Building the membership of the small community proved difficult. Though various small groups of followers could be found in several cities, the NOI was by no means a sizeable religious community when Louis encountered it. Indeed, his home temple in Boston had less than a dozen members in 1954.[79] The NOI sourced its funds directly from its small businesses and mandatory donations from its members. The annual Saviours' Day convention that celebrated the birth of its founder was also an opportunity to enhance finances through further donations from followers. Such donations to the community are still actively encouraged at the convention.

Louis's attendance at the 1955 Saviours' Day convention in Chicago came about after an invitation was extended from his friend, Rodney. Louis appears to have known little about the NOI beyond his earlier inclinations that it was a "hate" group. The Saviours' Day convention in 1955 proved life changing for Louis. He attended the event with his young family and was immediately separated from them upon entering the event in Chicago, as was normal process for male and female members. At the suggestion of Malcolm X, Louis was seated in the balcony area of the temple. Elijah's message and speech left Louis unimpressed to say the least. By his own admission he was dismissive of Muhammad until he addressed him directly, noting: "Brother, I didn't get that fine education that you got, when I got there the school door was closed … don't you pay no attention to how I'm saying it, you pay attention to what I'm saying then take it and put it in that fine language that you know."[80] Muhammad's comments frightened Louis and he came to believe that Elijah had read his mind until later discovering that Malcolm had advised Muhammad of Louis's attendance and potential. Indeed, in a recent lecture, Louis noted that Muhammad had instructed Malcolm to sit Louis beside the New York FOI captain Yusuf Shah so that he would know where to look when addressing him.[81] Betsy immediately got up to join the organization when the call for acceptances was given at the end of Muhammad's address. However, Louis was more reluctant and was in fact pushed to get up from his seat and join his wife after being shamed into doing so by his uncle. Betsy's decision to join the NOI independently of her husband is noteworthy and indicates that she was one of thousands of women to do so. Upon registering as an NOI member, Betsy and Louis both received their "X" to replace their slave names. Betsy began attending local NOI temple meetings back in Boston while her husband continued to travel and perform. Not until he realized how much time his wife was spending at the temple did Louis start to attend himself. It was not until Malcolm X visited the Boston Temple and invited Louis to provide his testimony in the temple that Louis began to take the NOI more seriously. His lack of initial commitment to the NOI may well stem from the fact that he was not a religious seeker—as many NOI converts were. In copious interviews, Louis has noted that he had little interest in changing his religion. While he has often conceded that he found the hypocrisy of white Christians more than troubling, he was not concerned with or troubled by the religion itself:

> I wasn't looking for a change in religion. I wanted a change in the status of black people. I was disillusioned with the Church. I couldn't understand why when Jesus would preach so much love, there was so much hate demonstrated by white Christians against black Christians.[82]

Louis's journey into the ranks of the NOI and leadership of the Boston Temple in 1957 was eased by the fact that he received little pushback or protest from his family regarding his membership in the NOI. As his earlier comments indicate, it was his uncle and his wife who shamed him into joining the faith community. Moreover, Sarah was accepting of his decision to become a follower of Muhammad's and no doubt recognized some of Garvey's teachings in what Louis relayed to her:

> When I decided to become a Muslim I went home to my mom. Now mom always did the talking; I always did the listening. But this time I said, "Mom, I don't want you to talk, I want you to listen. I ran down the history of what I had heard of how we were brought to America, the taking away of our names, our language, our culture and our religion, and how God had come to deliver us. When I had finished, I asked her, "What do you think, Mom?" She was a very reserved, strong woman, and she said, "It's very interesting," and didn't say yea or nay.[83]

Louis's conversion narrative is atypical for a number of reasons. First, as noted, he was not a religious seeker. Second, his early religious life was relatively positive, and he maintained a "love" for the church of his childhood. Third, the NOI's gospel of Black Nationalism and attacks on the church were not the driving force behind his conversion. Fourth, the NOI's membership was almost exclusively African American and thus Louis was certainly one of few West Indians to join the community. Lastly, his membership was not protested by his family. Thus, unlike other converts, Louis retained a healthy relationship with his family following his decision to join. Louis's love for the NOI and commitment to it were not immediate. Instead, it developed over time as his familiarity with and understanding of Muhammad's teachings developed. His conversion to the NOI changed the trajectory of his life but brought full circle the formative lessons of self-sufficiency and upliftment that he had been taught in his maternal home.

Louis's journey in to the NOI may be atypical but it was also something that his childhood lessons had helped direct him to. Sarah's modest commitment to Garveyite teachings and the church's reinforcement of lessons in racial upliftment and economic independence ensured that NOI norms were comfortably familiar to Louis when he embraced them more fully in Elijah Muhammad's NOI. Sarah was undoubtedly the most influential figure in Louis's life. She instilled in both her children a strong sense of racial pride and an understanding of the politics surrounding the US racial hierarchy. Understanding broader politics in the United States, Black America and the NOI later ensured Louis's elevation within the group. Accepting the teachings of the NOI in 1955 may have seemed inconsequential to Louis at the time. Unlike other NOI converts, the teachings of the NOI did not offer an immediate psychological "liberation" or instill in him a new sense of self and confidence.[84] The NOI's message of self-reliance, independence, and broader critiques of America sat reasonably comfortable with Louis. He was to spend the remainder of his life perfecting and marketing Muhammad's program and theology.

Notes

1 Abdul Wali Muhammad, "Nation Reflects on Death of Minister's Mother," *The Final Call*, December 30, 1988, 6.
2 John C. Walter, "West Indian Immigrants: Those Arrogant Bastards," *Journal of Black Studies*, vol. 5, no. 2 (September 2008): 2.
3 Farrakhan, "The Murder of Malcolm X: What Really Happened?" Speech delivered at Malcolm X College, Chicago, February 21, 1990.
4 "Louis Farrakhan on the Rock Newman Show," April 27, 2013.
5 Ibid.
6 Louis Farrakhan, "Justice or Else! The Twentieth Anniversary of the Million Man March: Main Address." Speech delivered at the U.S. Capitol Steps on the National Mall, Washington, DC, October 10, 2015.
7 Farrakhan, "A Saviour is Born for the Whole of Humanity."
8 Farrakhan, "The Murder of Malcolm X: What Really Happened?."
9 Jabril Muhammad, *Closing the Gap: Inner Views of the Heart, Mind & Soul of the Honorable Minister Louis Farrakhan* (Chicago: FCN Publishing, 2006), 325–6.
10 Ibid.
11 "Garvey Preaches Faith In Black God: Negro Leader Makes Plea for Free African Republic with a New Religion. Cheered By Big Audience Says White Man Can

Have America and Europe, But 'We Are Going to Have Africa,'" *New York Times*, August 4, 1924, 7.
12 Louis Farrakhan, "Have No Fear For the Future: The Future Is Ours: Part 1." Speech delivered at the Joe Louis Arena, Detroit, February 19, 2017.
13 Muhammad, "Nation Reflects on Death."
14 Michael J. Klarman, *From Jim Crow to Civil Rights: The Supreme Court and the Struggle for Racial Equality* (New York: Oxford University Press, 2004), 9.
15 Stephen Tuck, *We Ain't What We Ought to Be: The Black Freedom Struggle from Emancipation to Obama* (Cambridge, MA: Belknap Press of Harvard University Press, 2010), 145.
16 D'Weston Haywood, *Let Us Make Men: The Twentieth-Century Black Press and a Manly Vision for Racial Advancement* (Chapel Hill: University of North Carolina Press, 2018), 23.
17 Joe William Trotter, *The African American Experience* (Boston and New York: Houghton Mifflin, 2001), 381.
18 Ibid., 390.
19 Mark Ellis, "J. Edgar Hoover and the 'Red Summer' of 1919," *Journal of American Studies*, vol. 28, no. 1 (1994): 40.
20 Jan Voogd, *Race Riots and Resistance: The Red Summer of 1919* (New York: Peter Lang, 2008), 19.
21 Haywood, *Let Us Make Men: The Twentieth-Century Black Press*, 52.
22 Phillip Kasinitz, *Caribbean New York: Black Immigrants and the Politics of Race* (Ithaca and London: Cornell University Press, 1992), 19.
23 Nancy Foner, "West Indian Identity in the Diaspora: Comparative and Historical Perspectives," *Latin American Perspectives*, vol. 25, no. 3 (May 1988): 180.
24 Kasinitz, *Caribbean New York: Black Immigrants*, 24.
25 Magida, *Prophet of Rage*, 2.
26 Melissa E. Wooten and Enobong Branch, "Defining Appropriate Labor: Race, Gender, and the Idealization of Black Women in Domestic Service," *Race, Gender and Class Journal* vol. 19, no. 3/4 (2012): 302.
27 Tuck, *We Ain't What We Ought to Be*, 160.
28 John Henrik Clarke, "Marcus Garvey: The Harlem Years," *Transition*, no. 46 (1974): 14.
29 Nicholas Patsides, "Allies, Constituents or Myopic Investors: Marcus Garvey and Black Americans," *Journal of American Studies*, vol. 41, no. 2 (August 2007): 282.
30 Beryl Satter, "Marcus Garvey, Father Divine and the Gender Politics of Race Difference and Race Neutrality," *American Quarterly*, vol. 48, no. 1 (March 1996): 48.
31 "Garvey Preaches Faith in Black God."

32 Randall K. Burkett, *Religious Ethos of the UNIA in Cornel West and Eddie S. Claude, African American Religious Thought: An Anthology* (London: John Knox Press, 2003), 557.
33 Patsides, "Allies, Constituents or Myopic Investors," 283.
34 Ellis, "J. Edgar Hoover and the 'Red Summer,'" 48–9.
35 Louis Farrakhan Interview with Jamaica Radio, RJR Kingston, June 17, 1996.
36 Louis Farrakhan, *A Torchlight for America* (Chicago: Final Call, 1993), 110–11.
37 Louis Farrakhan, "The Black Man Must Do for Self or Suffer the Consequences," *The Final Call*, October 28, 1991, 21.
38 Louis Farrakhan, "Satan and the Mastery of Sexual Urges." Speech delivered at the Final Call Administration Building, Chicago, April 8, 1987.
39 Ibid.
40 Ibid.
41 Louis Farrakhan, "The Immeasurable, Limitless Value and Beauty of a Woman." Speech delivered at Mosque Maryam, Chicago, May 10, 2009.
42 Fatima Abdul-Tawwab, "Doing for Self: The Nation of Islam's Temple No. 11 and Its Impact on Social and Economic Development of Boston's African American community, 1948–1968" (MA Thesis, Temple University, 2001), 23.
43 Ibid.
44 Author telephone interview with representative from St. Cyprian's Episcopalian church in Boston, July 23, 2019.
45 Ibid., 24.
46 Farrakhan. "A Saviour Is Born for the Whole of Humanity."
47 Author telephone interview with representative from St. Cyprian's Episcopalian church in Boston, July 23, 2019.
48 Douglas Martin, "Nathan Wright Jr., Black Power Advocate, Dies Age 89," *New York Times*, https://www.nytimes.com/2005/02/24/obituaries/nathan-wright-jr-black-power-advocate-dies-at-81.html (accessed June 10, 2019).
49 "Boston Victory," *Jet Magazine*, April 2, 1959, 16.
50 Nathan Wright, Jr., *Black Power and Urban Unrest: Creative Possibilities* (New York: Hawthorn Books, 1967), 59.
51 *The Crisis*, May 1956, 269.
52 Minister Larry X, "To Serve His Own: Thumbnail Sketch of Minister Louis Farrakhan," *Saviour's Day 1981 Historic Souvenir Journal*, February 21–22, 1981.
53 Ibid.
54 Editorials, "Now Is Not the Time to Be Silent," *The Crisis*, January 1942, 7.
55 Simon Topping, "'Supporting Our Friends and Defeating Our Enemies': Militancy and Nonpartisanship in the NAACP, 1936–1948," *Journal of African American History*, vol. 89, no. 1 (Winter 2004): 17.

56 Ernest L. Perry, Jr., "It's Time to Force a Change: The African American Press' Campaign for a True Democracy during World War II," *Journalism History*, vol. 28, no. 2 (Summer 2002): 86.
57 Harvard Sitkoff, "Racial Militancy and Interracial Violence in the Second World War," *Journal of American History*, vol. 58, no. 3 (December 1971): 671.
58 Henry Louis Gates, "Farrakhan Speaks," *Transition*, no. 70 (1996): 146.
59 Muhammad, *Closing the Gap*, 111.
60 Gates, "Farrakhan Speaks," 146.
61 Muhammad, *Closing the Gap*, 109.
62 Gates, "Farrakhan Speaks," 146.
63 Farrakhan, "A Saviour Is Born for the Whole of Humanity."
64 Ibid.
65 Louis Farrakhan interview with Jamaica Radio, RJR, Kingston, June 17, 1996.
66 Ibid.
67 Gates, "Farrakhan Speaks," 148.
68 Ibid.
69 Berg, *Elijah Muhammad and Islam*, 11.
70 Ibid., 13.
71 Kambiz GhaneaBassiri, *A History of Islam in America* (New York: Cambridge University Press, 2010), 163.
72 Ibid., 164.
73 Berg, *Elijah Muhammad and Islam*, 19.
74 Jacob S. Dorman, *The Princess and the Prophet: The Secret History of Magic, Race and Moorish Muslims in America* (Boston: Beacon Press, 2020), 6.
75 Ibid., 15.
76 Ibid., 16–17.
77 Hakim, *The True History of Elijah Muhammad*, 39.
78 Manning Marable, *Malcolm X: A Life of Reinvention* (New York: Viking, 2011), 90.
79 Abdul-Tawwab, "Doing for Self: The Nation of Islam," 102.
80 Louis Farrakhan, "A Swan Song." Speech delivered at Mosque Marayam, Chicago, February 27, 2022.
81 Ibid.
82 Gates, "Farrakhan Speaks," 149.
83 Ibid., 148–9.
84 Dawn-Marie Gibson, "Making Original Men: Elijah Muhammad, the Nation of Islam and the Fruit of Islam," *Journal of Religious History*, vol. 44, no. 3 (September 2020): 2.

2

The Rise of Minister Louis Farrakhan

Louis found a receptive audience for his artistry within Elijah Muhammad's small Muslim community. The fruits of his creativity aided the NOI's broader promotional efforts and raised Louis's visibility within the religious community's close-knit hierarchy. Louis's most well-known works for the NOI were his early plays, *The Trial* and *Orgena*, and his music, particularly "White Man's Heaven Is a Black Man's Hell." His success with such works earned him a personal audience with Elijah Muhammad. Louis soon devoted himself entirely to the Boston Temple where he assumed the position of temple minister in 1957. His elevation within the community occurred amid the turmoil and upheaval produced by the Second Reconstruction and the NOI's exposure to national and international audiences. Such exposure intensified condemnation and persecution of the small Muslim community. Efforts to destroy the NOI from within met with some success. The fruits of which manifested in externally manufactured power struggles and attempts to discredit the legitimacy of the NOI's leadership. Malcolm X's exodus from the NOI in 1964 was no small feat for the NOI's tormentors. Louis's involvement in and contribution to Malcolm's exodus from the Nation was by no means insignificant. Yet, it is also true that he did not exercise the same influence in the NOI's structures to rival Malcolm or to be necessarily considered his heir apparent. Louis's rise within the NOI in the aftermath of Malcolm's exodus was hard won. His tireless efforts to rebuild trust in the NOI in Malcolm's former power base in Harlem were particularly impressive. Louis's involvement in the ploy to oust Malcolm from the community in 1965 came back to haunt him in 1975 when Muhammad's seventh son, Wallace, succeeded his father as the NOI's spiritual leader. Wallace quickly moved to transform the NOI into a Sunni Muslim and racially diverse body of believers. Louis was subsequently demoted and relocated. Yet, his time in service under Wallace was undoubtedly important in broadening his knowledge of Sunni Islam and connecting him with Black churches.

The Early Years in Boston

Louis's initial commitment to the NOI was questionable. Yet, in Boston he found a community of believers with similar interests in Black music and entertainment. The most detailed research on the early years of the Boston Temple was conducted by historian Fatimah Fanusie. According to Fanusie, the Temple was "formally organised in 1954 just one year prior to Louis's conversion."[1] As such, he found in Boston a small community of new believers and converts who however sincere were no less infants in their understanding of the NOI's belief systems. Fanusie notes that it was Boston's African American musicians who laid the groundwork for the formation of a NOI temple in Boston:

> Boston's Temple Number 11 represents a departure from the depression-era temples of the Midwest that previous scholars of the NOI have focused on and serves as a case study for the unique role of local musicians as both transporters and innovators of twentieth century religious and cultural ideas.[2]

Boston's first African American converts to Islam were not NOI adherents. Rather, they belonged to the Ahmadiyya movement. The Ahmadiyya movement was the most significant missionary group to appeal to African Americans and Jazz musicians. Boston's immigrant Muslim community had little direct contact with its African American neighbors. Islam, as presented and taught by Elijah Muhammad, was a religion that Boston's African American community knew little about.

Exposure and Persecution

The NOI's growth in the late 1950s was facilitated, in part, by the group's efforts to reach potential converts via the print press and the mass media. Historian Jamie J. Wilson notes that between 1956 and 1962 four leading

African American newspapers "featured over 300 weekly columns by Elijah Muhammad or Malcolm X."[3] The columns were published in the *New York Amsterdam News*, the *Pittsburgh Courier*, the *Los Angeles Herald Dispatch*, and the *Westchester Observer*. The press coverage of the NOI in African American newspapers differed significantly in tone and content. Thus, it would be wrong to conclude that all coverage was damning or critical. Indeed, in an article penned for the *Pittsburgh Courier* in 1956 Chicago Editor Ted Watson observed that "the followers of Islam in Chicago are part of some 500 million Moslems the world over … people from all walks of life have accepted the teachings of Islam in Chicago and have become owners of various business establishments."[4] Watson's apparent failure to distinguish between the teachings of Elijah Muhammad and those of "orthodox" Muslims was not unique. Moreover, his comments concerning NOI members venturing into business enterprises reflected the group's pro-ownership agenda. The NOI's outward appearance of Islamic legitimacy likely contributed to Watson's error. It is equally possible, however, that Watson chose to consciously overlook the NOI's more questionable teachings due to the *Courier*'s relationship with the NOI. Historian Patrick Bowen, for example, notes: "Watson and the Courier worked out an agreement with the NOI wherein they would publish a weekly column by Muhammad in exchange for having NOI members sell the newspapers on street corners."[5]

Watson's coverage of the NOI remained positive throughout 1957 also. In an article covering the annual Saviours' Day convention, for example, Watson described Muhammad as "a leader with exceptional power and influence" while also providing readers with a list of the NOI's then nineteen temples and their respective locations.[6] In short, Watson presented the NOI and its leader to his readers as a self-made man with a growing portfolio of properties and businesses. Such an image contrasted starkly with Muhammad's presentation as a "black supremacist" in other publications. Muhammad's column, "Mr. Muhammad Speaks," set out the NOI's theology and critiques of Christianity, as understood and practiced separately by African Americans and their white counterparts. In one such article in 1957, Muhammad noted that African Americans were "spiritually blind" and suffering as a result of a "wrong understanding of the Bible."[7] Moreover, in an article in 1959 he excoriated whites noting:

> Since the truth of the devils has been revealed, the devils are still trying to hide their true selves in order to fool the black man and woman and especially the American so-called Negroes, whom the white man has fooled for 400-years—and mean to keep them fooled regardless to the truth … white is not a superior color by nature to black, but it is inferior.[8]

Muhammad's censoring of whites and Christianity provoked a mixture of intrigue, condemnation, and praise. Readers used their voices to share their opinions on Muhammad and his community of believers. Indeed, despite the *Courier*'s relationship with the NOI, they did publish opinion pieces that denounced the group and condemned its theology. In 1956, for example, the paper published two letters to the editor in which Muhammad was accused of being a "fake." In one such letter Yusef Ahmad noted:

> It is a shame that so many people have let themselves be fooled by this man, Elijah Muhammad. Anyone with common sense should realise that the way he plays up the "race" angle in trying to win followers, he could not be anything but a fake. I would like to make it plain that Muslims in other parts of the world do not accept him or his followers as members of the Muslim brotherhood. By preaching race hatred and other things which are contrary to the principles of Islam, he has cut himself and his followers off from the Muslim world. It would be highly dangerous for any of them to get to any Muslim country … if they are foolish enough to try it.[9]

In the same issue, Abdul M. Fazl cautioned readers about Muhammad's teachings. He noted:

> In regards to the articles by the man who calls himself Elijah Muhammad, which appears in your paper, I would like to say that those articles do not reflect the true teachings of Islam. First of all, Islam is not a "race" religion, nor does it teach racialism. Muslims are taught to regard all men as equal in the sight of God. Anyone who desires to know the truth about Islam and what it teaches should write to: The American Fazl Mosque 2141 Leroy Pl., NW, Washington 8., DC.[10]

Such uncoordinated interventions by other Muslims proved insufficient at either delegitimizing the NOI or challenging its growing membership. Elijah Muhammad made occasional efforts to court Muslims beyond the fold of his own faith community. In 1957, for example, the NOI hosted a feast of the followers of Messenger Muhammad. About 2,000 individuals, including Muslim diplomats, attended the event.[11] Moreover, in late 1959 and early 1960, Muhammad made a lesser pilgrimage and traveled throughout Africa and the Middle East.[12] Muhammad's followers claimed that his reception in Muslim nations served as a clear rebuke to his critics in the United States.[13] Muhammad had intermittent dialogues with other Muslims including a Pakistani journalist, Abdul Bassit Naeem, whom he later employed at the *Muhammad Speaks* newspaper.[14] It is not clear, however, that Naeem's influence had any impact on Muhammad's own teachings or understanding of Islam.

The mass media exposure that the NOI needed to increase its reach and appeal arrived in 1959 when *The Hate that Hate Produced* aired. Historian Garrett Felber notes that the program was "singularly responsible for launching the NOI into national discourses of race."[15] The program ran for five episodes and included interviews with the NOI's leaders particularly Malcolm X. African American journalist Louis Lomax conducted the research for the program while Mike Wallace presented the series. The program was dramatically edited to highlight the NOI's most sensationalist aspects and to alarm viewers. Muhammad's small community of devout, unarmed, and hard-working followers were presented to the American public as radical black supremacists. Through the lens of Wallace and Lomax, the NOI appeared as a dangerous and less desirous alternative to the respected voices of the NAACP and the emerging mass civil rights movement. Condemnation from such voices disguised the growing willingness of their followers to entertain and even support NOI activities. Malcolm X addressed this predicament when he remarked:

> On the Mike Wallace program Roy Wikins was anything but in favour of our movement ... yet one of his members comes up and makes a donation of $100. Doesn't this show that even the efforts of Wikins and the others to discourage their members can not work ... We appeal to the little people on the street. The big people don't go along with us. They are afraid of losing respect of the white man which means loss of jobs and prestige.[16]

The NOI's presentation in the mainstream media proved troubling enough to convince Malcolm X and Muhammad in 1960 that the NOI should produce their own news organ in the form a newspaper entitled *Muhammad Speaks*. The newspaper served a number of purposes, which included challenging the group's image in the national media, promoting the organization's work, connecting members scattered across its 19 temples, and growing the community's financial prowess.[17] The newspaper succeeded expensive and short-lived NOI publications including *Supreme Wisdom* and *Messenger Magazine*. The newspaper was sold by the FOI and offered readers an inside look at Muhammad's growing community. The paper shared members' stories of conversion, advertised businesses and employment opportunities, offered advice to women, and set out the community's dietary and religious laws. In short, it offered a powerful corrective to the malign presentation of the group in the 1959 documentary. The paper offered all members of the community an opportunity to participate in the war to transform their image in the popular imagination of potential converts. In contributing their success stories and trials in the paper, rank and-file members made the community and its community of close-knit followers at once relatable and aspirational. It was in this context and with this understanding of the power of representation that Louis X developed the NOI's two most well-known plays, *Orgena* (A Negro Spelt Backwards) and *The Trial*.

It should be noted that there is some degree of debate over the authorship of Louis's plays. According to Louis, he wrote *The Trial* in 1956 and added to *Orgena* thereafter. However, Fanusie notes that several members of the Boston Temple were involved in the creation of the plays.[18] Regardless of the play's origins, it is evident that Louis received full credit for the success of the plays. *Orgena* was performed entirely by the Boston community of believers. The play, according to *Muhammad Speaks*, told the "true history of Afro-Americans." The three-hour musical offered viewers a "dramatization of the history, plight, and the 'prophetic salvation' of the American Negro." The first act of the play introduced viewers to what life in Africa was like prior to the arrival of "white colonial powers." *Muhammad Speaks* noted that this act in the play revealed that "the Negro once had a happy, prosperous, cultured and highly refined civilization." The play went on to present the experience of the Middle Passage in "particularly graphic" scenes.[19] *Orgena* was utilized by Louis and members of the Boston Temple as a didactic tool. The play offered an important corrective to popular representations of Africa as underdeveloped and to slavery as benign or paternalistic. In short, the play presented its audience with a revisionist and much-needed critique of ahistorical narratives that presented enslavers as saviors and Africa and its diverse populations as uncivilized. Louis's goals for *Orgena* were threefold. First, he used the play to educate and correct. Second, the play was an opportunity to encourage pride in and love for the African ancestry of its viewers. Third, it further propagated and vindicated Muhammad's attacks on whites, and lastly, it offered an outlet for the combined talents of the Boston community and its minister.

Orgena was followed by *The Trial*. The play was performed exclusively again by members of the Boston Temple and Louis starred as the prosecutor. The play presented a series of witnesses who testified against Mr. White Man. The key witnesses included an African character, Jomo Nkomo, a Native American character, Charlie Strongbow, and an African American woman, Thelna X Griffen, who described slave auctions and rape. Louis presented the charges to Mr. White Man as follows:

> I charge the white man with being the greatest liar on earth! I charge the white man with the being the greatest drunkard on earth … I charge the white man with being the greatest gambler on earth. I charge the white man, ladies and gentlemen of the jury, with being the greatest peacebreaker on earth. I charge the white man with being the greatest adulterer on earth. I charge the white man with being the greatest deceiver on earth. I charge the white man with being the greatest troublemaker on earth. So therefore, ladies and gentlemen of the jury, I ask you, bring back a verdict of guilty as charged.[20]

The Trial's judge and jury are exclusively Black. As such, Louis's play presented its viewers with an opportunity to witness a judicial process that was composed of their peers and where justice was delivered. This representation, of course, stood in stark contrast to the reality of the audiences' experiences of and encounters with the US justice system. The outcome of *The Trial*, as reported in *Muhammad Speaks*, is also noteworthy:

> The UNMASKED DEVIL then taunts the Negroes for having willingly followed him, telling them not to blame him for their troubles, but to blame themselves. He reminds them that their present plight is really their own fault, for he had no real power over them. He had never compelled them; he only called and they came. With shouts of "kill the beast, kill the beast,"

ringing in his ears, the audience goes wild as shrieking white devil, Mr. White Man, is led away by two huge African-Asian guards to be cast into the LAKE OF FIRE. (emphasis in original)[21]

The end of the play presented its audience with both a contrast and a challenge. Justice in this trial was delivered and thus the contrast, for the audience, was clear. The challenge was presented to the audience in the realization that Mr. White Man had "no real power." Thus, those who continue to fall under his influence are complicit in their own oppression and suffering. Here, Louis presents in dramatic terms Muhammad's indictment of whites and promise of justice for their victims. *The Trial* drew large audiences beyond Boston. According to *Muhammad Speaks*, an audience of 2,000 people attended the Christmas Eve performance of the play in 1960.[22] Both plays proved that Louis was a capable conduit through which Muhammad's teachings could be interpreted and relayed. Louis's efforts to perfect the performance of the star prosecutor did not end with his plays. Indeed, it is a role he has performed ever since.

Louis's performances and the successful delivery of the plays earned him a personal audience with Elijah Muhammad. The meeting between Louis and his teacher proved life changing in that it resulted in Louis giving up his music and the entertainment industry. Why Muhammad requested Louis's retirement on this occasion is unknown. He may well have sought to test his devotion or to guide his career in the NOI more closely. Louis recounted the request in a recent speech in which he noted that Muhammad remarked:

> "Brother, I was in the audience last night and I saw your performance, you're very good at what you do but your greatest gift is in the spiritual." He said, "would you give all of that up for me?" I said quickly "Yes sir," as if he might have been surprised that I answered so quickly. He said, "do you mean that you will give all of that up for me?" and I said it again, "Yes sir." And that was the end of my musical journey but the beginning of a spiritual journey that makes me the man that I am today.[23]

Louis's retirement from the entertainment industry reshaped his career and likely further fueled his complete devotion to the work of building and strengthening the Boston Temple. Louis's work at the temple earned him a place on the FBI's list of the NOI's "most active" ministers.[24]

Persecution

The NOI's heightened visibility and debate concerning its meaning for America in the local and national media intensified the FBI's efforts to monitor, disrupt, and discredit the group. Indeed, the bureau were so concerned about the tone of newspaper coverage of Muhammad and his followers that they included clippings from such papers in their investigative files. The file the bureau compiled on Elijah Muhammad and the Muslim Cult of Islam, for example, is replete with clippings from newspapers concerning the NOI. As noted elsewhere, the NOI proved difficult to infiltrate for several reasons. The religious community's ban on whites coupled with the fact that all but one of its national officials were family members made infiltration difficult. Indeed, the bureau observed in its profiles of NOI national officials that only John Ali (formerly John Simmons) was a non-family member among leaders. According to their intelligence, John joined the organization in 1954 and was a former accountant and part-time teacher and had previously served in the US army. According to Muhammad's son and grandson, Ali was an "opportunist," "completely untrustworthy," and "loose morally."[25] The bureau circumvented obstacles to infiltration and amassed a wealth of intelligence on the community. The bureau construed the group to be both fanatical and dangerous, and intent on overthrowing the government. In their description of the group, they noted:

1. The MCI is a fanatic Negro organization purporting to be motivated by the religious principles of Islam, but actually dedicated to the propagation of hatred against the white race. The services conducted throughout the temples are bereft of any semblance to religious exercises.
2. Organizationally, the MCI is a collection of autonomous temples bound by a tremulous personal relationship between the heads of the temple and the headquarters of the cult in Chicago, Illinois.
3. The MCI, although an extremely anti-American organization, is not at the present time either large enough or powerful enough to inflict any serious damage to this country; however, its members are capable of committing individual acts of violence.
4. The aims and purposes of the MCI are directed at the overthrow of our constitutional government, inasmuch as the cult members regard it as an

instrument of the white race; therefore, it is obvious that this group, as long as it retains the ideas now motivating it will remain an investigative problem for the FBI.[26]

The contents of the FBI's extensive surveillance files on the NOI and its leaders have been available to scholars and the public alike, via the Freedom of Information Act, for over two decades. The large sections of material that are heavily redacted leave questions about the extent of the FBI's, at times illegal, activities unanswered. However, the files do confirm that the bureau placed informants within the group and moreover placed them incredibly close to the community's spiritual leader. The files also evidence the extent to which the bureau was determined to destroy the community from within.

The FBI's intensified campaign of harassment and disruption coincided with the NOI's expansion, economic development, and newfound willingness to engage with larger societal discussions about race in the US context. Louis's career in the NOI in the early 1960s continued to blossom. Regardless of his growing stature and ambition, however, he remained very much subordinate to the community's first national minister, Malcolm X. Malcolm's work on behalf of Muhammad and his faith community earned him the adoration of thousands of rank-and-file members. According to Malcolm, Muhammad publicly lauded him as his "most faithful minister" at the 1963 Saviours' Day convention.[27] It is important to note, however, that the community's allegiance, and the allegiance of its ministers, lay with Muhammad and not Malcolm. Muhammad actively encouraged and enjoyed the cult of personality and loyalty that surrounded him. Likewise, his ministerial body and staff at the *Muhammad Speaks* printing plant encouraged complete and unquestioning devotion to Muhammad. Such devotion is evident in the articles, and in particular the poetry, that *Muhammad Speaks* printed. In one such poem, for example, Ruth X referred to Elijah Muhammad as "Allah, God to me."[28] Ruth's elevation of Muhammad to Allah in the above poem is particularly noteworthy. It suggests, for example, that by the time of its publication many NOI Muslims considered Muhammad to be equal to Fard Muhammad and therefore beyond question, refute or censure.

The adulation of women in the community likely facilitated and masked Muhammad's abuse of his female followers. It is not entirely clear when Muhammad's campaign of predatory abuse commenced. However, we know that his extramarital affairs with his female followers resulted in the births of illegitimate children during his time as the NOI's spiritual leader. It is evident that several ministers and confidants knew of his predatory behavior and consciously chose to turn a blind eye to the sufferings of Muhammad's victims. Extramarital sex was prohibited within Muhammad's community. Indeed, sexual immorality was punishable with expulsion. The silence of NOI ministers and affiliates regarding Muhammad's behavior is difficult to fathom. Fear of rebuke, punishment, or loss of position may well have been enough to silence those who were sickened by Muhammad's affairs. It may well also be the case that many assumed that Muhammad's actions were divinely ordained and therefore beyond criticism or questioning. It is important to note that it appears there was some precedent within the NOI for Muhammad's behavior. Erdmann Beynon's pioneering research on the NOI in the 1930s reveals that ministers were permitted to engage in extramarital relationships. This arrangement was limited to ministers of the faith and ministers alone.[29] Thus, it may be possible that Muhammad's behavior was condoned because there was an awareness that this was at some stage permitted in the community. Rumors regarding Muhammad's relationships began to surface within the faith community in the 1950s. Malcolm X recalls, for example, hearing "rumors" regarding Muhammad's relationships in 1955. Magida notes that Muhammad fathered children with six women who produced thirteen illegitimate children.[30] News of Muhammad's philandering reached Malcolm X via Muhammad's sixth son, Wallace. As noted by numerous scholars, Wallace relayed news of his father's transgressions personally to Malcolm following his release from prison on account of draft evasion. Marable's comments concerning the conversation that occurred between Wallace and Malcolm is particularly interesting. In his revisionist biography, for example, Marable notes that Wallace told Malcolm in 1963 that Muhammad's philandering was as "bad as it ever was."[31] Such comments indicate that news of Muhammad's abuse was not entirely new, and that Malcolm had therefore known of and remained silent about his spiritual father's penchant for young secretaries. Marable notes that upon hearing this news:

> Malcolm now had a choice. He could have stayed silent, continuing to give biblical and Qur'anic analogies to explain away Muhammad's errors in judgement. However, he felt a more aggressive approach was needed,

both to protect Muhammad and to stop the hemorrhaging of disillusioned members. He consulted with six or seven ministers whom he trusted. Among their number was, of course, Louis X- who knew more significantly more than Malcolm suspected. Malcolm's initial conversation with Louis about the Messenger's transgressions had occurred in New York; as was his custom after their meeting, Malcolm drove Louis to the airport. According to Farrakhan, as Malcolm was driving to LaGuardia airport, Louis casually told him that he would have to inform Muhammad that Malcolm had been discussing the infidelities with other ministers. There was a brief silence. Then Malcolm, looking straight ahead, said "Give me two weeks." Malcolm wanted to explain his contacts with NOI ministers about the scandal first. Louis consented to Malcolm's request.[32]

Marable's account of Malcolm's and Louis's conversation on the way to the airport is consistent with the latter's narrative of events, as expressed publicly in his 1992 lecture at Malcolm X college and numerous interviews in which he has repeatedly explained and sought to justify his actions.[33] It is likely the case that Louis was deeply concerned that news of the meeting would reach Muhammad via either another minister or the bureau. Thus, he may have wanted to protect his own position by assuring Muhammad, first and foremost, of his loyalty. Louis likely construed Malcolm's discussion with him as an effort to sabotage Muhammad's reputation or as revenge for his silencing, following unauthorized comments about President Kennedy's assassination. In a lecture from Mosque Maryam in 1992, for example, Farrakhan noted that Muhammad had silenced Malcolm in order to protect him "from being assassinated" and that Malcolm misconstrued Muhammad's motive. Moreover, he noted that Malcolm had referred to the women whom Muhammad had impregnated in Boston as "wives." Malcolm's revelations did not shake Louis's faith in Muhammad. Indeed, he recalls that when Malcolm asked him what he thought, he responded: "There is no God but Allah and Muhammad is his Messenger."[34] Louis's comments lack any indication that he was in any way disturbed by or anxious concerning his spiritual father's behavior. This may well be because he understood that polygamy is permitted in Islam or because he already knew of Muhammad's relationships and considered the women "wives" rather than vulnerable victims.

Malcolm's course of action following his discussion with Wallace can at best be said to be a serious error of judgment. Louis was very much Malcolm's junior at the time and therefore Malcolm may not have anticipated Louis's threat to tell Muhammad about the content of their meeting. Nevertheless, Louis and other ministers were also potential rivals to Malcolm and may well have questioned his devotion to Muhammad given that he had already disobeyed Muhammad's orders not to comment on Kennedy's assassination. Malcolm's relationship with the NOI's ministers and Muhammad continued to sour until he publicly announced his departure from the faith community in March 1964. In a telegram to Muhammad, published in the *New York Amsterdam News*, Malcolm laid the blame for his exodus solely at the feet of jealous ministers who sought to oust him:

> You are still my leader and teacher, even though those around you won't let me be one of your active followers or helpers. In order to save the national officials and Captain Joseph the disgrace of having to explain their real reason for forcing me out, I announced through the press that it was my own decision to leave. I did not take the blame to protect these national officials but to preserve the faith of your followers have in you and the Nation of Islam. I've never spoken one word of criticism to them about your family. I will always be a Muslim, teaching what you have taught me, giving you full credit for what I know and what I am. The present course I am taking is the only way I can circumvent their obstacles and still expediate your program.[35]

Malcom's telegram to Muhammad is noteworthy for several reasons. First, it suggests that Malcolm remained fully committed to Muhammad despite his predatory behavior. Indeed, this appears to have had no influence whatsoever in his decision to depart from the NOI. Second, it reveals that his exodus was forced not by Muhammad but by ministers such as Captain Joseph. Third, that he sought to assure Muhammad that rumors of criticism regarding his family were unfounded. Malcolm's telegram and some of his later comments to the national media indicate that he did not leave the NOI of his own accord. In a later article concerning death threats he remarked: "I never left the Muslim movement on my own. Those who envied my increasing successes conspired together to force me out."[36] Malcolm continuously pointed to Captain Joseph and his assistant Minister Henry X as two of the key figures in orchestrating his isolation from the NOI. Indeed, he alleged that Captain Joseph had since sent "Brothers from his 'special squad' out to try and kill me in cold blood."[37]

The NOI's campaign to discredit Malcolm continued after his departure from the community. Malcolm's embrace of Sunni Islam and efforts to establish his own religious and political organizations was clearly construed by the NOI as a potential threat. The NOI's efforts to remove Malcolm from his home in New York, which the NOI owned, and further efforts to harm him likely facilitated Malcolm's public censure of the NOI.[38] Such censure included public revelation of Muhammad's infidelities and efforts to discredit the NOI's theology. The NOI responded by launching a series of attacks on Malcolm through their publications. Indeed, dozens of articles in the *Muhammad Speaks* newspaper portrayed Malcolm as a hypocrite and traitor. In one such article, John Shabazz noted: "I would have referred to you as an 'Uncle Tom,' Malcolm, except that it would have been an insult to all the Uncle Toms on earth to class you with them. The worst Uncle Toms you yourself ever criticised look ten feet tall beside you now."[39] Attacks on Malcolm's character came from several NOI ministers and Malcolm's brother, who remained within the fold of the NOI. In a letter in the *Muhammad Speaks* newspaper, for example, Philbert referred to his brother as a "great user of people, especially women." In his attack, Philbert went on to suggest that Malcolm was suffering from the same mental illness that had afflicted his mother.[40]

The impact of the very public feud between Malcolm and his former mentor on rank-and-file NOI members is difficult to gauge. The community did not suffer a mass exodus of members and therefore it is likely that many chose to ignore Malcolm's public attacks. The impact on Muhammad's ministers is easier to assess. Indeed, many ministers were at pains to defend Muhammad and effectively demonize Malcolm. For his part, Louis has since portrayed himself as a child torn between two divorcing parents.[41] Yet, at the time, he very publicly rebuked Malcolm. Louis joined the choir of other ministers who sought to vilify Malcolm and defend Muhammad's reputation in the *Muhammad Speaks* newspaper. In an often-quoted article Louis wrote:

> Only those who wish to be led to hell, or to their doom, will follow Malcolm. The die is set, and Malcolm shall not escape, especially after such evil, foolish talk about his benefactor (Elijah Muhammad) in trying to rob him of the divine glory which Allah has bestowed upon him. Such as man as Malcolm

is worthy of death, and would have met with death if it had not been for Muhammad's confidence in Allah and victory over the enemies.[42]

Louis's attack on Malcolm nullifies his later suggestions that he was like a child caught between divorcing parents. Indeed, as the above-quoted article makes clear, Louis threw his full support behind the NOI's efforts to discredit Malcolm and to uphold Muhammad's reputation. Louis's article has often been misquoted to make it appear as though he was calling for Malcolm's death. Louis's depiction of Malcolm as a hypocrite was much in line with similar articles penned by ministers.

Malcolm's assassination at the Audubon Ballroom on February 21, 1965, and the implication of individuals associated with the NOI in his murder have forever damaged the NOI's reputation. As noted, it an accusation they have repeatedly sought to challenge.[43] Debates concerning responsibility for Malcolm's death have raged for decades. The NOI, under Farrakhan, have repeatedly laid blame for Malcolm's death at the hands of the FBI.[44] Their arguments are not without merit. Moreover, as noted earlier, recent revelations that the NYPD withheld evidence in the trials of Malcolm's alleged assassins have, if anything, added credibility to the NOI's position. Elijah Muhammad's reputation had clearly suffered somewhat as a result of Malcolm's very public exodus, assassination, and Wallace's brief departure. Yet, his community continued to grow, and by 1975 Muhammad had been awarded several accolades for recognition of the NOI's community work. The NOI's continued success was in small part due to the sacrifices and hard work of Muhammad's followers and ministers. It is also important to note, however, that the frustrations and failings of the Civil Rights Movement also played an important role in changing perceptions of Muhammad and his followers. Louis's sudden elevation within the NOI following Malcolm's assassination was not quite as glamorous as one might imagine. His appointment as national minister and minister of Harlem Temple Number 7 required much of the young minister.

Louis as First Minister

Louis's move to Temple Number 7 came at a time when the NOI's reputation was in ruins in Harlem. Far from basking in his appointment there, Louis was acutely aware that it would take much time and work to rebuild the trust and admiration of the community. Indeed, Louis once remarked that Muhammad told him that "New York will either make a man out of you or boy out of you."[45] Former NOI Temple Number 7 member, James Najiy notes that Louis's task in Harlem was "frightening" and that he was certainly not "a bundle of confidence."[46] Moreover, the work invited economic hardship and sacrifices on the part of his young family. In a lecture outlining his early struggles, for example, he remarked:

> For nine years as a Minister, I never bought a new suit, for nine years, I used to wear old suits, I don't know whether they came off a dead man or what … you should have seen your brother, I was a wreck. But I was a Muslim, I was jamming hard … The FOI had to get some money together to buy me a pair of shoes. Nine years I was like this, but I kept going. My wife couldn't have no new bedroom suit. We didn't have no money, I don't like debt. I don't like no white man telling me "You owe me."[47]

Louis's work as minister of Temple Number 7 and national minister followed a course similar to that of Malcolm's in that he oversaw the affairs of the temple, spoke on behalf of Muhammad, and represented the Muslim program to believers and nonbelievers alike. Louis's job was demanding but it also helped him to perfect his ministry and convey Muhammad's message to diverse audiences. Louis was acutely aware that rumors regarding his spiritual father's domestic life had the potential to damage the Nation's representation among Black women. In his early speeches concerning the NOI's gender norms, Louis emphasized to his audiences that women were the foundation of their civilization. In a speech in 1966, for example, he noted:

> The Honorable Elijah Muhammad teaches us that men are the builders of civilizations, but, that the woman is the foundation upon which a civilization is built. The family, which is the basic unit of a civilization, is built around the woman; therefore, anything that will destroy a woman is a destroyer of civilization. The so-called Negro has nothing to call a civilization. He can not even claim a peaceful home. Why? Because the unity between the black man and the black woman has been destroyed by the slavemaster. We realize that an oppressed people cannot gain freedom from a base of weakness. And we realize that our unity is basic to our strength. Thus, we must come to see the black man and woman have to come together in order to build a

lasting Nation. Mr. Muhammad teaches the black man that the woman is part of us—she is ourselves. Therefore, if the black man disrespects the black woman, he is divided against himself. As a consequence, our homes break down, and our attempt to build a civilization fails.[48]

Much like Malcolm before him, Louis accepted invitations from colleges and universities to address the matter of race relations in the United States and to defend the NOI's position of nonengagement with civil rights and Black Nationalist organizations. In 1971 Louis was invited to Wayne State University to address their student body. In an article concerning his lecture at the university, it was reported:

> He made it obvious that since the Honorable Elijah Muhammad is building schools, creating jobs, and providing food, clothing and shelter for his people in a way that excels the efforts of all the other leaders combined, then he must be the leader we are looking for. Concerning the non-violent movement and the Armed Revolutionary Movement, Minister Farrakhan proved that they were produced as a result of the white man's education. The white man has also fooled us into following dead leaders. This dynamic spokesman pointed out the way the white man cleverly uses his knowledge of tricks and lies to divide Black leaders against themselves here in North America in much the same way as he has already done in the Congo, Nigeria, Viet Nam, China, Korea and other places.[49]

Louis's remarks in this speech suggest that he sought out to present before his audience, tangible evidence of Elijah Muhammad's effectiveness as a leader. His remarks concerning the NOI's gains in building educational settings for their children and providing employment opportunities for members may well have contrasted rather sharply with the slow and less tangible grassroots gains made by civil rights activists. The speech also reveals that Louis was eager to demonstrate to his audience that the NOI was concerned about liberation struggles beyond America's borders. Thus, Louis, much like his predecessor, was cognizant of the fact that Muhammad's message could transcend borders and broaden the NOI's base of support.

Representing the teachings of Elijah Muhammad in educational settings no doubt helped challenge malign portrayals of the group in the national media. Moreover, such appearances may have contributed to more college-educated men and women joining the NOI. Indeed, in a discussion with Joe Walker in

1974, Louis noted: "In my travels throughout the country, I have noticed that Black students really want a Black Nation. They want to see the Black man free and independent. In the 1970's Black students are very enthusiastic in their response to the Teachings of the Honorable Elijah Muhammad."[50]

Louis's appearances at college campuses across the United States may well have aided the NOI's quest for respectability and recognition as an independent entity among the pantheon of civil rights and Black Nationalist organizations. Such recognition appeared to be increasingly forthcoming in the 1970s, in particular. For example, in 1974, the Mayor of Gary, Indiana, declared December 12–22 to be "Muhammad Week."

> WHEREAS, The Honorable Elijah Muhammad has for the past forty-three years worked for the development of a positive self-image and self-determination for the Blacks of America; and
>
> WHEREAS, Largely as a result of his teachings, American Blacks are increasingly becoming more independent in the areas of education, medicine and economics; and
>
> WHEREAS, The Honorable Elijah Muhammad has adamantly rejected all attempts to be co-opted either politically or morally; and
>
> WHEREAS, The Honorable Elijah Muhammad has built within the American society an independent national school system in order to enable Blacks to meet the standards of the civilized societies of the world without losing their heritage and in a manner worthy of universal and international recognition;
>
> NOW, THEREFORE, I, Richard Gordon Hatcher, Mayor of the city of Gary, Indiana, do hereby proclaim the week of December 15–22, 1974 "HONORABLE ELIJAH MUHAMMAD APPRECIATION WEEK" in the city of Gary.
>
> IN TESTIMONY WHEREOF, I have hereunto set my hand and caused to be affixed the great seal of the City of Gary, in the state of Indiana, this 13th day of … December …. 1974.
>
> RICHARD G. HATCHER
Mayor of Gary[51] (emphasis in original)

Similar accolades were awarded throughout the 1970s. In 1972, for example, the association of Black social workers presented Muhammad with a National Service award and in 1974 the Association of Black Psychologists also presented

Muhammad with an award.[52] Similarly, in 1975, Oakland and Berkeley declared January 26 The Honorable Elijah Muhammad day.[53] There can be little doubt that Muhammad yearned for such recognition. However, Louis was wary of the praise that the NOI was receiving. In 1975 the *Muhammad Speaks* newspaper offered a summary of a speech Louis delivered in Oakland in which he

> stressed that while Messenger Muhammad is being honored death hangs over America and that the more He is honored the more people will come to Him. But, he added, "The honor sometimes can be subterfuge to throw you off." He said the progress of the Honorable Elijah Muhammad is a threat to white America and yet they will honor Him … Minister Farrakhan again emphasized that as Blacks become more independent as producers and consumers of their own goods, the threat to the economic security of white America will appear more imminent. He urged Oakland Blacks not to again be taken in by the subtle tricks and games that could result in Blacks thinking that they have arrived at the valley of progress while having to come to the mountain top of great decision. Min. Farrakhan then noted that only one direction was left for Blacks now that all other entities have been destroyed. "And that's the Honorable Elijah Muhammad and the Nation of Islam," he said. "And you are not going to honor us to death or life; we are going to work ourselves to life."[54]

The unease Louis felt in regard to praise of his mentor from actors outside the faith community may also have been due to an awareness of the "tactics" employed by the bureau to monitor, disrupt, and infiltrate the NOI. Indeed, the community noted and made members aware of the FBI's campaign of disruption via articles and announcements in their newspaper. In 1973, for example, they noted that Muslims in Boston had been harassed by the FBI.[55] It is entirely unclear how aware NOI ministers were of FBI infiltration or influence in the group. Articles such as the aforementioned, however, indicate at the very least a basic awareness of the bureau's desire to disrupt the community and intimidate its members.

Louis's speech in Oakland was not the first or last occasion on which he addressed the apparent lessening criticism of the NOI and Muhammad. In part, he appears to have attributed the NOI's newfound acceptance as a result of the lesser influence of Jewish Americans in civil rights organizations:

> In 1959 Jews were in control of every major Black organization, the NAACP, the Urban League, CORE, SNCC, and SCLC headed by Martin Luther King. So, at that time, they were able to get Mr. Wilkins, Dr. Bunche, Thurgood Marshall, A. Phillip Randolph, Bayard Rustin, Martin Luther King, Whitney Young and others to speak against the Honorable Elijah Muhammad very strongly and very vehemently … but since that time, the Honorable Elijah Muhammad's positive accomplishments have silenced his critics and since that time, there has been a lessening of Jewish power and influence over the Blacks in these groups. The Black leaders are not able nor willing to speak against Messenger Muhammad as they did back in 1959.[56]

It is important to note that there remained widespread opposition to the growing recognition of the NOI among African American organizations. The various proclamations and service awards that Muhammad received did little to convince more conservative and politically orientated groups of the NOI's cause. In 1972, for example, the second National Black Political convention declined to extend an invitation for Louis to address their gathering.[57]

Elijah Muhammad's failing health resulted in Louis addressing more national and international audiences on his behalf. Such events afforded Louis the opportunity to develop a wealth of contacts in both professional organizations and to address international state actors. Behind the NOI's facade of respectability and growing acceptance, however, the faith community was beset by questions over Muhammad's successor, abuses by the FOI, and financial mismanagement. In his public addresses, Louis lauded and gloated over the love that NOI Muslims showed one another. In his address to the National Association of Black Social Workers in New York in 1973, he remarked:

> Elijah Muhammad is the greatest teacher of Black love that has ever stood in America. He is the only Black man to have gotten together thousands of Black people and welded them together in bonds of love and brotherhood. Muslims love each other, live for each other and die for each other. We don't look at you as non-Muslims but as Muslims too … we believe that all Black people are Muslims.[58]

In his public representations and defense of the NOI, Louis can at least be said to have been complicit in upholding an image of the faith community that was very far from the lived experiences and reality of some members.

Indeed, in later speeches, Louis acknowledged that the FOI had become a law onto itself. In his later efforts to explain the NOI's fall, for example, he reasoned that Allah had allowed the community to fall because it had lost the "love of the brotherhood."[59] Louis's position as a national minister should have enabled him to reign in the FOI or at least confront their abuses. It is entirely unclear whether he did so. Indeed, Louis's rather intense schedule of speaking engagements alongside managing the administration and affairs of Temple Number 7 may have precluded him from dealing with the FOI.

1975 was a year of deeply personal highs and lows for the NOI's first national minister. In January 1975, Louis traveled to his father's country of birth to present the NOI's program and Muhammad's message to Jamaicans. Louis was part of a NOI delegation to present the NOI to the Caribbean. During his brief time in Jamaica, he appeared on the television show *Focus* and spoke at a rally for Muhammad Ali.[60] Only weeks later, two of his daughters married into Elijah Muhammad's family.[61] The personal joys of the early months of 1975, however, were followed by a tragic and irreplaceable loss for Louis. The death of Elijah Muhammad on February 25 and the succession of his son, Wallace, profoundly impacted Louis, his faith, and his family.

The Fall of the NOI

Wallace Muhammad officially assumed leadership of the NOI at the 1975 Saviours' Day convention. His succession came at a time when the faith community was already divided somewhat along theological lines.[62] Wallace was known within the community for his adherence to Sunni Islam. He demonstrated little tolerance for the NOI's unconventional beliefs and disliked the abuses and flamboyance of some NOI staff and senior FOI figures, in particular. Wallace's succession effectively ended the NOI's isolation from the American Muslim community. Indeed, Wallace introduced structural reforms and imposed Sunni Islam at rapid speed. His path to doing so was made easier by a number of actions including his decision to disband the FOI, cap ministerial salaries, remove ministers from NOI business enterprises, and relocate ministers who could effectively challenge him. In many ways, Louis's career and livelihood as a NOI minister was a casualty of Wallace's succession. The former prodigal son's inheritance of his father's position in 1975 ended Louis's career within the community.

Wallace's succession was never approved publicly by Elijah Muhammad. Muhammad had refused for many years to either privately or publicly nominate a successor. He remarked that it was foolish to try to "designate" someone to replace him because he was appointed by God.[63] As such, the Royal Family's decision to select Wallace as their father's successor was never one that could be said to be officially sanctioned. Wallace's succession ensured that their father's wealth and property would remain within the family. Moreover, it provided the family with some reassurance that the NOI's theology would be significantly amended in order to bring the community into relationship with other US and non-US Muslim groups. The former prodigal son's ascension was something of a surprise to a number of NOI ministers, members, and outsiders. After all, it was Louis who had represented the NOI nationally and internationally since 1965. The fact that the Royal Family overlooked Louis as a possible successor is telling. Wallace's succession was even more surprising for some given that he had been suspended from the faith community on a number of occasions by his father.[64] Indeed, some scholars have suggested that Wallace's succession was desired and aided by the FBI. Islamic studies scholar Edward Curtis IV, for example, remarked:

> In 1968, the FBI's field office in Chicago identified Wallace Muhammad as "the only son of Elijah Muhammad who would have the necessary qualities to guide the NOI in such a manner as would eliminate racist teachings." How much the FBI actually assisted Wallace in his bid for the position cannot be known due to key deletions in their files. But the Bureau seemed to do what it could. In a January 7, 1969 letter from the Director's office to Chicago Agent Marlin Johnson, a Bureau official stated that after the death of Elijah Muhammad "a power struggle can be expected … We should plan now to change the philosophy of the NOI to one of strictly religious and self-improvement orientation, deleting the race hatred and separate nationhood aspects." The Bureau also reiterated that it viewed Wallace Muhammad as uniquely qualified to fulfil this task.[65]

The extent to which the FBI may have aided Wallace's succession remains largely unknown. It is evident, however, that his succession was the most desirable outcome for them. Wallace provided clear indications of the sweeping changes he would make as the NOI's new spiritual leader just days after his father's death. At the 1975 convention, he noted:

> I want you to know we are not a people to harp upon color and racism. The Honorable Elijah Muhammad says this is not a race; He says this is a nation … The Honorable Elijah Muhammad is a mind, a spirit, a morality, that is from God Almighty, that is filling the Nation of Islam, that is called a nation because a new people are coming into birth, who start of like an Adam and an Eve, and grow into a family and into a tribe, and on and on into a nation. This is a nucleus; this is a beginning; this is a small community, but the nation of Islam is the whole earth … this is a house formed by knowledge, and men of knowledge just don't fall down to the floor and weep and moan and cry like babies when the wind of emotion comes.[66]

Wallace's speech at the convention sought to forewarn the faith community that change was imminent. His comments relating to color and racism, for example, clearly indicated that his father's censure of whites would not be part of the NOI's discourse moving forward. Moreover, his remarks relating to the community's size and new beginning suggested that an evolution within the community should be expected. The rather matter of fact tone of Wallace's remarks contrasted sharply with Farrakhan's tears at the event. Indeed, Wallace's speech is also noteworthy for the complete lack of emotion or feeling it communicated.

Wallace addressed questions over his ascension in the weeks that followed his speech in an interview with the *Muhammad Speaks* newspaper. In an interview that covered questions relating to his father's death, potential schisms, and his grooming, Wallace offered confident reassurances that he was born to one day lead the community:

> The Honorable Elijah Muhammad was a wise leader. And a wise leader does not make death a question in the minds of the people, or put this question constantly in the minds of the people. He did, however, mention his passing, but as hints to the wise. He also said that He would not die, that He would live and be with His God in the end … I have been groomed because it was necessary … He prepared and taught many. He prepared and taught each member of His immediate family and many outside of the immediate family who are also members of the family … But there was never any doubt in His mind that I would be the one who would come to this office.[67]

The theological reforms that Wallace introduced were immense, far reaching, and swift. Wallace's personal journey to Sunni Islam commenced during his time as a minister in his father's community. Indeed, his father punished his theological diversions with suspension. Wallace sought to guide his father's faithful away from the community's founding doctrine and justified the new theological teaching as in line with his father's wishes. Wallace found introducing Sunni Islam more difficult than structural reforms because it involved telling members that his father was not a Messenger of Allah.[68] Wallace sought out to remake the community in the eyes of its followers and outsiders. As such, he renamed the community, the World Community of Al-Islam in the West (WCIW) and instructed members to refer to themselves as Bilalians. It appears that this term was employed as it was a direct reference to Bilal Ibn Rabah, a Black companion of Prophet Muhammad. In honor of this new ethnic term, the *Muhammad Speaks* newspaper was renamed, *Bilalian News*. The introduction of Sunni Islam brought with it a clear need to open the community and membership to others. While it is fair to say that whites did not rush to join the community in large numbers, the community did highlight the conversion and membership of whites in their publications. In a September 1977 issue of *Bilalian News*, for example, the conversion and membership of a white couple, Gary Paarlberg and his wife, was highlighted. In an interview with the paper, Paarlberg noted:

> Joining the WCIW gives me an opportunity to learn both about the faith of Islam and to educate myself with the problems of contemporary America. I want to take this opportunity to make an expression of public gratitude for the way the people at the masjid have so kindly accepted us. The great friendliness they have shown from the very beginning, from my very first visit, and all the help and kindness they have given us is very truly appreciated.[69]

The welcoming of members such as Paarlberg evidenced the faith community's evolution and quickened their efforts to move beyond their history of race baiting, criticism of the US government, and embrace and acceptance of their rights as US citizens.

Wallace's rather formal approach to leadership was evident in the manner in which he introduced sweeping reforms. The structural and theological changes he introduced were carefully and very clearly designed to transform the community to a point where it was no longer recognizable. Wallace anticipated resistance to such change from the FOI and his father's ministers. As such, he disbanded both the FOI and MGT and relocated or demoted ministers who might seek to stage a coup.

Wallace's disdain for the FOI was evident throughout his time as a minister in the NOI. Indeed, he referred to the group in unfavorable terms and clearly disliked several leading FOI figures.[70] His decision to disband the FOI and the MGT was delivered in the same formal manner in which other significant changes were arrived at. The MGT and the FOI were important spaces in which NOI members could work together and support one another. While it is true that some captains were known to be abusive, it is also the case that for many members the MGT and the FOI provided structure, routine, a place of belonging, and a sense of purpose. Disbanding both structures enabled Wallace to weed out abusive captains and remove long-standing hierarchies within the community. In doing so, Wallace also mitigated potential attempts for his adversaries to unseat him. Indeed, it is notable that few high-profile defections occurred.

Wallace was acutely aware that some of his father's senior ministers, including Farrakhan, were wary of him. As such, he sought to strategically relocate some of his father's most loyal aides, including Farrakhan and his associates in New York. In the months that followed his succession, Wallace relocated Farrakhan, his former assistant in Harlem, Larry Muhammad, and the New York FOI captain, Yusuf Shah. Farrakhan was relocated to Detroit and Larry (then known as Karriem Abdel Aziz) was sent to as a minister and administrator. Aziz was kept busy with the affairs of the Chicago followers and with international travels on behalf of the community. Indeed, between 1975 and 1976, Aziz traveled to a number of countries including Saudi Arabia, Barbados, Trinidad, and Algeria. Publicly, Aziz and Farrakhan praised Wallace's work. In issues of the community's newspaper, Farrakhan lauded the changes Wallace introduced:

> These changes demonstrate the Honorable W.D. Muhammad's honesty, integrity, and moral character. These changes also demonstrate the ability of membership of the Nation of Islam to accept these changes and come

more strongly behind the dynamic leadership of the Honorable W.D. Muhammad.[71]

Likewise, Aziz noted in a 1976 issue of the paper that the changes Wallace introduced had been "positive":

> The Chief has taught us that the real "you" is the inner person, the mind. He has rapidly accelerated the growth of the individual. He has actually pushed us out into the greater community, telling us, "Your service is not just to Muslims because if you believe in God, then know that God is concerned with all of humanity."[72]

Public praise of the theological and structural reforms may well have helped other believers to follow Wallace. Privately, however, some ministers struggled to stomach the changes. In a later speech regarding the reforms, Minister Farrakhan conceded that by the time he was relocated to Detroit he had lost himself and purchased guns.[73] Farrakhan publicly accepted the embrace of Sunni Islam. It would be wrong, however, to suggest that he himself was a convert to Sunni Islam.

Louis did embrace and approve of some of Wallace's initiatives. Indeed, he actively sought out the fellowship and assistance of Christians in Wallace's new initiative: the Committee for the Removal of All Images of the Divine (CRAID). CRAID was an interfaith initiative and as such brought Farrakhan into frequent contact with African American churches. It required the active support and willingness of Christians to remove images of God from their various churches. Farrakhan proved to be a popular speaker at Black churches. As part of his work for CRAID, for example, he was invited to address Christians at First Baptist Church of Rocky Mount in Virginia and Norfolk's Unitarian Church. Minister Farrakhan's interfaith work was reported in early copies of *Bilalian News*. Such articles indicate that he was popular with Christian audiences and that he had found favor with members of Rev. Jesse Jackson's Operation PUSH (People United to Save Humanity).[74] Minister Farrakhan's time in CRAID evidenced the willingness of Black Christians and clergy to work alongside former NOI members on programs that were considered to be mutually beneficial. It appears that Minister Farrakhan particularly relished this work. Indeed, interfaith outreach among African Americans would later become a preoccupation for him.

Despite his success with CRAID, Wallace was particularly cautious of Farrakhan. It appears he sought to neutralize his authority by removing his key aides firstly from New York and then sending him to the Caribbean to spread the WCIW's teachings. According to Farrakhan's former assistant in Harlem, Wallace was reluctant to utilize Farrakhan's talents but agreed to his deployment to the Caribbean. Farrakhan's time in the Caribbean came to a swift end when it was reported that he had cursed at someone who had criticized Elijah Muhammad.[75] In a subsequent meeting with Wallace, Farrakhan told him that he agreed with 60 percent of his teachings but did not agree with the remaining 40 percent. In response, Wallace is alleged to have told him that he should concentrate on teaching the 60 percent he agreed with and offered him five mosques at which he could minister. Farrakhan declined the offer stating that he feared that while teaching it would become apparent to an already "confused people" that he did not subscribe to Wallace's teachings. At that point, Farrakhan informed Wallace that he planned to go back to show business and end his career as a minister.

Farrakhan's time in service to Wallace was trying at best. He both publicly and privately accepted Wallace's leadership because he felt less than adequate to challenge him.[76] Such feelings of inadequacy may well have stemmed from the fact that Wallace was more well versed in the Islamic faith. Moreover, Wallace was Muhammad's biological son and challenging him could well have resulted in schisms in the faith community. Farrakhan did not subscribe to or agree with Wallace's move away from NOI teachings. Yet, for the sake of the community he kept his reservations and disappointments private. Such disappointment was felt by other ministers and members. The extent to which the reforms diluted or altered Farrakhan's faith is difficult to determine. It is clear, however, that the NOI's transition left him longing for a return to his pre-NOI life. Farrakhan's departure from the WCIW did not result in a mass exodus from the community. Indeed, it appears that Wallace was rather successful at neutralizing his powerbase. Minister Farrakhan left the WCIW with little intention of rebuilding the work of his spiritual mentor. Yet, at the prodding and intervention of his friends, particularly Jabril Muhammad, he determined that his life's mission was to continue and surpass the work of Elijah Muhammad. The decision to do so came during a brief trip to Mecca, which Farrakhan has at least publicly said little about. In setting out to rebuild the NOI, Farrakhan put himself on a collision course with the WCIW, Sunni Muslims in the United States, and the US government. Rebuilding Muhammad's work would consume the rest of Farrakhan's life.

Notes

1. Fatima Fanusie and Beboppers Ahmadi, "Veterans and Migrants: African American Islam in Boston, 1948–1963," in *The African Diaspora and the Study of Religion*, ed. Theodore Trost (New York: Palgrave, 2008), 40.
2. Ibid., 50–1.
3. Jamie J. Wilson, "Come Down Off the Cross and Get Under the Crescent," *Biography*, vol. 30, no. 3 (Summer 2013): 494.
4. Ted Watson, "The Rise of Muhammad Temple of Islam: Hard-Working, Thrifty and Dedicated Moslems in Chicago Are Showing a New Side of This Movement in America," *Pittsburgh Courier*, April 7, 1956, 3.
5. Bowen, *A History of Conversion to Islam in the United States, Volume 2*, 447.
6. Ted Watson, "Activity Plentiful at Muslim Convention in Chicago," *Pittsburgh Courier*, March 16, 1957, 20.
7. Elijah Muhammad, "'Mr. Muhammad Speaks': Jesus' History Misunderstood by the Christians," *Pittsburgh Courier*, November 9, 1957, 10.
8. Elijah Muhammad, "Mr. Muhammad Speaks," *Pittsburgh Courier*, July 4, 1959, 14.
9. Yusuf Ahmad, "Voice of the People—What Courier Readers Think: Thoughts on 'Muhammad Pro and Con. Is Mr. Muhammad a 'Fake'," *Pittsburgh Courier*, August 18, 1956, 10.
10. Ibid.
11. Marable, *Malcolm X*, 131.
12. Gibson, *A History of the Nation of Islam*, 47.
13. Ibid.
14. Abdul B. Naeem, "Explains Importance of and Reasons for Ignoring Muhammad's Critics," *Muhammad Speaks*, December 9, 1966, 19.
15. Felber, *Those Who Know Don't Say*, 18.
16. Garrett Felber, "Muslims Meet at St. Nick Arena," *New York Age*, August 1, 1959, 4.
17. Dawn-Marie Gibson, "Nation Women's Engagement and Resistance in the Muhammad Speaks Newspaper," *Journal of American Studies*, vol. 49, no. 1 (February 2015): 5.
18. Geoffrey Lokke, "The Muslims Present Orenga," *The Drama Review*, vol. 62, no. 2 (2018): 81.

19 Geoffrey Lokke, "Orenga Tells True History of Afro-Americans," *Muhammad Speaks*, December 1960, 7.
20 C. Eric Lincoln, *The Black Muslims in America* (Boston: Beacon), 1961.
21 C. Eric Lincoln, "'The Trial' Becomes Broadway Smash Hit," *Muhammad Speaks*, December 1960, 10.
22 Ibid.
23 Louis Farrakhan, "The Criterion: Worldwide Address." Speech delivered in Michigan, July 4, 2020.
24 "Muslim Cult of Islam FBI File: Part 3 of 3. IV: Leadership." Section A: National Officials, 29.
25 Ibid., 12.
26 "Muslim Cult of Islam FBI File, Part 1 of 2." Part B: Conclusions, iii.
27 Gibson and Karim, *Women of the Nation*, 15.
28 Sister Ruth 4X, "Elijah," *Muhammad Speaks*, October 7, 1966, 7.
29 Beynon, "The Voodoo Cult among Negro Migrants," 902.
30 Magida, *Prophet of Rage*, 76.
31 Marable, *Malcolm X*.
32 Ibid.
33 Farrakhan, "The Murder of Malcolm X: The Effect."
34 "Farrakhan speaks on Malcolm X's separation from the Honorable Elijah Muhammad." YouTube.
35 "Telegram to Muhammad," *New York Amsterdam News*, March 14, 1964, 1, 51.
36 "Malcolm X Tells of Death Threat," *Amsterdam News*, March 21, 1964, 50.
37 Ibid.
38 Gibson, *A History of the Nation of Islam*, 64.
39 John Shabazz, "Open Letter: Muslim Minister Writes to Malcolm," *Muhammad Speaks*, July 3, 1964, 9.
40 Philbert Muhammad, "Malcolm Exposed by His Brother," *Muhammad Speaks*, January 15, 1965, 15.
41 Farrakhan, "The Murder of Malcolm X: The Effect."
42 Minister Louis X, "Malcolm-Hypocrite," *Muhammad Speaks*, December 4, 1964, 15.
43 Muhammad, *"But, Didn't You Kill Malcolm?"*.
44 Gibson, *A History of the Nation of Islam*, 120.
45 Louis Farrakhan, "Let Us Make Man." Speech delivered in New York, 24 January 24, 1994.
46 James 7X Najiy, *The Nation of Islam's Temple #7 Harlem, USA: My Years with Louis Farrakhan and Malcolm X* (Atlanta: Rathsi Publishing, LLC, 2012), 215.
47 "Farrakhan Goes In! Talks about His Early Days as a Muslim." YouTube (accessed June 5, 2021).

48 "Young Gallowshaw's Mother Strengthened by New York Minister's Womanhood Talk," *Muhammad Speaks*, October, 21, 1966, 8.

49 Herman L. 2X, "Farrakhan Tells Wayne State Students of the Right Leader," *Muhammad Speaks*, June 4, 1971, 15.

50 Joe Walker, "College Students, Professionals Coming to Nation of Islam," *Muhammad Speaks*, February 3, 1974, 3.

51 James Hoard Smith, "'Muhammad Week' Proclaimed in Gary, Ind.," *Muhammad Speaks*, December 27, 1974.

52 Gibson, *A History of the Nation of Islam*, 68.

53 C. Lawrence X, and James Hoard Smith, "The Honorable Elijah Muhammad Day: Oakland and Berkeley Deliver Simultaneous Proclamations," *Muhammad Speaks*, February 14, 1975, 7.

54 C. X. Lawrence X and James Hoard Smith, "Farrakhan Warns Blacks 'Stay Vigilant,'" *Muhammad Speaks*, February 14, 1975, 7.

55 Kamal Majied, "FBI Fear Tactics Wasted on Muslims," *Muhammad Speaks*, June 15, 1973, 4.

56 Joe Walker, "Media Attempt to Undermine Muslim Progress Exposed," *Muhammad Speaks*, February 1, 1974, 3.

57 James Hoard Smith, "Delegates Get Disturbed Over Snub to Farrakhan," *Muhammad Speaks*, April 5, 1974, 10.

58 Joe Walker, "Farrakhan Addresses Conference," *Muhammad Speaks*, May 11, 1973, 3.

59 Louis Farrakhan, *The Meaning of F.O.I.* (Chicago: Elijah Muhammad Education Foundation, 1983), 18.

60 "Farrakhan in the Caribbean," *Muhammad Speaks*, January 24, 1975, 29.

61 Mary Eloise X, "Two Great Families Unite," *Muhammad Speaks*, February 14, 1975, 4.

62 Gibson and Karim, *Women of the Nation*.

63 Elijah Muhammad, "Victory of the Apostle," *Muhammad Speaks*, January 15, 1965, 3–4.

64 Gibson, *A History of the Nation of Islam*, 74.

65 Curtis, *Islam in Black America*, 112–13.

66 Annual Muslim Convention, 1975. Chicago, Illinois (FBI File: E. Muhammad, Section 16).

67 "First Official Interview with the Supreme Minister of the Nation of Islam, The Honorable Wallace D. Muhammad," *Muhammad Speaks*, March 21, 1975, 3.

68 "Valerie Linson, Inheritors of the Earth: This Far by Faith" (PBS, 2003), DVD.

69 "Study of Al-Islam Wins New Convert," *Bilalian News*, September 9, 1977, 12.

70 Gibson, *A History of the Nation of Islam*, 81.

71 "Unity, Stronger Than Ever," *Bilalian News*, March 19, 1976, 15.

72 Malik S. Hakim, "Serving the Community," *Bilalian News*, February 11, 1977, 13.
73 "Farrakhan Goes In! Talks about His Early Days as a Muslim." YouTube.
74 Gibson, *The Nation of Islam, Louis Farrakhan*, 125.
75 See, for example, Akbar Muhammad's comments in "Rebirth series," Never Fall Again Studios.
76 Muhammad, *Closing the Gap*.

3

Atonement

The NOI's transition in 1975 profoundly impacted Minister Farrakhan, his colleagues, and rank-and-file members. Indeed, Farrakhan has often spoken of the Nation's fall as a time in which he suffered "mentally."[1] The sheer pace at which Elijah Muhammad's theology was discarded left countless NOI members and ministers disillusioned and "confused."[2] Minister Farrakhan's decision to rebuild the work of Elijah Muhammad in 1977 came after a short time in Mecca and at the bequest of former ministers whom he trusted dearly. A number of these individuals are still part of his inner circle today. Minister Farrakhan came to see himself during this time as Muhammad's rightful successor and as a divinely appointed "warner" to the US government.[3] Earlier feelings of inadequacy dissipated when he came to reflect more deeply on Muhammad's public remarks at the 1972 Saviours' Day convention in which he referred to Farrakhan as one of his "strongest national preachers." Moreover, he remarked: "Everywhere you hear him, listen to him. Everywhere you see him, look at him. Everywhere he advises you to go, go."[4] Farrakhan's belief that he was Muhammad's chosen heir was further solidified in 1985 in Mexico when he encountered Muhammad in what was a profound religious experience for him. The destruction of the NOI's former structures and theology made any attempt at rebuilding the faith community problematic. Wallace had discredited the NOI's theology as heresy, both publicly and privately, and members either accepted Sunni Islam, lost faith altogether, or returned to the religion of their pre-NOI life.[5] Farrakhan spent a significant period rethinking, reflecting upon, and effectively reinterpreting Muhammad's theology before presenting it to potential members. The theology and structures that Minister Farrakhan instituted in the RNOI resembled closely those of the original community. Yet his faith community is also in many ways far removed from its earlier incarnation. Minister Farrakhan's willingness to engage in interfaith work, build political alliances, and set aside, when inconvenient, earlier NOI dictates enabled him to court a new generation of recruits. His ability to relate to and intimately understand the frustrations, anxieties, and aspirations of young Black men and women ensured that by 1995 he was a significant and influential religious actor and leader in his own right. The RNOI's success was helped along by the regressive racial climate of the 1980s and the subsequent failures of the New Democrats. Minister Farrakhan's road to national prominence with the MMM in October 1995 was paved with sacrifice, years of unpaid work, personal security risks, and a significant, though uncoordinated, effort on the part of the US media to isolate him. Yet his work and words continued to resonate deeply with his audiences. Minister Farrakhan's popularity owed much to the fact that he situated his faith community in no man's land. Indeed, the RNOI and its members belong neither to the American ummah (Muslim community) nor to the world of the Black church. Rather, they move fluently between both.

Reinterpreting and Rebuilding: The Early Years

Rebuilding the NOI caused Minister Farrakhan significant hardship. The bulk of his former followers in Harlem had been scattered as a result of the actions of Imam Mohammed. Moreover, he had neither the manpower, resources, nor networks required to successfully relaunch the NOI. Farrakhan utilized the power of the African American press to promote, explain, and justify the rebuilding of his spiritual father's work. In a series of articles penned for the *Chicago Defender* between 1977 and 1979, Minister Farrakhan set out his mission and critiques of existing relations between Black leaders and communities. Such writings indicate that Farrakhan and his ministerial associates subjected Muhammad's teachings to a healthy dose of revisionism. Farrakhan's atypical conversion to the NOI, coupled with his affection for the church of his youth, and his brief flirtation with Sunni Islam led him to reconsider and subsequently revise Elijah Muhammad's theology. Indeed, in 1979 he noted that he had had three years to "reevaluate" Elijah Muhammad.[6] References to Fard Muhammad as Allah in person and to whites as devils permeated Farrakhan's early writings and speeches. However, by 1979 he no longer espoused the exclusionary theology of his former mentor. He publicly lauded the Black church as an engine for progress rather than an "enslaver" or accessory to Black suffering. Several speeches and newspaper articles from 1979 onward indicate that Farrakhan sought to present new and old converts alike with a substantially revised version of Mr. Muhammad's theology. In an article for the *Chicago Defender* in June 1979, for example, Farrakhan praised the Black church and lamented Elijah Muhammad's inability to "get near to our Black clergymen":

> The Black Church has been and still is a major part of the Black experience. Much of the good that we have experienced and most Black progress has come through the Black Church … The Honorable Elijah Muhammad has always wanted to get near to our Black clergymen to share with you what Allah (God) had blessed him with for the good of our people but, for many reasons, was unable … We must as Ministers of God pull our knowledge for the good of those whom we serve.[7]

Minister Farrakhan's comments in the *Chicago Defender* may well have come as a revelation to readers familiar with Muhammad's rampant condemnation of the church, Christianity, and African American preachers. Indeed, Muhammad's writings for the *Muhammad Speaks* newspaper and his subsequent book, *Message to the Black Man in America*, were littered with insults and condemnation of African American preachers and their followers. In *Message to the Black Man in America*, for example, he described Christianity as "a curse to us."[8] Some of Muhammad's greatest derision was reserved for African American preachers whom he defined as the "greatest hindrance to the truth of our people."[9] Muhammad's critique of the Black church was considerable and consistent. Yet it is evident that following his death, his community's tolerance for Christian clergy improved somewhat. In the months that followed his passing, for example, the *Muhammad Speaks* newspaper featured an interview with Rev. Jesse Jackson. In an interview with newspaper editor Askia Muhammad, Jackson proved eager to differentiate himself and the church from earlier generations of preachers. He noted, for example, "you have a whole new generation of ministers now whose model is that of Dr. King's. Their model is social activism; their model is social change. The model is relating to other religions and other denominations."[10]

Farrakhan's writings for the *Chicago Defender* aided him in his efforts to bring the RNOI to the attention of its target demographic. Yet in 1979 he embarked on the task of launching the RNOI's national newspaper, *The Final Call*. The paper was named after the Original NOI's (ONOI's) first newspaper, *The Final Call to Islam*. *The Final Call to Islam*, was published irregularly in the 1930s and a small number of surviving copies are now housed at the University of Michigan's Bentley Historical library.[11] The RNOI's national newspaper was described as "A monthly message dedicated to the Black man and woman of America and the world." The first issue of the paper was sold for 50 cents in May 1979. The contents of the first issue of the paper set out in stark terms Farrakhan's revised theology and message to the WCIW. In one section of the paper, for example, the minister confessed that he self-identified as a Christian, a Jehovah Witness, a Moorish Scientist, and a Catholic. Yet, he offered nothing more than superficial explanations for identification with each faith community. In setting out why he identified as a Christian, for example, he noted: "Brothers and sisters, I am a Christian. I am a follower of the Honorable Elijah Muhammad, yet I am a Christian because I have been crystallized into oneness with God. The Honorable Elijah Muhammad said the best Christian is a Muslim and the best Muslim is a Christian."[12] In the same section of the paper, Farrakhan also made clear that his "conscience" forced him to depart from the WCIW. In addressing the WCIW, he noted: "My conscience dictates to me that the Honorable Elijah Muhammad's plan and program for Black people is the best plan and program … my conscience dictates to me that that program needs no changes, no alteration; no one should corrupt it."[13] It is important to note that in addressing his split from the WCIW, Farrakhan neglected to mention theological disagreements with Imam W. D. Mohammed. Rather, it appears from this piece that his efforts to rebuild were motivated entirely by recognition of the need for Elijah Muhammad's program and plan in African American communities. The early issues of *The Final Call* demonstrated, if nothing else, Farrakhan's efforts to align his small faith community more closely with various Black churches and leaders. He remarked in one issue, for example, that if the church opened "the doors to us" he would "certainly go in. And we will help the church grow, and the church will help us grow, for no more shall we recognize—or feed artificial barriers and divisions that keep Black people away from each other."[14] Farrakhan's public pronouncements and affection for the church led some clergy to invite him into their churches. In 1977, for example, Reverend Willie Wilson of Union Temple Baptist Church invited Farrakhan to address his congregation. In doing so, Wilson misread the temperament and tolerance of his congregation. Indeed, half of his congregation left as a result of Farrakhan's admittance to the church.[15] Despite resistance from his congregation, Wilson maintained his relationship with Farrakhan. Wilson and several other well-known African American pastors did much to assist Farrakhan in his efforts to rebuild the NOI. Indeed, Farrakhan's reevaluation of Muhammad's theology and efforts to secure the friendship of influential pastors significantly aided the RNOI. The support of Black churches has been and remains vital for the RNOI.

Time spent "reevaluating" Elijah Muhammad's teachings led Farrakhan to espouse a revised and amended theology—one that was more amenable to potential allies and converts alike. Farrakhan presented himself and his early followers as open to, accepting of, and in observance of all the Abrahamic faith traditions. In a speech at the University of Wisconsin in February 1980 he described his own belief system as simply "obedience to the will of God." It appears that by the late 1970s Farrakhan came to consider "labels" of religious traditions as destructive, unnecessary, and contrary to the teachings of the major faith traditions. In his address in 1980 he remarked:

> We're not as intelligent as winos because winos don't care about the label … all he's interested in is the content and here we are killing ourselves over labels. Yet, all of us say that God is one … He didn't send prophets into the world to bring all these different religions and the devotees are killing each other in the name of God … something is wrong somewhere … The scriptures do not mention a name of the religion for the prophets. All it says in many places is that they spoke peace … all the prophets … taught obedience to the will of God.[16]

Farrakhan's subtle revisions to Muhammad's theology may have resulted from a number of considerations. Firstly, as noted, Farrakhan loved the West Indian church of his youth and arguably felt some discomfort with the NOI's fierce attacks on Christianity. Secondly, many of the ONOI's members were former Christians and "fishing" for new recruits would need to take place in Christian settings. Lastly, as noted earlier, Farrakhan's experiences in CRAID brought him into contact with Black churches and their pastors providing opportunities for discussion about mutual socioeconomic programs and interfaith initiatives. Time spent courting the Black church and its members proved fruitful. Yet it should also be noted that such efforts had the potential to come at the cost of nation-building and gaining converts. Former RNOI member Lance Shabazz gave voice to this critique in his own book, *Blood, Sweat and Tears*, when he noted: "We were not converting Christians; we were joining them under Minister Farrakhan."[17]

Farrakhan personally financed the production of the early issues of *The Final Call*. It is evident that he underestimated the cost and time required to produce the newspaper. Indeed, the second issue of the paper was sold for one dollar and the paper was no longer described as a "monthly message." Rather, the paper was published irregularly, and Farrakhan continued to promote his small faith community via articles in well-established African American newspapers. Indeed, in the same month that he launched the first issue of *The Final Call*, he also wrote an article for the *Chicago Defender* in which he set out the FBI's campaign to destroy the ONOI and Elijah Muhammad's reputation:

> From my reading from certain FBI files gained through the Freedom of Information Act, it became clear to me that the FBI had found a way to destroy the Nation of Islam, but, they could not do it successfully as long as Messenger Muhammad was among us. Their files show that they wrote anonymous letters to the Honorable Elijah Muhammad's wife, Sister Clara Muhammad, and his daughters accusing Messenger Muhammad of adultery … When Malcolm X and Wallace D. Muhammad left the Nation in 1964 and began mud slinging at Elijah Muhammad, the FBI instructed their agents to "lay low" and watch the effects of their slander of Messenger Elijah Muhammad and the Nation … They also found that by attacking the credibility of second-line leadership accusing the Ministers, Captains and Secretaries of stealing, adultery, etc., which in some cases were true, this would weaken the confidence in leadership and begin the process of scattering the followers … J. Edgar Hoover said that the philosophy and direction of the Nation of Islam on the death of Elijah Muhammad had to be one of STRICT RELIGIOUS ORIENTATION with a FOCUS on SELF-IMPROVEMENT and that the BUILDING OF A SEPARATE NATION was to be dropped. If this could not be accomplished then plan B was to destroy the Nation completely through the promotion of fractional disputes. (emphasis in original)[18]

Farrakhan's summation of the FBI's intentions and tactics are generally accurate. Declassified intelligence files clearly indicate that the bureau set out to neutralize the community. Moreover, as noted earlier, some scholars suggest that the bureau assisted or facilitated Imam Mohammed's succession in order to ensure that future NOI teachings would be strictly religious. Minister Farrakhan's intentions with this article are explicit. He sought to convince readers that the changes the NOI experienced in 1975–7 were pre-planned and for the benefit of the faith community's tormentors. Though he did not mention Imam Mohammed by name, it is evident that he considered him a pawn, knowingly or not, in partaking in the NOI's demise. In doing so, Farrakhan effectively presented Imam Mohammed as an accessory to the FBI's plans and thus further legitimized his own leadership. It is important to note that Farrakhan also acknowledged the truth in some of the FBI's allegations. This article was neither the first nor last time that Farrakhan would admit that NOI officials and ministers abused their power or engaged in relationships that would be considered immoral by believers. Indeed, just weeks before the publication of the aforementioned article, Farrakhan conceded that some NOI officials had become "drunk" with power and "abused" members:

> We had many problems obeying Black authority because most of us who held authority as Black people never had the opportunity to hold any position of authority, consequently, many officials became drunk with their new-found "power" and abused Messenger Muhammad's followers, yet the discipline never broke down.[19]

Admissions relating to deviations and abuse within the community may well have served to assure potential converts that Farrakhan understood why some of the NOI's original members welcomed the demise of the FOI and the MGT. Equally, however, they also reveal that, as noted earlier, he was likely aware of such abuse as a national minister and refused to address the matter.

Attacks on Imam Mohammed, direct or indirect, were few and far between during Farrakhan's early ministry. Indeed, it is worth noting that even in the early issues of *The Final Call*, he refrained from attacking Mohammed and his followers directly. Farrakhan sought not to capture the hearts of former members but to convert a new generation of recruits. His decision to target new audiences rather than former members seems to have been due to an initial inability to find favor with former recruits or ministers. In addressing the Nation's fall and his early rebuilding efforts in a later lecture in 1994, he remarked:

> To tell people Elijah Muhammad deceived people made people cold ... We watched the Nation die ... Many of us with knowledge went back into the streets to become hustlers and drug pushers and criminals and low life with the knowledge of God in our heads ... I didn't steal members from Warith Deen Mohammed. The ministers said: "we ain't helping you" ... some of you had been hurt so deeply that you didn't want to try again."[20]

Testimonies contained in early issues of *The Final Call* suggest that many of Minister Farrakhan's followers had little knowledge of or exposure to the faith community of Elijah Muhammad. However, a few of these testimonies indicate that some of his followers had been children in the original community. In the May 1982 edition of the paper, for example, three new converts, Edward X, Cleotha X, and Wanda X Harrison, provided testimonies for the *What Islam Has Done for Me* section of the paper. In her short testimony, new convert Cleotha X remarked: "I am one of the many followers who have never seen the messenger of Allah in person. I have come to the Nation of Islam on the faith of the word."[21] Similarly, Wanda X Harrison also conceded that she had limited knowledge of Muhammad before joining the RNOI: "People, black and white, tell us of Malcolm X, but they never tell you who raised Malcolm from the life of a drug user, or hustler. They never tell you of that Great Man, the Honorable Elijah Muhammad, who made Malcolm come to the knowledge of himself."[22] Later testimonies in the paper indicate that the RNOI had a particular appeal for individuals who had been exposed to Muhammad's community as children. In the July 1985 issue of the paper, for example, Khadijah X remarked:

> My parents came into the Nation in 1965 ... When I was old enough to go to school I went to Muhammad's University of Islam ... Muhammad's University was my life. When my third grade teacher told me that it was being closed down it brought about a horrifying feeling for the one true thing that I really loved was being taken away from me. When I started public schools this brought about an astounding transformation in my life ... I knew Islam was the only way for me.[23]

In the same issue of the paper the Mustafa family credited the ONOI and the RNOI with keeping their family together. They noted: "Islam has helped our parents stay through 25 years of marriage, raise nine children and be successful in our electrical business. Our family has stayed together through the good times and the bad times."[24] *The Final Call* lacked the staff and finances needed to keep the newspaper in regular circulation. Its dilemma was shared by countless African American newspapers in the post–civil rights era.[25] Minister Farrakhan construed the struggles of Black newspapers in the post-1968 years to be a result of integration. In one of his columns for the *Chicago Defender* in 1979, for example, he wrote:

> In the South, segregation forced us to be more self-reliant; now, with "integration," Black people are running to spend their hard earned money with whites, abandoning Black Enterprises, thus, many former thriving businesses of ours are closing down or have already ceased to exist. The Black Newspaper in most cities across America are weak because of a decline in our support. The Black newspaper is the only voice that we have in our Community that will actually tell "Our Story." If we lose the Black Newspaper through non-support and neglect we will lose a most vital instrument for our survival.[26]

Minister Farrakhan reached new audiences via his writings, lectures, and various speaking engagements. Doing so enabled him to gather a significant number of converts by the early 1980s. Indeed, in 1980 he held the RNOI's first annual Saviours' Day convention in Chicago. Shortly, thereafter, he was able to purchase what became known as *The Final Call* Administration Building in 1982. The building served as the faith community's main place of assemblage in Chicago for many years. The building was officially opened on September 9, 1982. In his opening remarks at the official opening, Farrakhan's long-time friend and associate Akbar Muhammad recounted the NOI's history, transition, and newfound success. In his address to members, he described the NOI's transition as a "terrible change" and lauded the "fruits" of the community's efforts:

> We went through a terrible change ourselves and we changed our direction. We saw that we didn't have the same effect to affect black people throughout America … we saw the things that we had falling apart, we had no control

> over things we controlled yesterday. We saw the wealth that God had blessed us with leaving ... so when Brother Farrakhan had three years to stand back and look at it, and he's not like a brother who is just in the Nation of Islam, he's a brother taught by the Honorable Elijah Muhammad ... He saw after studying certain things the reason that we are not doing what we were able to do yesterday is because we left the right path given to us by the Honorable Elijah Muhammad. When God blessed him to see his way back to that path, and begin to talk the words of the Honorable Elijah Muhammad, God made him see the fruits of that work.[27]

It is certainly interesting to note that Akbar's comments indicate that success, in his own estimation, was directly linked to visible signs of wealth in the NOI's community. His disdain for the "terrible change" the NOI experienced in 1975 appears to have little to do with the theological direction that Imam Mohammed led the community in. The purchasing of a small number of properties in the 1980s is testament to the toil and sacrifice of Farrakhan, his associates, and early converts. The purchasing of Elijah Muhammad's former home, known as the Palace, "excited" new members but also generated some annoyance from Imam Mohammed's followers. Current NOI Minister Abdul Muhammad, for example, remarks:

> The Bilalians did not want the Nation of Islam, under the guidance of the Honorable Minister Louis Farrakhan, to have The Palace ... during that time things were not at peace. Warith Deen's community sold The Palace to a fraternity, who turned it to a party house. The Fraternity reached a point where they could not keep up with the home, and the Honorable Minister Louis Farrakhan was able to buy it back. The Nation was so excited because the Minister was getting everything back that the Nation had during the time of the Most Honorable Elijah Muhammad.[28]

The RNOI's early followers, including Abdul, sacrificed much to assist Minister Farrakhan in his efforts to restore Elijah Muhammad's reputation, program, and work. Yet, the community remained relatively small and largely insignificant. Moreover, in its formative years it suffered from infighting among members over titles and positions of authority. Farrakhan addressed such infighting directly in 1982 in a message in *The Final Call* in which he requested all members, including ministers, to set aside their particular titles:

> The nation fell because of pride, because of envy, because of jealousy, because of striving for power and influence and wealth and domination of one another … when the Nation became untrue to the character of its function, then death set in and God gave the people leadership after their own corrupt desires which led them further in the path of destruction that they nation may be taught a Divine Lesson. That lesson is that we must submit to God, yield ourselves to His instruction and let Him guide us to the right path, the path of Divine favor. Therefore, I have asked that we set aside title, not because titles are unnecessary, but they become counterproductive if the underpinning, the support for title, is not yet in place. We must have the proper attitude, the proper mental view of the mission of the Honorable Elijah Muhammad. We must understand Allah's (God's) aim and purpose for bringing Elijah Muhammad into the world. If we indeed want to carry on His work, then we cannot put titles on ourselves … we must first study and qualify ourselves for the position that we desire to hold … we admonish you to strive no more for title, power, influence, position, of advantage, more than our brother, then let us serve our brother with love and humility and promote the brotherhood of the Blackman here, and throughout the world.[29]

Minister Farrakhan's efforts to rebuild and promote the NOI paid off rather slowly. In 1981, for example, he had approximately 4,000 followers in the United States.[30] The small, but growing, community held its annual Saviours' Day in 1981. During his keynote address, Farrakhan made a startling remark concerning his spiritual father. According to Farrakhan, Elijah Muhammad was still physically alive. In reflecting on the 1981 convention, he remarked:

> Forty-two years ago, the world thought that the Honorable Elijah Muhammad was dead. I came to understand that he really was alive, and the enemy had been deceived thinking that he killed that great Jesus. He was made to appear as such, as the Qur'an teaches, but Allah raised Him to Himself. So, in 1981, at our first Saviour's Day, to a small crowd of about, not even 4,000 at the time; after working underground for three years, the Nation of Islam popped up again. And I declared at our first Saviour's Day that Elijah Muhammad is alive and now in power. I suffered the loss of a lot of friendship when I made that statement. Some of my brothers that helped me while we were in the dark, growing underground, they said, "Farrakhan, you know Elijah Muhammad is dead. Why would you say such a thing?" But I made a declaration that took a lot of courage to state my belief. You say, "But there was a death certificate." Yes, you make them all the time.

> I offered the family to exhume the body. And I said, "If you can prove that that body is Elijah Muhammad, I will stop teaching." I sounded to many like a crazy man. But 39 Saviours' Days after, here we are, all over the world. The sad thing about this, they tried to bury my teacher, not only in a grave, but destroy his works to cut the Nation of Islam off, as it is written in the Psalms, that the name of Israel would no longer be remembered, or the name of the Nation would no longer be remembered in us. It was a conspiracy between the federal government of the United States of America, the hypocrites from among us, and members of the Arab Muslim world.[31]

It is not entirely clear what or who informed Farrakhan's revelation. However, it is likely that knowledge of the bureau's tactics to cripple the community informed to a considerable degree his thinking. Elijah Muhammad, for Farrakhan, became a messiah and the Christ figure prophesied in the Bible. Indeed, when Farrakhan has often professed his love for Christ in churches, his audiences have likely been unaware that it is Elijah Muhammad to whom he is referring. Farrakhan's pronouncement in 1981 became a central component of the NOI's revised theology. Indeed, the overwhelming majority of his student ministers currently refer to Elijah Muhammad as an "exalted Christ." Farrakhan's comments angered Imam Mohammed and Elijah Muhammad's family. However, his revelations were soon supported by Elijah Muhammad's "polygamous wife" Tynetta Muhammad.[32] Tynetta's embrace of Minister Farrakhan added legitimacy to his leadership. She ultimately became an important asset in his efforts to restore Elijah Muhammad's reputation. Minister Farrakhan discussed his beliefs concerning Elijah Muhammad's immortality in intricate detail with his advisor and friend, Jabril Muhammad. Jabril subsequently set out the NOI's argument in a short book entitled *Is It Possible that the Honorable Elijah Muhammad Is Still Physically Alive?*.[33] The book is advertised regularly in NOI publications and in their mosques.

Writings for leading African American newspapers and the production of *The Final Call* newspaper greatly assisted Farrakhan in promoting the existence of the RNOI. However, he lacked a national platform. The exposure that the small faith community desperately needed to grow arrived in 1984 when Minister Farrakhan publicly backed Rev. Jesse Jackson's presidential campaign. The historical significance of their brief alliance should be neither understated nor underestimated.

Antisemitism

It is unclear when or how Minister Farrakhan and Rev. Jackson first met. Jackson had achieved some degree of national standing as director of the Southern Christian Leadership Conference (SCLC)'s economic program, Operation Breadbasket in Chicago. Operation Breadbasket was "an outgrowth of Martin Luther King's evolving and maturing approach to America's racial injustices."[34] Addressing pressing economic concerns and injustices in Chicago raised Jackson's profile in the community and exposed him to the leadership and membership of Elijah Muhammad's NOI. Jackson's relationship with the leadership of SCLC soured and he subsequently established Operation PUSH in Chicago in 1971. Jackson's immense political ambitions became apparent in 1984 when he announced his intention to run for the presidency of the United States. His campaign forced his rivals to confront issues of racial inequality and President Reagan's rather dismal reputation in African American communities across the United States. Historian Iwan Morgan, for example, notes: "Most blacks regarded Reagan as the president of white America rather than of all Americans."[35] Reagan perfected the use of racially coded language to exploit racial divisions and garner the support of white conservatives as a presidential candidate and as president. Yet, as far as he was concerned, African Americans were doing better economically under his administration than at any time before:

> In 1983, 30 per cent of African Americans considered themselves middle class, double the level in the late 1960s, a trend reflected in increasing university enrolments, entry into the professions and suburban residence. There was also a growing black presence in the mainstream cultural media, exemplified by Michael Jackson's music mega-stardom, Oprah Winfrey's debut on a Chicago television station in 1984 and the launch of *The Cosby Show*—the most watched television series of the decade that focused on a black upper-middle-class family in the same year. Meanwhile black unemployment fell from its Reagan-era high of 19.5 per cent in 1983 to 11.5 per cent in 1988, when the economy was in a prolonged cycle of growth. For Reagan, all this was vindication of his vision that the well-being of blacks, like the well-being of every other American—is linked directly to the health of the economy.[36]

Jackson's candidacy was dismissed by many at the outset. Yet, he garnered significant support from African Americans, Hispanics, and white liberals. Jackson's success in 1984 should not be understated. His campaign faced sustained challenges including insufficient funding and limited advertising on a national scale. Such disadvantages made the fact that he managed to capture 19 percent of the primary vote all the more impressive. Jackson's progressive rhetoric and foreign policy positions on the question of the Middle East, and Palestine in particular, sat well with Black voters.

Minister Farrakhan traveled with Jackson to Syria to secure the release of US navy pilot, Lt. Robert O. Goodman, Jr. Minister Farrakhan's presence on the trip to Syria was generally omitted from mainstream coverage of the event. Yet, a few publications, including *Jet*, did mention and include photographs of Farrakhan with Jackson in Syria. In an interview with *Jet* covering his efforts in Syria, Jackson emphasized that his plea to President Assad for Goodman's release was made based on an appeal for peace. In recounting his plea, he remarked: "If I go back home empty-handed, people are able to see clearly that a humanitarian appeal does not work with you, but I think it does. It is important that you take a leap of faith and break the cycle of pain and return that boy to his parents and leave a good taste in the mouth of the American people."[37] Minister Farrakhan's role in securing Goodman's release may well have been omitted from mainstream coverage but his presence undoubtedly cemented his friendship with Jackson.

Minister Farrakhan's alliance with Rev. Jackson in 1984 is largely credited with exposing his disdain for America's Jewish community and what he perceives as their inordinate influence in American politics and African American politics, in particular. Jackson harbored antisemitic attitudes. Such attitudes were exposed when journalist Milton Coleman published what was supposed to have been an off-the-record conversation in which Jackson referred to Jews as hymies and to the New York as Hymietown. According to his associate, Askia Muhammad, Farrakhan confronted Jackson about the comments and he denied making them. Farrakhan then took Jackson at his word and vigorously defended him.[38] Jackson's antisemitic rant with Coleman was the greatest mistake of his campaign. Farrakhan's contribution to the controversy around Jackson's remarks was to forever taint his career and lead the ADL to brand him America's most notorious antisemite. Farrakhan's defense of Jackson was immense. Indeed, at one point he appeared to threaten Coleman's life: "One day soon, we will punish you with death. You say when is that? In sufficient time, we will come to power right inside this country. One day soon. This is a fitting punishment for dogs. He's a dog."[39] 1984 was certainly not the first time that Minister Farrakhan had given voice to or expressed feelings of hostility toward Jews. Indeed, in 1979 alone he addressed the issue of Black-Jewish relations in two separate articles for the *Chicago Defender*. In September 1979, for example, he wrote:

> The much talked of rift between Blacks and Jews is real … Blacks separating from Jews is the clearest sign of a beginning of a true movement towards freedom. For Jews have been in the forefront of the Black movement towards integration. They have generously financed many black leaders spiritual, political and civic and they have generously financed many black groups so that these leaders and groups have always been effective spokesman for the hurt of Jewish people and these leaders and their organizations have consistently oppressed all groups that their Jewish friends felt were not in the best intent of Jewish people.[40]

Farrakhan's comments here evidence an early preoccupation with Jewish interest in Black organizations. Indeed, his comments illustrate a deep distrust of Jews and a belief that their support for civil rights was directly tied to a larger goal of controlling Black leaders. Farrakhan turned his attention again to the matter of Black-Jewish relations in November 1979 when he wrote:

> For many years Jewish liberal money has financed black organizations and Jewish liberal brain power has been behind the organization and development of every major civil rights organization. We must remember the old saying, "He who pays the piper, calls the tune." These Jewish liberals have been calling the tune in the civil rights struggle for nearly sixty years. No wonder what we have gained is now a fading illusion … Why shouldn't Jesse Jackson and Joseph Lowery speak to the P.L.O. Why shouldn't blacks in America develop international ties of friendship with other oppressed peoples around the world … The Jewish liberals have now turned on Reverend Jesse Jackson and Reverend Joseph Lowery and they are putting great pressure on these men and their organizations. The Jewish liberals today as in the past pulled the strings on their black puppets to condemn the actions of these men.[41]

Farrakhan's comments reveal an eagerness to support Jackson from potential criticism regarding his position on the Palestinian Liberation Organization (PLO). Indeed, this piece suggests that both men shared a similar perspective on the question of the PLO and that both resented censure from Jewish Americans. Farrakhan's comments in his articles for the *Chicago Defender* were mild in comparison to his later verbal attacks on Jewish Americans. Following his efforts to support Jackson, Farrakhan went on to refer to Judaism as a "dirty religion."[42] The ADL retaliated by referring to Farrakhan as a Black Hitler. In his defense, Farrakhan remarked:

> The Jews don't like Farrakhan, so they call me Hitler. Well that's a good name. Hitler was a very great man. He wasn't great for me as a Black person, but he was a great German. Now, I'm not proud of Hitler's evils against Jewish people, but that's a matter of record. He raised Germany up from nothing. Well, in a sense you could say there's a similarity in that we are raising our people up from nothing. But don't compare me with your wicked killers.[43]

Minister Farrakhan's comments have often been deliberately shortened to a sound bite: "Hitler was a very great man." Indeed, his comments concerning Hitler's evils have often been omitted entirely. The origins of Farrakhan's antisemitism are unclear. It appears that nothing in his childhood provoked such intense feelings about Jewish Americans. Indeed, at the 2017 Saviours' Day convention, he noted that his mother had worked for Jews and that she never complained about them: "I didn't want no fight with the Jewish people … my mother worked for them. She never came home and complained about them."[44]

Jackson came under increasing pressure to distance himself from Farrakhan. On June 28, 1984, he publicly rebuked Farrakhan's comments as "morally indefensible."[45] Jackson's rebuke was short-lived. Jackson continued to work alongside Minister Farrakhan on numerous occasions. Not until he threw his weight behind Hillary Clinton's second presidential bid did his working relationship with Farrakhan appear to end. Indeed, Jackson was notably absent from the 2015 Justice or Else March when Farrakhan and civil rights activists commemorated the twentieth anniversary of the MMM.

Minister Farrakhan's rise to national prominence in 1984 aided the NOI immensely. However, the community was still without the muscle and assets that once made it a model of Black entrepreneurship. Minister Farrakhan's tireless work to increase the community's assets and economic prowess began to pay off in 1985. Farrakhan had long considered Libya to be a friend of the NOI. That friendship made national news in the United States when Qaddafi provided a $5 million interest-free loan to assist the community's economic initiatives in 1985. The NOI's membership was informed of the loan in early July 1985 via an article in *The Final Call*:

> I am here to say tonight that Brother Qathafi and the Libyan Arab Republic has given us a $5 million interest-free loan ... we must help ourselves ... but God has given us a brother to help us help ourselves ... America has been and is a land of bondage of the Blackman ... we must come out of the mind, the spirit, the ways, the values, the norms, the mores and the culture of our former slavemasters and their children.[46]

Minister Farrakhan utilized the money to kick-start People Organized and Working for Economic Rebirth (POWER). The success of POWER is debatable. However, its launch and the willingness of foreign nations to finance NOI initiatives gave the small faith community a degree of confidence and vigor that it had previously lacked. Minister Farrakhan eagerly sought out the support, financial and otherwise, of the Muslim World in 1985 and 1986. It appears, however, that Libya was its largest donor. Farrakhan's visits to Kuwait and Libya and reports concerning those visits reveal a willingness on his part to acknowledge the concerns that foreign nations had about his particularistic teachings. In May 1985, for example, Minister Farrakhan was interviewed for a Kuwaiti magazine. In recalling the interview, Minister Farrakhan's associate, Akbar Muhammad, wrote:

> Minister Farrakhan reviewed the historical background of the Nation of Islam, the approach that Master Fard Muhammad used, and how the Honorable Elijah Muhammad used that same approach in bringing Islam to Black people in America. He explained why certain things were done that were not understood generally in the Muslim world, but the approach was successful in reaching Black people throughout America.[47]

Akbar's recollection of the interview is telling. It suggests that when in conversation with the Muslim World Farrakhan is willing to play down his own unorthodox beliefs and instead explain the community's teachings as something of a method aimed at bringing African Americans to Islam.

Minister Farrakhan also traveled to Jamaica again in 1986. His fondness for the Nation is no doubt informed by his love for the people of the Caribbean and his personal search for information relating to his biological father. Minister Farrakhan was personally invited to speak at the National Arena in Kingston by Reverend Ernle Gordon, director of St. Mary's Anglican Church. Gordon appears to have had some knowledge of Farrakhan's paternal family in Jamaica. In his invitation, for example, he remarked that Farrakhan's uncle was a well-known teacher in Jamaica known as Teacher Clarke. Such an invitation evidenced Minister Farrakhan's growing appeal not only among Christians in the United States but also internationally. Minister Farrakhan utilized the speech to call for Jamaicans to "take your country back." Indeed, he remarked that current conditions in the Nation would leave "Marcus Garvey ... turning in his grave."[48]

Minister Farrakhan's rise to prominence in the United States opened the door to high-profile invitations to take part in television interviews. For his part, Farrakhan seems to have been more than willing to utilize the media for the benefit of the NOI. In 1985, for example, he appeared on *The Phil Donahue Show*. Moreover, he amassed an audience of 25,000 for a speech in Madison Square Garden in the same year. In his speech at Madison Square Garden, Farrakhan acknowledged the furor that surrounded him as a leader: "I seem to have become quite a controversial fellow ... Everywhere Farrakhan goes, there's controversy around this fellow. There has not been a black man in the history of America that has been as repudiated as Brother Farrakhan."[49] His appearance on *The Phil Donahue Show* solidified his growing stature in America and gave Americans an insight into the NOI's theology and its leaders. The appearance on Donahue afforded Farrakhan an opportunity to address his critique of race relations and charges of antisemitism. Indeed, in the interview he clarified that equality within the United States for African Americans would be more desirable than separation and that his "gutter religion" comments related to not only what "you profess" but what "you practice." Farrakhan remained composed throughout repeated and somewhat hostile questions from Donahue. Moreover, he appeared to relish the attention and limelight.

1985 Vision and Solidifying Support

Minister Farrakhan's belief in the immortality of his spiritual father is something that he consciously avoided discussing in his 1985 interview with

Donahue. According to Farrakhan, his belief was affirmed on September 17, 1985, when he encountered Muhammad in a vision while in Mexico. Minister Farrakhan's 1985 vision was a "profoundly religious event."[50] He recalled the event during a press conference in Washington, DC, in 1989. During the press conference, he revealed that he had been

> Taken in the night in an out-of-the-body experience, up to the top of a small, sacred mountain chain called Tepozteco Mountains in the Mexican town of Tepotzlan. Tepotzlan is located 40 miles south of Mexico City and some 19 miles from the city of Cuernavaca. It was there where the Honorable Minister Louis Farrakhan had his Vision-Like Experience being transported to the Great Mother's Wheel (a wheel within a wheel). Upon reaching this mighty craft, which the Honorable Elijah Muhammad described as being a man-made planet in the sky and is virtually a city in the sky and is described in the Bible as being dreadful to look upon. He had his first direct communication with the Most Honorable Elijah Muhammad, not seeing his person, but hearing his voice that he recognized as clear as crystal. The Honorable Elijah Muhammad told him about a war being planned by the President of the United States and his Joint Chiefs of Staff to take place somewhere on our planet. At the end of this experience, he was dropped off outside of Washington, D.C., and was further instructed by the Honorable Elijah Muhammad to hold a press conference in the Capitol and to tell those in attendance about this war being planned by the United States Government and its President.[51]

Minister Farrakhan has referred to and retold this event on many occasions. There can be little doubt of its significance to him and the NOI's faithful. More recently, Minister Farrakhan discussed his experience during the 2022 Saviours' Day convention. During his extensive keynote address entitled *A Swan Song*, Minister Farrakhan revealed that he was immediately fearful when he heard Muhammad's voice. His fear was due to concerns that Muhammad may rebuke him for having taken multiple polygamous wives.[52] According to Farrakhan, Muhammad was unconcerned about his wives. Little is known about Farrakhan's polygamous wives or indeed the children he has fathered as a result of these relationships. Indeed, not until 2022 did he even acknowledge to the NOI's faithful that he had polygamous wives. Polygamy is not tolerated within the NOI and is forbidden for FOI. It appears, however, that Farrakhan considers himself to be above the regulations that govern other members' behaviors. According to one high-profile NOI member, there has been "no reaction" within the NOI to Farrakhan's admission.[53] Farrakhan's Mother Wheel experience solidified his beliefs and bolstered his confidence in leading the NOI. Indeed, such confidence would lead him to call for a million men to march on Washington in 1995.

Farrakhan's rapport within African American communities was aided by the tireless work of his followers and the regressive racial climate on the late 1980s and early 1990s. Indeed, the community was recognized nationally in the 1990s for its work in cleaning up drug-infested neighborhoods. Such work was carried out by an affiliate of the FOI, known as Dope Busters. According to *The Final Call*, "national attention was first focused on the dopebusters, a name for the Muslims coined by a Washington newspaper, when they effectively reclaimed a drug infested housing development on Washington's far northwest side, Mayfair Mansions."[54] Dope Busters won a number of government contracts, which, according to the ADL, generated millions of dollars for the NOI.[55] Dope Busters was but one of the NOI's positive outreach initiatives in the late 1980s and 1990s. Their prison reform ministry was also lauded for the positive work that carried out in dozens of prisons across the United States.

America's prison population grew exponentially in the post–civil rights era. President Reagan's War on Drugs, as legal scholar Michelle Alexander notes, was launched at a time when drug use was declining in the United States. The language, images, and sentencing surrounding Reagan's War on Drugs did much to criminalize and incarcerate African Americans. Alexander explains:

> The impact of the drug war has been astounding. In less than thirty years, the US penal population exploded from around 300,000 to more than 2 million, with drug convictions accounting for the majority of the increase. The United States now has the highest rate of incarceration in the world … The racial dimension of mass incarceration is its most striking feature. No other country in the world imprisons so many of its racial or ethnic minorities. The United States imprisons a larger percentage of its black population than South Africa did at the height of apartheid. In Washington D.C., … it is estimated that three out of four young black men … can expect to serve time in prison. Similar rates of incarceration can be found in black communities across America.[56]

Drug use, as Alexander notes, cannot explain these statistics alone. Indeed, "people of all colors *use and sell* illegal drugs at remarkable similar rates" (emphasis in original).⁵⁷ America's War on Drugs disproportionately targeted African American communities. Minister Farrakhan construed the war on drugs as a means by which to criminalize and incarcerate Black men. Farrakhan laid the blame for the emergence and ready availability of crack cocaine in poor neighborhoods at the door of local police departments. Farrakhan was not alone in offering such blistering attacks on the police and the penal system. In short, his belief that the US government was consciously trying to harm African Americans was one that was widely supported. In 1990, for example, a poll conducted by the *New York Times* and WCBS-TV revealed that one-quarter of respondents agreed that the government "deliberately makes sure that drugs are readily available in poor Black neighbourhoods in order to harm Black people."⁵⁸ The expansion of the American prison population did not end with the Reagan administration and the Republican Party's reign. The Democratic Party of Bill Clinton worked with zeal to distance itself from identification with African American voters. Doing so paid dividends. As a New Democrat, Clinton focused his campaign on welfare reform and crime. Such themes found favor with traditionally republican voters. Clinton, unsurprisingly, outpolled his republican opponent among white voters. African American writer Toni Morrison dubbed Clinton "America's first black president." Yet, once in office, Clinton continued previous policies that aided mass incarceration. The passage of the crime bill in 1994, for example, carried a three-strikes provision. This, in effect, meant that anyone convicted of a violent crime with two previous convictions could be given a life sentence. Not until 2015 did Clinton publicly admit his role in worsening mass incarceration.⁵⁹

It was in this context that Minister Farrakhan rebuilt the NOI's prison reform ministry. Farrakhan has himself visited and delivered talks in numerous prisons. Indeed, the NOI has a presence in prisons across the United States. Under Farrakhan's guidance, local chapters of the NOI began to send their ministers into neighboring prisons to offer religious services and disseminate *The Final Call* newspaper. Farrakhan is undoubtedly proud of the NOI's work in prisons. Indeed, he has often boasted of the community's success in effectively transforming the lives of convicts. *The Final Call* newspaper became an important source of information about the NOI and Farrakhan for inmates. The newspaper also began to include prisoners' testimonies within the paper in the late 1980s and early 1990s. In April 1991, for example, the paper carried a short article by Keith Earmon in which he noted:

> I want to express my thanks to Minister Farrakhan and all who assist the Minister in his Mission. I am incarcerated in the U.S. penitentiary in Atlanta and in this place, most are depressed, confused and hopeless. The Nation of Islam has given me something to look forward to each day and in the future. I read The Final Call paper and I watch Minister Farrakhan on television each week … Accepting the message of the Honorable Elijah Muhammad, as taught by Minister Farrakhan, has changed my way of acting and my way of thinking, for the better. Thank you in the Nation of Islam, not just for the message that I receive but for the wonderful works you do for Black people all over the world. If it is Allah's will, I pray that I will be able to join the struggle to liberate our people. For now, I will study and heed the words of Minister Farrakhan.[60]

Likewise in 1994 an article appeared that lauded the NOI's ability to settle internal conflicts between prisoners:

> We wish to thank and commend Brother Minister Abdullah Muhammad … for his very successful work here at Western Pen in Pennsylvania. On December 6, 1991 Minister Farrakhan sent a letter to the Deputy Superintendent David J. Good of the State Correctional Institution in Pittsburgh, Pa, to introduce Min. Muhammad to the prison administration to help them "settle internal conflicts" that existed among the Believers who are under the leadership of Minister Farrakhan … We are beginning to really know the Divine Blessings and Mercy of Allah through our growth and development. Also, the brothers who are striving to become true believers are very obedient to the divine instructions given to us from our leader and father, Min. Farrakhan through Min Abdullah.[61]

The NOI's prison reform ministry is often perceived as a positive force in correctional institutions. Such work has earned the NOI funding from the federal government. In 2018, such funding was made public when the *Washington Examiner* reported that the Bureau of Prisons had awarded the NOI funding from 2008 onward for religious services. In 2012, the NOI received $47,000 in contracts from the federal government. In 2018, they received $17,000 and in 2019 they received $8,250.[62]

Minister Farrakhan was, by and large, a popular and well-respected leader in sections of the United States in the early 1990s. His theology was certainly questioned and ridiculed by Sunni Muslims. Nevertheless, his community's social reform and prison reform ministries earned the NOI a great degree of prestige and respect. Minister Farrakhan's growing rapport concerned American Jewish communities and Jewish organizations, many of whom felt that Farrakhan's reputation as an antisemite was being glossed over by those voicing support for him. Minister Farrakhan's and the NOI's relationship with Jewish Americans deteriorated further in 1992 when, with his blessing, the historical research department (HRD) of the NOI published the book *The Secret Relationship between Blacks and Jews*. The book's publication in 1992 horrified the ADL. *The Secret Relationship* is officially authored by the HRD of the NOI. However, it was penned by NOI convert Allen Muhammad.[63] The book is based on the works of discredited Jewish authors and sets out to present Jews as the primary architects and beneficiaries of Black exploitation in the United States.[64] The book's publication did little to dampen Minister Farrakhan's rapport. Indeed, he was celebrated by music artists and hailed by rap artists such as Snoop Dogg, Sista Souljah, and The Fugees. Farrakhan's antisemitic rants were also aided by his ministers and in particular by his national minister, Khalid Muhammad. Khalid enjoyed a close relationship with Farrakhan until November 1994 when he was suspended. The suspension came after Khalid delivered a vile speech at Kean college in which he referred to Jews as "crackers" and "Bloodsuckers." Farrakhan's decision to suspend Khalid took almost three months. His delay in speaking out is telling and evidences a failure to control the conduct of his ministers.

Minister Farrakhan's rapport with young Black men was unrivaled. Yet, his stature was threatened in 1992 when Spike Lee released his biopic, *Malcolm X*. Spike Lee was widely celebrated for his movies prior to the release of *Malcolm X*. The movie followed rather closely Haley's flawed and incomplete *The Autobiography of Malcolm X*. It is worth noting, for example, that Malcolm never had an opportunity to approve the final manuscript for his autobiography. Moreover, chapters that outlined Malcolm's political testament were removed.[65] Lee's epic movie starred Denzel Washington and was, in part, financed by Black America's elites including Oprah Winfrey, Michael Jordan, and Bill Cosby. The movie gave rise to what Russell Rickford termed "Malcolmology."[66] Malcolm's famous *X* was commercialized and printed on baseball caps and T-shirts. Lee's movie reopened questions about the NOI's role in Malcolm's assassination. Moreover, it raised questions about Elijah Muhammad's domestic life and his sexual relationships with young women. Lee avoided making any direct reference to Farrakhan in the movie. Nonetheless, it compelled Minister Farrakhan to explain the NOI's role and his role in particular in the demise of his former teacher. Farrakhan met with Lee prior to filming. He also delivered a series of lectures both at Malcolm X College and at other venues where he described in detail the events leading to Malcolm's split from the NOI. Minister Farrakhan categorically denied any direct involvement in Malcolm's exit from the NOI or his assassination. Rather, he argued vigorously that the FBI set out Malcolm's assassins and that their agents had exploited differences between Elijah and Malcolm. In his extensive lecture at Malcolm X College, Minister Farrakhan portrayed Malcolm as a political disciple and himself as a spiritual disciple. He also conceded that ministers in the NOI had been jealous of Malcolm. Farrakhan, as noted, denied any direct involvement. However, he did concede that he had participated in creating a hostile atmosphere in the NOI surrounding Malcolm.[67] Spike Lee's biopic did not portray Muhammad's relationships. Nonetheless, the movie led to questions about the NOI's treatment of women and the nature of Muhammad's relationships with several women. Minister Farrakhan devoted his 1993 Saviours' Day address to such questions. During his lecture, he presented Muhammad's "wives" on stage. Each woman offered a brief testimony aimed at persuading the NOI's faithful that Muhammad had not exploited or abused them.[68] Minister Farrakhan's best efforts failed to settle questions about his relationship with Malcolm, Malcolm's assassination, and Muhammad's wives. Indeed, in the decades that followed, Minister Farrakhan was required to repeatedly address these issues. Farrakhan's plight in 1992 was not helped by the fact that Malcolm's widow, Dr. Betty Shabazz, held him and the NOI responsible for her husband's death.[69] Minister Farrakhan made numerous efforts to reach out to the Shabazz family. Yet not until 1995 did Dr. Shabazz publicly reconcile with Farrakhan. Dr. Shabazz was compelled to appear publicly with Minister Farrakhan following her daughter Qubilah's indictment on charges of conspiring to kill him. Qubilah had discussed arranging Farrakhan's murder with a government informant, Michael Fitzpatrick. Rather than criticize Qubilah, Farrakhan rushed to defend her as misguided by a government informant. As such, he arranged a benefit for

Qubilah in Harlem. On May 6, 1995, Minister Farrakhan and Dr. Shabazz shared a stage at the Apollo theatre in Harlem.[70]

Minister Farrakhan's NOI did not emerge from the events of 1992 unscathed. However, the community continued to grow not only in the United States but in Ghana, Trinidad, and Britain. All three chapters of the NOI were launched in the years preceding the MMM. Minister Farrakhan had eagerly sought out a home for the NOI on African soil. As such, he sent his former international representative, Akbar Muhammad, to launch a NOI mosque in Ghana. The NOI mosque in Accra was construed as a huge feat for the NOI. Indeed, the community held their annual Saviours' Day convention in Ghana in 1994.[71] Their apparent success in Ghana was short-lived and the NOI's presence there, as discussed later, dissipated. The study groups and mosques initiated in Trinidad and London had greater success and remain small but nonetheless operational. The UK chapter of the NOI was led by Hillary Muhammad. In 2001, he traveled to Chicago with 500 followers to meet Minister Farrakhan.[72] The UK chapter of the Nation has survived despite the fact that Farrakhan has been banned from entering the UK since the 1980s. It is worth noting, however, that his followers in the United Kingdom often travel to the United States to commune with their African American counterparts. The Trinidad chapter likewise was formed in 1992 by David Muhammad. The chapter is smaller than its British counterpart but its existence evidenced for Farrakhan interest in his community beyond the United States.

The Million Man March

Minister Farrakhan exploited to maximum effect worsening race relations in the United States to fuel support for what became the Million Man March in October 1995. The Holy Day of Atonement, as it was officially known, witnessed the largest gathering of African American men in US history. Minister Farrakhan and his ministers worked tirelessly to fundraise and promote the march. Women and homosexuals were excluded from the march. The exclusion angered feminists and women outside the NOI. Nation women, however, eagerly worked together to organize, fundraise, and make the march possible. Their efforts have been documented within the NOI by Angela

Muhammad.⁷³ Minister Farrakhan delivered a series of women only and men only events to raise money for the march. Such events were published widely in the community's literature. Moreover, the number of men attending such events reassured Farrakhan that he could indeed call one million Black men to Washington. The organizational success of the march does not belong to the NOI alone. Indeed, several organizations including the NAACP, the National Black United Front, and the Rainbow Coalition worked together to organize the march. Minister Farrakhan depended greatly on his friends and colleagues in Black churches to support and help organize the march. The momentum that the planned march gathered in 1994 panicked observers who tried to separate support for the march from support for Farrakhan. Farrakhan worked to appease the interests of his colleagues. In a nod to the political activism of other groups supporting the march, he consented to the registering of voters before the march.⁷⁴

The agenda for the march was conservative in nature. It called not for government action but for personal responsibility and atonement. Indeed, the pledge that Minister Farrakhan asked men to repeat reflected this emphasis:

> I PLEDGE that from this day forward I will strive to love my brother as I love myself. I, from this day forward, will strive to improve myself spiritually, morally, mentally, socially, politically and economically for the benefit of myself, my family and my people. I pledge that I will strive to build businesses, build houses, build hospitals, build factories and enter into international trade for the good of myself, my family and my people. I PLEDGE that from this day forward I will never raise my hand with a knife or a gun to beat, cut, or shoot any member of my family or any human being except in self-defense. I pledge from this day forward I will never abuse my wife by striking her, disrespecting her, for she is the mother of my children and the producer of my future. I pledge that from this day forward I will never engage in the abuse of children, little boys or little girls for sexual gratification. For I will let them grow in peace to be strong men and women for the future of our people. I WILL never again use the 'B word' to describe any female. But particularly my own Black sister. I pledge from this day forward that I will not poison my body with drugs or that which is destructive to my health and my well-being. I pledge from this day forward I will support Black newspapers, Black radio, Black television. I will support Black artists who clean up their acts to show respect for themselves and

respect for their people and respect for the ears of the human family. I will do all of this so help me God. (emphasis in original)[75]

Minister Farrakhan considered the MMM to be a success and a demonstration of himself as a leader in Black America. In his keynote speech at the march, he addressed attempts to portray him as a bigot and a hate monger. Farrakhan's speech was certainly not enough to undo such accusations. However, this does not appear to have been his goal. The march was intended to give Black men a safe space in which to atone for their personal failings and shortcomings. It presented conservative gender norms, as advocated in the NOI, as a solution to strained male–female relationships and it highlighted the importance of unity, brotherhood, and family for march participants.

The MMM had a profound and lasting impact on some of the men who attended. Damon Jones, for example, comments:

> We stood as a solid wall of strength and brotherly love. There was no violence amongst us that day. There was no discord that day. My life was forever impacted by this historic moment in time. I saw the government close down and get outta town that day.[76]

Likewise Vincent Muhammad remarks:

> I will always remember October 16, 1995 as the best day of my life. I was 24 years old and eager for a life changing adventure. It was the first and only time I got on a plane and almost everyone on the flight was a black man. It was the first time I stood in a sea of hundreds of thousands of black men with no one using profanity, arguing, or fighting. The crowd was full of men greeting each other, smiling, crying, laughing, hugging, and showing respect to one another. Most of all I felt the spirit of love and peace blowing through the air like a warm breeze across the mall.[77]

Conclusion

The MMM demonstrated to national and international audiences that Minister Farrakhan and the NOI were a force to be reckoned with. It evidenced Minister Farrakhan's esteem and showcased the diligence and hard work of his followers. In many ways, the march and its success do not belong to

Farrakhan alone. Indeed, it would be entirely inaccurate to suggest that the event was a one-man show. Minister Farrakhan captured the hearts and minds of hundreds of thousands of Black men. Moreover, the majority of these men were not Muslim, and the event did not result in a surge of membership in the Nation. Minister Farrakhan's goal with the march was not mass conversion to the NOI. It was personal atonement and responsibility. The march evidenced the willingness of Black men and leaders to turn inward to find solutions to problems blighting their families and communities. It is thus impossible to determine the extent to which the march impacted the lives of those who attended. Minister Farrakhan's ascendancy to the position he assumed in 1995 was neither smooth nor welcoming. He left the WCIW in the late 1970s with little. His writings, speeches, and tours elevated his profile. His willingness to court Christians has been fruitful. Indeed, without the support of Black churches, Minister Farrakhan may well have remained a largely unknown figure. His involvement in Jackson's campaign ultimately harmed his candidacy. Accusations of bigotry and antisemitism did not impact Farrakhan to any considerable degree in the late 1980s and early 1990s. Indeed, he seemed to relish the attention and headlines his antisemitism invited. In the post-1995 period, Minister Farrakhan's antisemitic remarks would cost him and the NOI greater leverage and contribute to the community's decline.

Notes

1. Farrakhan, "Let Us Make Man."
2. Akbar Muhammad's comments in Rebirth of a Nation (Part one) in The 1981 Re-birth of a Nation: This is how it all began (DVD: Final Call Publishing: 2022)
3. Louis Farrakhan, "The Final Call," *Chicago Defender*, December 16, 1978, 7.
4. Elijah Muhammad, *The Theology of Time* (Chicago: Secretarius Publications, 2002), 164–5.
5. Farrakhan, "Let Us Make Man."
6. Louis Farrakhan, "The Ultimate Challenge: The Survival of the Black Nation," *The Final Call*, May 1979, 3.
7. Louis Farrakhan, "Insight," *Chicago Defender*, June 9, 1979, 6.
8. Elijah Muhammad, *Message to the Black Man in America*, 285.
9. Ibid., 18.

10 "Muhammad Speaks Interviews the Rev. Jesse Jackson, President of Operation PUSH and Outspoken Civil Rights Activist," *Muhammad Speaks*, June 6, 1975, 22.
11 Patrick D. Bowen, "Propaganda in the Early NOI," in *New Perspectives on the Nation of Islam*, ed. Dawn-Marie Gibson and Herbert Berg (London: Routledge, 2017), 135.
12 Farrakhan, "The Ultimate Challenge," 12.
13 Ibid., 13.
14 Ibid., 12.
15 Nisa Islam Muhammad and Askia Muhammad, "A Legacy of Brotherhood and Unity: Reverend Willie Wilson Celebrates 37 Years of Faith in Action," *The Final Call*, May 11, 2010, 2.
16 Farrakhan, "The Sentence of Death on America."
17 Lance Shabazz, *Blood, Sweat and Tears: The Nation of Islam and Me* (North Carolina: Lulu Publishing Services, 2015), 116.
18 Louis Farrakhan, "Insight," *Chicago Defender*, May 5, 1979, 6.
19 Louis Farrakhan, "Insight," *Chicago Defender*, April 14, 1979, 10.
20 Farrakhan, "Let Us Make Man."
21 Cleotha X, "Has Not Seen Messenger, Yet," *The Final Call*, May 2, 1982, 16.
22 Wanda X Harrison, "Islam Addresses Questions Church Cannot Answer," *The Final Call*, May 1982, 16.
23 Khadijah X, "Family Saved By Islam," *The Final Call*, July 1985, 27.
24 The Mustafa family, "Islam Works," *The Final Call*, July 1985, 27.
25 Patrick S. Washburn, *The African American Newspaper: Voice of Freedom* (Evanston, IL: Northwestern University Press, 2006), 202.
26 Louis Farrakhan, "Final Call: Institutional Destruction," *Chicago Defender*, June 23, 1979, 6.
27 Akbar Muhammad opening remarks at the historic opening of *The Final Call Administration* Building, Chicago, September 9, 1982.
28 Abdul Sharrieff Muhammad, *A Soldier in the Movement of Christ* (Atlanta: Independently Published, 2020), 49.
29 Louis Farrakhan, "Memorandum to the Black Nation," *The Final Call*, vol. 2, no. 5 (May 1982): 10–11.
30 Farrakhan, "The Unravelling of a Great Nation."
31 Ibid.
32 Azizah Muhammad, "A Son's Testimony: The Biological Son of the Most Honorable Elijah Muhammad Shares His Story of Faith, Findings, and Prayers for the Future," *Rise Magazine*, December 2021.
33 Jabril Muhammad, *Is It Possible that the Honorable Elijah Muhammad Is Still Physically Alive?* (Phoenix: Nuevo Books, 2007).

34 Martin Deppe, *Operation Breadbasket: An Untold Story of Civil Rights in Chicago, 1960–1971* (Athens: University of Georgia Press, 2017), xiv.
35 Iwan Morgan and Mark White, *The Presidential Image: A History from Theodore Roosevelt to Donald Trump* (London: I.B. Tauris, 2020), 175.
36 Ibid., 182.
37 Michael Cheers, "Untold Story of How Jesse Jackson Won Navy Flyer's Freedom," *Jet*, January 1984, 14.
38 Gibson, *The Nation of Islam, Louis Farrakhan*, 40.
39 Magida, *Prophet of Rage*, 146–7.
40 Farrakhan, "Final Call."
41 Louis Farrakhan, "Final Call," *Chicago Defender*, November 10, 1979, 12.
42 Gardell, *Countdown to Armageddon*, 216.
43 Ibid., 252.
44 Farrakhan, "Have No Fear for the Future."
45 Jon Margolis, "Jackson Denounces Farrakhan Remarks," *Chicago Tribune*, June 29, 1984, 1.
46 Abdul Wali Muhammad, "$5 Million Loan Announced in D.C.; Col Qathafi Helps Launch P.O.W.E.R.," *The Final Call*, vol. 5, no. 2 (July 1985): 3–4.
47 Abdul Akbar Muhammad, "Arab World Welcomes Farrakhan," *The Final Call*, vol. 5 no. 2 (May 1985): 4.
48 Abdul Wali Muhammad, "Jamaican Welcomes Native Son," *The Final Call*, January 13, 1986, 3.
49 Bob Herbert, "In America, Endless Poison," *The New York Times*, August 29, 1999.
50 Stephen C. Finley, "The Meaning of "Mother" in Louis Farrakhan's "Mother Wheel": Race, Gender, and Sexuality in the Cosmology of the Nation of Islam's UFO," *Journal of the American Academy of Religion*, vol. 80, no. 2 (June 2012): 440.
51 Mother Tynetta Muhammad, "Revisiting Minister Farrakhan's Vision-Like Experience on September, 17 1985—The Magnificent Wheel within a Wheel—The Mother's Wheel," *The Final Call*, vol. 32, no. 51, 15.
52 Farrakhan, "A Swan Song."
53 Interview with NOI representative, July 7, 2022.
54 "Community Outraged; D.C. Police Assault 'Dopebusters,'" *The Final Call*, October 3, 1988, 3.
55 Gibson, *A History of the Nation of Islam*, 122.
56 Michelle Alexander, *The New Jim Crow: Mass Incarceration in the Age of Colorblindness* (New York: New Press, 2011), 6.
57 Ibid., 7.
58 Gibson, *A History of the Nation of Islam*, 107.

59 Gibson, *The Nation of Islam, Louis Farrakhan*, 59.
60 Keith Earmon, "Thanks for Minister," *The Final Call*, April 22, 1991, 16.
61 "N.O.I. Prison Ministry Helps Settle Differences," *The Final Call*, July 20, 1994, 17.
62 https://www.washingtonexaminer.com/politics/nation-of-islam-defends-federal-funding-for-prison-lectures-as-a-blessing-to-prisoners (accessed February 1, 2020).
63 Gibson, *A History of the Nation of Islam*, 122.
64 Historical Research Department of the NOI, *The Secret Relationship between Blacks and Jews* (Chicago: NOI, 1991).
65 https://www.democracynow.org/2005/2/21/the_undiscovered_malcolm_x_stunning_new (accessed September 10, 2006).
66 Manning Marable, "Recovering Malcolm's Life: A Historian's Adventures in Living history," *Souls: A Critical Journal of Black Politics, Culture and Society*, vol. 7, no. 1 (2005): 22.
67 Farrakhan, "The Murder of Malcolm X: The Effect."
68 Maureen O'Donnell, "Farrakhan to Muslims: Honor Elijah Muhammad," *Chicago Sun-Times*, February 22, 1993, 10.
69 "Malcolm's Murder: His Widow Says 'Of Course' Farrakhan Was Involved," *Philadelphia Daily News*, March 14, 1994, 7.
70 Gibson, *A History of the Nation of Islam*, 120.
71 "Saviours' Day Convention on the Continent of Africa," *The Final Call*, July 20, 1994, 15.
72 Gibson, *A History of the Nation of Islam*, 134.
73 Gibson and Karim, *Women of the Nation*.
74 Gibson, *A History of the Nation of Islam*, 127.
75 http://www.finalcall.com/national/anniversary/mmm-pledge.html (accessed November 4, 2019).
76 "Remembering the Million Man March: Testimonies from People Who Attended" *Virtue Today Magazine*, October 2021, 11.
77 Ibid., 12.

4

Aftermath

The MMM was a "triumph" of unparalleled scope" for Black nationalists, Minister Farrakhan, and his faith community.[1] Twenty-seven years after the march, Minister Farrakhan and his faith community are much diminished in both number and stature. The faith community he leads today is in many ways a shadow of its former self. Minister Farrakhan now stands ready to hand over the reins of his beloved community to his national assistant Ishmael Muhammad and the Executive Shura Council. In a recent address at the NOI's annual Saviours' Day convention, Minister Farrakhan noted: "Ishmael has a burden on him. He got to beat history because his brother [Imam W. D. Mohammed] gave us our first examination and we failed it. He's in that position now as the face of the teachings."[2] Ishmael, as Minister Farrakhan notes, carries a "burden." As the biological son of Elijah Muhammad, his succession would meet with acceptance from NOI purists. The community that Ishmael is set to inherit is theologically divided, racially diverse, and numerically small. Moreover, its financial prowess appears to have weakened. Minister Farrakhan's overtures to Sunni Muslims and Christians, coupled with his flirtation with the COS in the years that followed the MMM has resulted in a broad set of religious beliefs and practices coexisting within the NOI with relative fluidity. Indeed, such a scenario has resulted in some confusion, even among ministers as senior as Ishmael, regarding whether NOI members pray to Fard Muhammad.[3] Ishmael is cognizant of the magnitude of the challenge he will face when his mentor departs. In his comments at the 2021 Saviours' Day convention, for example, he remarked that "we have a lot in front of us, we got to stay together, let's work out whatever needs to be worked out …

we got to stand as a solid wall … as long as we are united … we will be ok."[4] Minister Farrakhan and his team of thirteen ministers in the Executive Shura Council have adapted and diversified to survive in the post-MMM period. Their efforts have ensured the survival of the NOI. The NOI's teachings still resonate. Yet, it is undeniable that the community has dwindled in numbers and that it no longer generates national headlines. Indeed, the 2022 Saviours' Day convention, a highlight in the NOI's calendar, was poorly attended in comparison to previous conventions. Minister Farrakhan and his community have been plagued by charges of antisemitism, blasphemy, homophobia, and bigotry in the years since the march. The accusations are not without merit. The deeply unpopular tours that Minister Farrakhan undertook after the MMM followed by his brief reconciliation with Imam W. D. Mohammed after 9/11 and later engagement with the COS have led the community to a place where it accepts and tolerates diversity of religious practice and belief within its own mosques. The community's decline was not, however, inevitable. Minister Farrakhan and the NOI remain popular in pockets of the United States, and they have retained their presence and power in many US prisons where their ministry is welcomed, albeit reluctantly.[5] Association with Minister Farrakhan remains problematic for many public figures and politicians. The uproar created by his apparent endorsement of Barack Obama in 2007 and his sharing a stage with Bill Clinton in 2018 at the funeral of Aretha Franklin evidences widespread disapproval of his yet underexamined links with figures in the Democratic Party, for example. Moreover, the NOI's place in the American Muslim community remains peripheral. Minister Farrakhan and his followers have limited engagement with Sunni Muslims. Yet, the community continues to attract young members and in doing so secures its future. The recent results of the "Mosque in America" report in 2021 illustrate that African American mosques and African American attendance at Mosques has dwindled since 2010. According to the report's author Ihsan Bagby, the cause of the decline is the "inability of mosques to attract and maintain African American young adults."[6] Unlike their mainstream counterparts, the NOI continues to appeal to young people and give voice to their frustration. Minister Farrakhan and the NOI's story in the post-1995 period is one of decline, adaptability, and diversification.

The Post-1995 Years

The MMM was both a personal and professional achievement for Minister Farrakhan. Minister Farrakhan left the WCIW in the late 1970s with little in the way of assets, finances, or followers. In his 2020 address to his faith community, he lamented that he "started with nothing, no followers, no money."[7] Twenty-years later he entered the history books of the United States for bringing together the largest gathering of Black men in the nation's history. His feat in 1995 was no small achievement. Farrakhan is not far wrong when he remarks that the "most powerful government" in the world "tried to destroy" the NOI.[8] Moreover, his ability to bring secular and Christian groups on board to support the march evidenced both his ability to be humble, when required, and his skills as a community leader. The success of the MMM does not belong to Farrakhan alone. Indeed, he has often acknowledged as much. Farrakhan delivered the main address on October 16, 1995, but it was far from a one-man show. The march elevated Farrakhan to great heights in the United States. However, he and his coworkers failed to build on the unity of the day. Rather than commit to organizing and building networks at home, Farrakhan embarked on a series of deeply unpopular tours. The effect of which was a loss of some support at home and further condemnation and isolation from more traditional Muslim communities.

In his memoir entitled *Inside the Nation of Islam*, author and professor Vibert White argues that Minister Farrakhan embarked on tours abroad because he was depressed by negative press coverage of his October 16 address.[9] Regardless of his motive for doing so, Farrakhan and a delegation from the NOI embarked on a series of tours in the post-1995 period that brought them to South Africa, Ghana, Libya, Iraq, and later Zimbabwe. Minister Farrakhan construed the tours as an opportunity to internationalize the NOI and capitalize on his growing reputation. Many in the United States, however, construed the tours as "thug fests" and nothing more than an opportunity for Farrakhan to enrich himself.

Minister Farrakhan visited South Africa, Ghana, and Libya in January and February of 1996. Farrakhan was no stranger to Ghana. Indeed, he held the NOI's Saviours' Day convention in 1994 in Ghana and had enjoyed a warm relationship with President Jerry Rawlings. His trip to South Africa generated greater interest and criticism. Indeed, President Nelson Mandela had come under considerable pressure regarding his planned meeting with Farrakhan. It was commonly reported that white South Africans felt some degree of anxiety about Farrakhan's motives for visiting the country. Such anxiety was no doubt informed by press coverage that presented Farrakhan as divisive. Mandela, however, was undeterred and met with Farrakhan at his home in Johannesburg. Farrakhan remarked:

> All of the principles that President Mandela outlined [to us] we agree with totally. Islam is a religion which, if practiced, disallows racialism, racism, injustice, tyranny and oppression, said the controversial Muslim cleric after his meeting with Mr Mandela. President Mandela said: Our meeting has been very short and we were able to cover only those things that were considered to be fundamental. And there was no issue which arose on which there was disagreement.[10]

Farrakhan's time in South Africa enabled him and his entourage to network with leading figures in the African National Congress. Such networking in the short-term was beneficial. Indeed, the NOI secured Winnie Mandela as a keynote speaker for the Million Woman March in 1997.[11] However, Farrakhan's time in South Africa and Ghana had no long-term benefit for the NOI. The NOI's small mosque in Accra, Ghana, no longer exists. The 1994 Saviours' Day convention was the only such event that the NOI has held beyond the United States. Scholars De-Valera Botchway and Mustapha Abdul-Hamid argue that "by bringing the Saviours' Day celebration to Ghana, Farrakhan hoped to establish the NOI firmly in Ghana. However … that never happened, and today the NOI barely maintains a presence in Ghana."[12] Minister Farrakhan's visit to Libya in 1996 and acceptance of monetary gifts in the form of a $250,000 cash injection from Colonel Gadhafi did nothing to abate speculation that his tours were a self-enriching exercise.[13] Minister Farrakhan's tours appear to have had little impact on his own understanding of or critique of the race problem in the United States. The NOI's major initiatives on US soil in the post-1995 period included the Million Woman March in 1997, the Million Family March in 2000, the Millions More Movement in 2005, and the Justice or Else March in 2015. Each march helped raise the NOI's profile and showcased its capacity and skill for organizing on a national scale. Moreover, each march reminded American civil rights and Black Nationalist groups of the NOI's prowess and esteem in local communities where the work of the FOI and MGT is known to make a tangible difference in communities where drug use, violence, and conflict are rife.[14] Minister Farrakhan's grip on the NOI and his ability to capitalize on the momentum of subsequent marches were limited as a result of health problems and prostate cancer in particular.

The Million Woman March witnessed the largest gathering of African American women in the history of the United States. Estimates of attendance at the march varied greatly. *Jet Magazine* claimed that "two million women" attended the march in Philadelphia while more modest estimates of 300,000 were offered by the *New York Times*.[15] The march focused on themes of sisterhood and family, in particular. Women in the ranks and leadership of the MGT worked diligently to promote the march. Their efforts paid dividends. The march, in itself, did little to propagate the NOI's theology. However, it did give a platform to its conservative gender norms. The NOI's program was given female voice at the march through speeches delivered by Tynetta Muhammad and Khadijah Farrakhan. Khadijah reiterated the MGT's adage: "A nation can rise no higher than its women … We focus on women but cannot lose sight that we must rise as a family: men, women and children."[16] Khadija's remarks may seem rather insignificant, and her presence was certainly overshadowed by Winnie Mandela's keynote address. Yet, her choice of words, however few, offered women in attendance a powerful reminder that the faith community's gender ideology was not about oppressing women but elevating them.

Events such as the MMM and the Million Woman March evidenced the NOI's relevance and ability to galvanize the masses. They did not, however, result in the masses joining the NOI or endorsing it as a faith community. The theme of unity and family was also dominant in the Million Family March in 2000. The march itself was of particular importance for Minister Farrakhan's faithful. Recollections of the march and its meaning for NOI members were recently published in a November 2022 issue of *The Final Call* in which Abisayo Muhammad reported:

> It was the Million Family March that my husband Marcus Muhammad and I were blessed to work, attend and recite wedding vows given by Min.

Farrakhan. So, five years after the initial Million Man March, I had the honor and privilege of being among 10,000 other couples who participated in blessing or renewing our marriages in front of the world. It was exciting to travel to Washington, D.C., with my mother, sister and cousin while my husband's father, stepmother and brother prepared to enjoy this unique occasion along with us. The Minister required every couple to have a marriage license prior to the event. So, though we had a wonderful, small ceremony prior to the march at Mosque Maryam in Chicago by our marriage counselor and officiator, Student Minister Amin Muhammad; every year in addition to celebrating the Holy Day of Atonement, we also honor this day as our official wedding anniversary. Married couple Gregory and Sheryl Muhammad also remember the renewal of their vows on this special day. This couple celebrates 48 years of marriage and has a rich history in the Nation of Islam. Bro. Gregory Muhammad remembers that the march was a special day but says he could not have been there without acknowledging another impactful day back in 1972. "We had no plans of getting married because we were just close friends and college classmates. I invited my friend Sheryl to the 'Black Family Day' celebration at Randall's Island in New York. There we witnessed the beauty of a man who expressed the importance of family, the love, respect, and protection for the Black woman. That beautiful man was the Honorable Minister Louis Farrakhan. In fact, the speech was so invigorating that we were encouraged to get married seven months and one day later, on December 28, 1974," he said.[17]

The Million Family March came at a time of increasing uncertainty for Minister Farrakhan and his faith community. His prolonged absence from the NOI on account of treatment for prostate cancer created panic about the future of his faith community. Minister Farrakhan's illness forced him to reassess not only his own theological perspectives but the leadership structures within the NOI.[18] Outside observers of the NOI rightly remarked that Minister Farrakhan's illness had "set off a new wave of anxiety among his followers" and that "no clear hierarchy" existed in the community.[19] Farrakhan's illness compelled him and other ministers to contemplate the community's prospects for surviving his exit. Such contemplation appears to have personally moved Farrakhan away from the NOI's foundational theology. Indeed, in February 2000, Minister Farrakhan publicly reconciled with Imam W. D. Mohammed. While the reconciliation with Imam Mohammed should not be read as an embrace of Sunni Islam by Farrakhan, it is nonetheless important to note that both his tone and emphasis did change.

The Nation's fall in 1975 and the emergence of the RNOI only a few years later created deep wounds in families that had been effectively torn apart over opposing theological understandings of Elijah Muhammad's teachings. Former NOI member, Sonsyrea Tate, for example, recalled that the split between the WCIW and the RNOI had been deeply hurtful for many families: "Each side sharply criticized the other. Nation of Islam members berated former members for embracing the traditions of Arabs … and former Nation of Islam Muslims who converted to Sunni Islam condemned those who lined up behind Farrakhan to rebuild the old Nation of Islam as people stuck in the past."[20]

The February 2000 Saviours' Day convention was billed as a reconciliation of family. The event brought together members of Imam Mohammed's American Muslim Mission and Minister Farrakhan's RNOI in Chicago. The event was attended by delegations from abroad and witnessed Farrakhan embrace, at least in public, a revised interpretation of Fard Muhammad and Elijah Muhammad's teachings. Farrakhan's embrace of Sunni Muslims had been encouraged by the Islamic Society of North America (ISNA) and its national director, Dr. Sayyid Syeed in particular. Dr. Syeed, for example, notes that Minister Farrakhan first reached out to the ISNA as early as 1994 for assistance with moving his followers closer to Sunni Islam. He also ordered his followers to fast during Ramadan rather than in December, as early NOI members had done. Dr. Syeed remarks that he talked rather "extensively" with Farrakhan prior to his national address at the February 2000 Saviours' Day convention.[21]

In the run up to the event, Farrakhan had a number of conversations with members of the Imam W. D. Mohammed community. In conversation with Imam Mohammed's brother, Akbar, for example, Farrakhan remarked:

> Our greatest teacher, Prophet Muhammad, Salla Allahu Wassalam, taught us to worship Allah and Allah alone do we worship. Master Fard Muhammad taught us to worship Allah and Allah alone. The Honorable Elijah Muhammad taught us to worship Allah and Allah alone. We believe in the finality of Prophet Muhammad Bin Abdullah of Mecca as the last prophet and Messenger of Allah. Fard Muhammad was the messenger of the messenger of Allah to us, to our people.[22]

Minister Farrakhan's response to Akbar appears to be the closest he has ever come to publicly repudiating the notion that Fard Muhammad was God in person. His comments here, for example, stand in stark contrast to his feedback to Ishmael concerning NOI members praying to Fard Muhammad.[23] Minister Farrakhan's personal gravitation to more traditional Islamic teachings was no doubt a serious concern for some of his followers. Yet, his alignment and his community's newfound acceptance with sections of the American ummah was to be further strengthened by the 9/11 terrorist attacks.

The terrorist attacks on US soil on September 11, 2001, led to far-reaching changes in US foreign and domestic policy. President Bush's War on Terror and the passage of the Patriot Act six weeks after the attacks forever changed America's relationship with the Muslim world and its own domestic Muslim population. American anti-Muslim sentiments are, as Kambiz GhaneaBassiri notes, as "old as the United States."[24] Such sentiments have been helped by malign portrayals of Islam in the national media and an unfortunate ignorance about the religion itself:

> While favorable opinions toward Muslims have declined since the time immediately after 9/11, an overview of public opinion surveys conducted since 9/11 reveals a polarized nation divided down the middle within a 5–10 percent margin in terms of its opinion toward Muslims. Given that this division persists, even though the majority of Americans admit that they do not "have a good basic understanding of the teachings and beliefs of Islam," it seems clear that attitudes toward Islam have less to do with the religion and its practitioners than it does with current events and media reports, which have indelibly associated Islam with violence in the American public square.[25]

America's troubling relationship with its Muslim population has deep roots. Local police departments and intelligence agencies treatment of NOI members and their leaders in the 1930s and thereafter revealed the extent to which the government was willing to persecute and vilify its own Muslim population. Thus, as Edward Curtis rightly notes: "By the time of the 9/11 attacks, the association of all Muslims and Islamic religion with violence, misogyny, and general backwardness had already become an entrenched form of conventional wisdom in some policy circles, especially among neoconservatives."[26]

Minister Farrakhan and his faith community immediately condemned the 9/11 attacks. In a press conference delivered from Mosque Maryam on September 16, 2001, Minister Farrakhan stood before NOI members and representatives from the national and local press to condemn the attacks:

> I, like millions of people around this earth, watched in amazement, shock, and horror, the events of September 11, and the unfolding of the ripple effect of this terrible tragedy. I have listened with great care to the leaders of this nation, political and spiritual. I have read the condolences of leaders from around the world who stand with the United States of America in this hour of her greatest national tragedy. I have listened and watched the President of the United States with his eyes filled with tears, feeling the pain of the countless numbers of Americans affected by the tragedy of events on the morning of September 11. I, on behalf of all the members of the Nation of Islam and on behalf of many millions of Muslims here in America and throughout the world, lift our voices to condemn this vicious and atrocious attack on the United States. In this very dark hour in American and world history, the greatest need for us and for the leadership of this nation is Divine Guidance … We mourn the loss of the many who have perished in this national and international tragedy. We commend the firemen and the policemen and women who risk their lives on a daily basis to keep an ordered society and a society free from the danger of fire and crime. These police and fire persons should be looked upon as heroes, notwithstanding the fact that we have issues of police brutality and racial profiling. Yet, it must be understood that these police and fire persons leave their homes everyday to do their duty in an ever-increasingly violent society, never knowing whether they shall return home to their families.[27]

Minister Farrakhan's condemnation of the attacks was both passionate and tactical and further evidence of a shift in his theological influences. For decades, Farrakhan riled against the US government, its judicial system, and police departments that disproportionately targeted African Americans. Further, he personally held the US intelligence community responsible for the Nation's power struggles in 1965 and its fall in 1975. Moreover, he had enjoyed the friendship of nation's hostile to US interests. Minister Farrakhan's condemnation of the attacks was also tactical. Farrakhan was and remains cognizant of the might and willingness of the US government to crush entities considered to be a threat or threatening to US interests. Had he failed to condemn the attacks, Minister Farrakhan would have left his followers vulnerable to attack and his faith community open to further intrusive surveillance and ultimately destruction. Minister Farrakhan's condemnation of the attacks and his prayers for the victims placed him alongside other Sunni Muslim communities and organizations.

The rise of rampant Islamophobia in the United States and Farrakhan's public embrace of more traditional Muslim teachings led him to pursue closer ties with organizations such as the Council of Islamic Organizations of Greater Chicago (CIOGC) and leading Imams in Chicago including Imam Siraj Wahhaj and Imam Abdul Malik in New York. These relationships remain positive, despite Farrakhan's oscillation between Sunni Islam and heresy. Indeed, Imam Siraj Wahhaj's "bond" with Minister Farrakhan is as "strong as ever." Moreover, Imam Malik served as Farrakhan's tour guide during hajj.[28] Minister Farrakhan also returned his attention to tours of Africa and the Middle East in the early 2000s. In 2002, for example, he traveled to Zimbabwe for a private meeting with President Robert G. Mugabe. Farrakhan's meeting with Mugabe was significant given that by 2002 the former liberation hero and his country were under intense sanctions. Farrakhan's meeting with Mugabe appears to have been amicable but his visit failed to generate much interest from Zimbabweans. It was not, for example, reported in the country's leading newspaper, *The Herald*. Farrakhan's willingness to meet with heads of state who were openly critical of the US and the Bush administration, in particular, revealed a determination not to be hampered by the hostile climate at home. Minister Farrakhan's addresses to audiences beyond America's borders were not always hostile in tone. In an address to students at the University of the West Indies in March 2002, for example, he spoke of his hope that censure of the United States would move the country to "a more humane posture." In the same speech, he spoke of his gratitude to live in the United States:

> America means that much to me. It is a very great Nation with great potential ... thank God that I live in America ... I live in a democracy that allows me the freedom of expression that I would be free to criticise my government and hopefully move the government of the United States to a more humane posture that she will not be drunk with the arrogance of wealth and power ... I must speak boldly this truth ... because America means that much to me.[29]

Minister Farrakhan's embrace of a more traditional and indeed universal understanding of Islam also led to changes within the NOI. In 2005, for example, Minister Farrakhan launched the Millions More Movement. Unlike, earlier marches, the Millions More Movement was considerably more inclusive, and its appeal directed specifically at native Americans and Latinos. Farrakhan's adventures abroad in the years between 1995 and 2005 certainly cost him leverage. Indeed, even his longtime friend Rev. Jeremiah Wright from Trinity United Church of Christ expressed misgivings about the MMM.[30] Ultimately, the march failed to generate the same support or coverage as the 1995 march. The devastation caused by Hurricane Katrina in 2005 and the Bush administration's ineptitude in the face of such tragedy provided Farrakhan with plenty of ammunition to justify the need for the MMM. Yet, his support had very clearly dwindled. Farrakhan did receive a BET Person of the Year Award in 2005.[31] However, the events of 2005 illustrated very clearly that he had lost ground.

Farrakhan's leadership of the NOI in 2005 and the years that followed was again stifled as a result of health problems. In 2006, Farrakhan traveled to Cuba where he underwent a series of medical tests. Such tests revealed that his cancer had returned. Farrakhan's health scare forced him to hand control of the NOI to his subordinates, as discussed later in the chapter. Not until 2008 did Farrakhan return his attention to the NOI. His fresh health scare once again moved him closer to Sunni Islam. Indeed, when he rededicated Mosque Maryam on October 19, 2008, it was evident that he had further embraced a revised understanding of Elijah Muhammad's teachings:

> When Elijah Muhammad came among us he taught what you could call a Black theology. A lot of people were offended by that; turned off by that. In the Muslim world they were angry; they said: "Islam does not teach colour; what's wrong with you people?" But they don't know what happened to us ... here's a people that have been in America over 450 years and foreigners come to America and within a few days they have money, they have businesses, they have economic standing, they're proud of being an American because they came here with nothing and they have what they have. We've been here longer than anyone else except the Native indigenous peoples ... but we have some stars among us, we do, we have people that have shaken the world ... but the Honorable Elijah Muhammad said: "you can never, no one man, can

ever escape being identified with the condition of his people … ." The man that came to us from Mecca, we call him Master Fard Muhammad, he had a Black father and a White mother. That man came to us first because our condition was worse. He was so skilful, he developed a methodology along with an ideology, that would start a process of transformation in our lives. … This may shock some of you, but he wanted to help, eventually, both people.[32]

Minister Farrakhan's comments during his speech at Mosque Maryam were significant. In them, he offered not condemnation of foreign Muslims, but understanding of their misgivings. Moreover, he referred to Fard Muhammad as a mere mortal and suggested that what he taught was part of a methodology aimed at starting a process of "transformation." Farrakhan's suggestion that Fard wanted to help both African Americans and whites was significant. Yet, it also panicked his followers. In the weeks that followed his address, Minister Farrakhan was required to reassure his followers that the NOI's mosques were primarily, though not exclusively, for African Americans.[33]

Minister Farrakhan's addresses to his followers throughout 2008 and 2009 were largely aimed at quieting their concerns over what appeared to be his public embrace of Sunni Islam and efforts to extend membership of the NOI. Farrakhan's addresses also evidenced his growing preoccupation with Jewish American attitudes toward him and what he construed to be an orchestrated campaign to silence and ostracize him. In the post-2005 period in particular, association with Minister Farrakhan could prove damaging for public figures. Farrakhan's promotion of the NOI research department's 2010 book, *The Secret Relationship between Blacks and Jews (Volume 2)*, invited further censure from the ADL. Indeed, this appears to have been Farrakhan's goal. The ADL, for example, notes that the NOI mailed copies of the book to Jewish organizations.[34] Farrakhan's reputation in the United States soured as a result of his frequent attacks on Jewish Americans and his support for nation's that the United States considered to be pariah states. As the decade progressed, it became increasingly evident that public support for Farrakhan had waned. Yet, he remained, beyond any doubt, a significant figure in sections of the United States.

Senator Barack Obama's bid for the presidency in 2008 was something that the NOI and their leader watched with cautious optimism. Their national paper produced frequent reports about Obama's campaign while also giving a fair amount of coverage to his opponents. Minister Farrakhan offered his endorsement of Obama at the 2008 Saviours' Day convention. During his address he labeled Obama "the hope of the entire word."[35] Obama was subsequently asked if he would both "denounce" and "reject" Farrakhan's support during an awkward debate with Hillary Clinton and Tim Russert. Obama conceded.[36] For his part, Farrakhan continued to voice his support. Unbeknown to American voters at the time, Farrakhan had already met and been photographed with Obama. Indeed, when Obama left office, Farrakhan informed his followers that Obama had sought him out in Chicago when he was first elected as a senator. Moreover, he was photographed with Obama by his longtime associate Askia Muhammad in 2005.[37] The photo was taken at the Congressional Black Caucus and shows Obama smiling happily beside Minister Farrakhan. Minister Farrakhan was aware of the photo and requested that Askia "bury" it until Obama was no longer in office.[38] Minister Farrakhan addressed the controversy surrounding the photo during a community rally at the faith community of Saint Sabina in Chicago on May 9, 2019:

> I'm a hated man today, you can't event have a picture with me. Poor Barack, we helped him win in Illinois and at the Congressional Black Caucus he was now a senator, and he had a beautiful smile on his face, and somebody had that picture ... I don't mind saying it was one of our brothers. You can't say you like Farrakhan ... They are angry with me because I exposed their hatred of Jesus ... I don't have no army, I just know the truth and I'm here to separate the good Jews from the satanic Jews. I have not said one word of hate. I do not hate Jewish people ... I'm not a misogynist, I'm not a homophobe ... don't be angry with me if I stand on God's word.[39]

Obama was by no means a regular visitor at Farrakhan's home. However, the two men had crossed paths on at least a few occasions and Obama, by his own admission, attended the MMM in 1995. Minister Farrakhan was a longtime friend of Obama's pastor, Jeremiah Wright. Wright led Trinity United Church of Christ in Chicago for decades. He officiated Obama's marriage and baptized his children. Moreover, his church awarded Farrakhan the Dr. Jeremiah Wright Trumpeter Award.[40] Unlike Obama, Wright refused to denounce Farrakhan and instead defended him as a friend.

President Obama's inauguration was celebrated widely in the NOI. Indeed, their national newspaper covered the inauguration in considerable detail. Obama's election unleashed deeply flawed arguments that the United States was "post-racial." Moreover, the election induced hysteria among those desperate to maintain the racial hierarchy. Obama faced an onslaught of intense opposition, political efforts to stifle his agenda, and personal insults.[41] For much of his presidency, Minister Farrakhan was restrained in his criticism. However, that changed in 2011 when Ghaddafi was killed.[42] Farrakhan laid the blame for Ghaddafi's death squarely at the hands of an aggressive US foreign policy bent on removing him from power through regime change. In discussing his response to the loss of Ghaddafi, he remarked:

> I feel like I have lost a very, very important member of my own family. I can't take the assassination of Muammar Gadhafi lightly, as I could not take the assassination of my brother, or my mother, or my wife or my children lightly. That's the kind of relationship that we had and that we have ... I come to say to the world that the Nation of Islam mourns the loss of a great brother, leader, the Lion of the Desert, the Lion of Africa, and those who rejoice at his death, your laughter will turn to tears and your joy will turn to sorrow and great pain because of what the Western world and those collaborators will lose as a result of his betrayal and his ultimate assassination.[43]

Minister Farrakhan's criticism of Obama and his administration intensified further from 2012 onward. High-profile cases of police brutality, miscarriages of justice, and deteriorating race relations enabled Farrakhan to network extensively alongside his ministerial counterparts to build support for the twentieth anniversary of the MMM. Moreover, the emergence of the Black Lives Matter movement helped Farrakhan galvanize the support of young students and individuals who were too young to remember the MMM.

The Justice or Else March in October 2015 was promoted primarily among Christians. Indeed, Minister Farrakhan's promotional tour for the planned march included just one speaking engagement at a mosque. He also utilized his relationships with rappers including Snoop Dogg and Kanye West to promote the march. Farrakhan has known both men for quite some time. He shared a stage with Snoop Dogg at the funeral of Stanley Tookie Williams and in 2005 the NOI had awarded West its Million Man March Image award.[44] West has a particular fondness for Minister Farrakhan. In 2015, for example, he told

Rolling Stone magazine that he was working on a documentary with Minister Farrakhan and that he specifically requested that Minister Farrakhan give him his BET award. In the same interview he defended Minister Farrakhan from charges of bigotry: "He's a classically trained violinist, and he's also one of the most humane people. And now he got that stamp—in the same way my wife was stamped with the sex tape, the minister was stamped with [bigotry]. It's important that while he's still alive, he has to see the people appreciate his message … There's a lot I can learn from him."[45] Minister Farrakhan's rapport with rappers only went so far in promoting the march. Farrakhan's efforts to raise awareness of the planned march left him exhausted and unable to fast during Ramadan.[46] The march itself brought together representatives from Black Lives Matter, the Southern Christian Leadership Conference, the NAACP, and well-known pastors including Rev. Jeremiah Wright. Local media reports suggested that thousands attended the march. However, figures for march attendance are not available. Indeed, the march received very little coverage in the national news.

Minister Farrakhan depended greatly on his network of Christian allies to support the Justice or Else March. The fact that his speaking engagements were delivered exclusively in Christian settings speaks volumes about Farrakhan's standing in Sunni Muslim communities. Minister Farrakhan has in recent years welcomed engagements with Sunni Muslims. His willingness to support the work on the DIA is evidence of this. Moreover, representatives from the CIOGC have met with Farrakhan multiple times and attended numerous events held by the NOI. Yet, Sunni Islam and Christianity are not the only theologies at work in the NOI. Minister Farrakhan's relationship with the COS has bemused and baffled many. Farrakhan introduced his followers to Dianetics Auditing in 2011. He promoted the practice among his followers as a means to help them overcome traumatic experiences. According to Jacob King, Farrakhan was introduced to the COS formally in 2006. However, its teachings were made known to him much earlier via contacts in the music industry.[47] King argues: "It should … be emphasized that it is not Scientology that Farrakhan is embracing. Scientology, in affirming past lives, an immortal soul, and the alien origins of human neuroses, is clearly at odds with the NOI's core tenets."[48] As noted, Dianetics Auditing is a common practice within the NOI's mosques. Minister Farrakhan has consistently denied rumors that he accepted money from the COS. Moreover, his followers are not likely to abandon the NOI for the COS. Yet, their willingness to wholeheartedly embrace Dianetics Auditing reveals that there is flexibility and openness within the RNOI.

The Justice or Else March was something of a success for the NOI and Minister Farrakhan. However, his high-profile engagements since have been limited. With the exception of his appearance at Aretha Franklin's funeral in 2018 and smaller engagements within the NOI, he has kept a relatively low profile. Minister Farrakhan's attendance at the funeral of Franklin generated headlines not because he was there but because of who he was seated beside. According to Farrakhan, it was a friend in the clergy who asked him to sit on the stage beside Bill Clinton and Jesse Jackson. Clinton is not a stranger to the NOI or its staff. While Hillary Clinton chided Obama for not speaking out sooner to reject Farrakhan's support, she herself was likely aware that her husband had invited the NOI's chief of protocol to serve on his national steering committee for his reelection in 1996.[49] Farrakhan and his followers do appear to have extensive links with political actors in the Democratic Party. Such links are, however, largely underexamined and thus not publicized. Minister Farrakhan is not himself a fan of Clinton's politics. During her second presidential run, Farrakhan appeared to suggest that Trump would better serve the interests of the NOI and African Americans.[50]

Minister Farrakhan's leadership of the NOI was further restricted with the emergence of the Covid-19 pandemic. The pandemic visited havoc on religious communities and forced many such communities to move religious services online. As noted, NOI members have benefitted from online services and programs for many years. Thus, the move to online services was something they were arguably more prepared for. Minister Farrakhan's followers worked tirelessly throughout lockdowns to provide for and educate their communities.[51] Minister Farrakhan himself made only one speech regarding the pandemic. In a lecture entitled "The Criterion" delivered on July 4, 2020, Minister Farrakhan set out his own understanding of the pandemic. In his extensive address delivered in front of a small outdoor delegation, he referred to Fard as the Messiah and to Covid-19 as a pestilence from God:

> Our iniquitous behavior is a pestilence on the earth so God answers with a pestilence. His anger is at a point where He has to punish the inhabitants of

the earth for their iniquity. So punishment from God's pestilence is to turn against you the things that you depend upon for your sustenance.[52]

Minister Farrakhan later revealed at the 2022 Saviours' Day lecture that both he and his wife had contracted Covid-19 and that neither had been vaccinated.[53] That Farrakhan would construe the pandemic to be the result of some form of divine punishment is rather unsurprising. Minister Farrakhan and his ministers have cautioned their followers against the Covid-19 vaccine. Their writings in *The Final Call* concerning the vaccine evidence a measure of fear and suspicion regarding its safety. Weekly issues of the paper often carry at least one page dedicated to cautioning readers about the vaccine. According to Farrakhan, the vaccine is part of a depopulation conspiracy. In place of the vaccine, he urges his followers to use "fourteen therapies" to fight the disease. Each page of the paper also carries a warning, noting: "Brothers and Sisters: Do not take the Covid-19 Vaccine. It is unsafe, ineffective, and it is not even a vaccine. It does not stop infection and it does not stop transmission of the pathogen known as Covid-19." In place of the vaccine, it encourages readers to take ivermectin.[54] It is entirely unclear whether NOI members have taken the vaccine. It is safe to assume that many such members regard the decision as a personal one and therefore Farrakhan's recommendations are taken as advice rather than regulation.

The NOI's ministers delivered weekly addresses online throughout the pandemic. Ishmael and members of the executive board worked tirelessly to provide online services for eighteen months. Minister Farrakhan was, by and large, absent from such services. Indeed, more often than not, it was Ishmael who delivered weekly messages. The NOI's mosques reopened in November 2021. The reopening was advertised in the national paper:

> "Those of you who are present today at Mosque Maryam, all of you who are watching via webcast on your various electronic devices, we want to invite all of you who have been listening to us for the last 18 months, that by Nov. 14, you can come to your local mosque and study group in the cities where you live, that we may embrace you, welcome you, receive you and continue this great work of the Honorable Elijah Muhammad in the transformation of our lives. So, extend the invitation to the public," Student Minister Ishmael joyfully announced ct. 31. The pandemic-driven, physical closure of mosques had been unprecedented in the NOI's 91-year history,

noted Student Minister Demetric Muhammad, who is also a member of the Nation of Islam Research Team. The only possible exception was the government incarceration of the Honorable Elijah Muhammad, the Eternal Leader of the Nation of Islam, and many of his male followers in the 1940s during World War II, he said. One of the most significant consequences of the reopening of the Mosque will be the social interaction in a spiritual place, Demetric Muhammad said. "It's good that the mosques are opening because from the perspective of the Believer, you know, Allah (God) says in the Holy Qur'an that the Believers are friends of one another, and humanity is referred to as social beings," he continued. "So ultimately among spiritual communities, when the building is no longer open, there is a longing and a yearning for community life, where co-religionists can assemble in a place of shared values, a shared culture, shared belief system, which strengthens each other to go through difficult periods."[55]

Minister Farrakhan's frail condition during his *Criterion* lecture and his absence from online weekly services ensured that the work of the NOI's ministry was left to the Executive Shura Council.

The Executive Shura Council and the Future of the NOI

Minister Farrakhan has remained the public face of his faith community since its formation in the late 1970s. Privately, he has relied on the counsel of several long-serving members and aides for decades. Such individuals are incredibly close to Farrakhan and offer him practical, spiritual, and professional guidance. Yet, Farrakhan remains the sole religious authority in his faith community and all matters concerning the community's direction ultimately rest with him. The one-man show that the community presented itself as changed drastically, although temporarily, in 1999 when Farrakhan was diagnosed with cancer. The minister's deteriorating health and need for recovery forced him to delegate power and effectively reconsider and reorganize the community's hierarchy. Subsequently, in 2001 he announced the formation of the Commission for the Reorganization and Restructuring of the Nation of Islam. In discussions with his colleague and advisor, Jabril Muhammad, in the early 2000s, Farrakhan conceded that he formed the commission due to fears that, in its current configuration, the NOI would not have survived his death.[56] The formation of such a commission provided a rare opportunity for Minister Farrakhan's subordinates to shine and in particular Elijah Muhammad's son Ishmael.

Ishmael's position in the community and close relationship with Minister Farrakhan were highlighted in *The Final Call* in 2001 in an article entitled "Taking on the Mission."[57] In his interview with the community's national paper, Ishmael noted that Farrakhan had been a "mentor," a "teacher," and an "example" to him throughout his life. He further noted that his position as an assistant minister had brought "struggle" and "trials":

> I believe I have come a long way and it has taken this many years for me to finally accept the position I hold in the Nation of Islam as assistant minister, and the tremendous responsibility of leadership. It has been a tremendous struggle. It certainly has had its trials and setbacks, but I'm more determined now than ever before to help Min Farrakhan in this work and to help the Black community out of the condition it suffers.[58]

Ishmael's time as an assistant minister provided him with a unique opportunity to demonstrate his administrative talents within the community. In 2001 Farrakhan noted publicly that he was "proud" of Ishmael's "development."[59] Ishmael has remained positioned close to Farrakhan and the Nation's nerve center at Mosque Maryam since 2000. His closeness to Minister Farrakhan and Farrakhan's growing dependency on him has been evident since 2000. Indeed, rarely has Minister Farrakhan attended a speaking engagement without Ishmael by his side. At such engagements, it is Ishmael's job to introduce his mentor as Elijah Muhammad's only qualified successor.

Ishmael's emerging profile as a potential successor to Farrakhan was evidenced in 2006 when his mentor suffered fresh health problems. Farrakhan's battle with cancer became public knowledge on September 11, 2006, when he published a letter to the "Believers of the NOI" in *The Final Call* newspaper. In his letter, the minister outlined his personal health problems and informed his followers that the executive board of the NOI would be available "to solve the problems of the Nation" during his absence.[60] The executive board was almost certainly the same in size and compositions as its earlier incarnation. Farrakhan's yearlong break from the NOI throughout 2006 illustrated how unprepared his ministers and followers were for the task of collectively managing the community. Moreover, the weekly lectures that his ministers delivered highlighted that while some were more attune to Sunni Islam, others held dearly to the community's founding theology.[61] Farrakhan's Executive Board appear to have confronted serious challenges in his absence. First, the board was composed of ministers who were themselves at odds in their understanding of the NOI's theology and mission. As noted earlier, NOI members offer diverse interpretations of the NOI's theology and mission. For some, the NOI's founding doctrine is interpreted quite literally. Others, however, believe that the founding theology was simply a "method" by which Fard Muhammad could somehow lead his followers to a more traditional and universal understanding of Islam. Second, the board confronted and failed to effectively quell efforts by some ministers to grandstand in Farrakhan's absence. Such individuals clearly construed Minister Farrakhan's absence as an opportunity to vie for greater influence and leverage in the community. In response to such instances, Farrakhan removed prestigious titles from ministers, and all, regardless of years of service and distinction, were simply given the title "student minister."[62] Farrakhan has noted on at least a few occasions that "some" of his staff "don't like" the title "student minister."[63]

Farrakhan's efforts to effectively humble egotistic ministers and root out individuals with aspirations to replace him seem to have met with some success. The community has suffered little in the way of power struggles since 2008. However, it is also true that the composition of his executive board has since changed. Ishmael's mother and former "wife" of Elijah Muhammad, Tynetta Muhammad, passed away in 2015. Her passing has no doubt proven difficult for Farrakhan given that she was one of his "principal supporters" in his rebuilding efforts.[64] Moreover, Tynetta's public testimony regarding her relationship with Elijah Muhammad was something that Farrakhan and the NOI's faithful relied on to refute notions that Elijah Muhammad was a sexual predator.[65] Questions and criticism of Muhammad's domestic life remain an ongoing challenge for Minister Farrakhan's community. Indeed in 2019, *The Final Call* staff writer Richard B. Muhammad took to task filmmaker Dream Hampton for her series *Surviving R. Kelly*. According to Muhammad, Hampton "injected an ugly lie and nefarious slander" into the series with the comment that "Malcolm X was assassinated because he lifted his voice to call out a predator. Malcolm X died fighting for adolescent Black girls who were being exploited by a man he once loved. Doing the right thing is never easy and may cost you your life. Long Live Malcolm." In refuting Dream's allegation, Muhammad referred to and included an image of Tynetta and other wives testifying in 1993 that their "husband" had been an honorable man.[66] The notion that Malcolm was assassinated because he exposed Muhammad's behavior is flawed. Nonetheless, it evidences the extent to which Malcolm's own writings and comments concerning his exit from the NOI have been misunderstood and misinterpreted. As noted earlier, Malcolm likely knew of Muhammad's behavior as early as the 1950s. Moreover, his initial efforts to justify and explain Muhammad's behavior certainly suggest that he did not condemn, at least initially, his mentor's apparent predatory behavior. Tynetta's loss has been felt dearly not only by Farrakhan but by the many women in the community who regarded her as a role model.

Likewise, Ava Muhammad who served as Minister Farrakhan's attorney passed away in early September 2022. Perhaps more than any other minister, Ava gave voice to the NOI's separatist mandate. In the last several years, she participated in multiple interviews, events, and tours calling for racial separation in the United States. In May 2022, for example, she was introduced on WVON radio as heading "project separation" within the NOI.[67] Ava's speaking engagements and tours in the immediate years before her death indicate that she remained committed to an almost fundamentalist interpretation of Fard Muhammad's theology. Indeed, her addresses at NOI events and mosques evidenced, if nothing else, her contempt for whites, Christianity, and all forms of racial integration. Throughout 2019 Ava toured the United States promoting racial separation as a "solution" to racial strife and inequality in the United States. In an address at Muhammad Mosque Number 32 in January 2019, for example, she remarked:

> We have been shaped and moulded into a state of involuntary servitude ... we have to shed the badge of inferiority, we have to shed this inclination, this need to have everything that a Black man tells us confirmed by a white man ... we have difficulty accepting the authority of Black people ... separation is the best and only solution ... The menu in God's restaurant has one option: separation ... it is the only solution to the problem between Black and white and our problem is we keep trying other solutions, none of which have worked. Islam comes when all else fails ... we thank Allah for Donald

Trump because if Hillary had gotten in it would have stretched it out … she would have a bunch of Negroes in her administration … now we are being forced to go for self. as long as we live with white people we will live under white people.[68]

Ava's reception at Mosque Number 32 suggests that she is far from alone in her fundamentalist interpretation of Fard Muhammad's theology. Her death has thus removed another fundamentalist voice from Minister Farrakhan's body of advisors. It is unlikely, however, to have a significant impact on the NOI's direction or the decision-making processes that occur within the community.

Minister Farrakhan's advanced age and ailing health have hampered his efforts to effectively lead the NOI. In 2015, for example, he remarked publicly that he had been left "exhausted" by his efforts to promote the Justice or Else March.[69] Farrakhan's frail condition has been more evidenced in recent years and particularly during his addresses at the annual Saviours' Day convention. Indeed, in 2021 he delivered his closing remarks while seated and in 2022 he delivered his entire speech seated. During both addresses, he was effectively aided to and from his seat by senior FOI including his son, Mustapha Farrakhan.

Any doubt that NOI members may have had about Ishmael's prominence within Minister Farrakhan's inner circle were abated in February 2021 when he delivered the community's annual Saviours' Day address on behalf of Farrakhan. It is important to note that 2021 is the only instance in which Minister Farrakhan has not delivered the address himself. Owing to the Covid-19 pandemic, the 2021 convention was held virtually rather than in person. NOI members and readers of the national paper were informed of the decision to hold the event online in late February. In conveying the decision to hold the event online, Ishmael noted:

> Saviours' Day over the years has always been public and the public has been invited to attend and participate in the informative and educational and inspiring workshops and, of course, the keynote address delivered each and every year … So, the Executive Council took our historic template and we just applied that to the virtual world now so that all of the activities would be—exception of the annual drill competition—will be done in the same manner but it will be virtual. … It is our desire to transmit and convey to all who attend guidance in a time of great trouble … We have chosen the theme

that the Honorable Elijah Muhammad lifted in the early 70s, I believe in the Muhammad Speaks newspaper where he asked the question: How Strong is the Foundation? Can we survive? … The foundation of something is that which supports. It's the basis for support. So, we have designed Saviours' Day to help, to strengthen the foundation of the Believer in God and the human being that needs knowledge and guidance to get through this great time of trouble and dark hour that the scriptures are told would be visited upon the face of every inhabitant of the Earth.[70]

The task of pulling off such a large and international convention online was no small feat for the executive council. However, the NOI was very much "ahead of the curve" in the move to online programming because "it was already" offering such events pre-pandemic.[71]

The 2021 convention was very much a team effort on the part of the executive council. However, it was Ishmael who appeared front and center at the event. In his closing remarks at the event, Minister Farrakhan conceded that he had given Ishmael a "a few months" notice and that he did not "feel it was for me to give" the address himself but rather that it was his heartfelt desire that Ishmael should "carry" the day. He did, however, offer Ishmael some advice, noting: "Don't go out there thinking of me, you go out and teach what God has put on you to teach."

In his opening remarks, Ishmael conveyed how daunted he was at the prospect of delivering the main address. His fears, however, appear to have been unfounded as his mentor was notably pleased by the address. In his closing remarks, for example, Minister Farrakhan commented:

I'm comforted … because the teachings will keep the Nation thriving through the upcoming hour … I'm happy, I'm satisfied because you did a wonderful job … I wanted to thank the executive council, I wanted to thank the labourers, all of you. And I wanted to thank Brother Ishmael and those who work with him … for making a virtual Saviours' Day so phenomenal.

Minister Farrakhan utilized his closing remarks to hint at his own departure from the community and to call for unity among his followers. Minister Farrakhan is aware that his departure will cause divisions within the community. Indeed, his refusal to explicitly name Ishmael as a successor may well be due to fears that it would cause internal strife. Equally, however, it may well indicate that Farrakhan considers himself irreplaceable:

> My forty years is up now and by the grace of God, I have survived but look at we did survive, now I'm going away … well it's not around the corner … I'm going to be with Him … I finished the course, I kept the faith, now is laid up for me a crown and I go to my father to get the crown, that's fulfilling the scriptures … I am feeling that sense of being alone … time is calling me to another level … I want what happened Saviours' Day to be a template for how we are going to move through the darkness of the hour with greater unity, greater thought of how to plan our moves and above all knowing that you are really capable of bringing your nation through this hour, don't doubt, God has made you … be the good person that you have the capacity to be, don't mistreat the people under your charge … drive the people for national gain … brothers and sisters go after the lost found … my cupboard was bare when the nation fell, we had a beautiful refrigerator … nothing in there … when I came back to Allah … I put all that foolishness aside and came fully back to my teacher … so you do the same, put away the foolishness, come back home, do the work and watch your God amplify whatever you have.

Farrakhan's call for unity within the community was echoed by Ishmael in his final statement: "Beloved brothers and sisters we have a lot in front of us, we got to stay together, lets' work out whatever needs to be worked out … we got to stand as a solid wall … as long as we are united and on those solid foundations we will be ok." Ishmael's comments about the community having "a lot in front of us" are no doubt a reference to how the community will navigate the loss of Farrakhan.

Ishmael's performance at the 2021 Saviours' Day convention has no doubt further elevated him in the eyes of the community as Farrakhan's successor. Yet, he is not above correction. In the weeks that followed his address, Minister Farrakhan pointed to a number of errors Ishmael had made in his lecture and asked that he correct them. Ishmael conceded in a short address to the "Believers of the NOI" on March 3, 2021, that it was the "greatest honor" to deliver the speech but that he had felt under "tremendous pressure." More tellingly, however, he noted "this was not some anointing of me … this was a test for me and a test for our nation … no one person has it all." Farrakhan's remarks at the 2021 event certainly fell short of a full endorsement of Ishmael and his request that he correct his errors evidenced that he is still his mentor's subordinate. Ishmael made one serious error during the Saviours' Day convention. In conversation with the well-known African American Imam Siraj Wahhaj, he remarked that Elijah Muhammad did not instruct his followers to pray to Fard Muhammad. It was this particular error that he was asked to correct. In conceding his error, he remarked: "We do pray to master Fard Muhammad … he is Allah."[72] That someone as senior as Ishmael appears unsure and unclear about who NOI members pray to seems inconceivable. Yet, it is beyond doubt that there exists within the community diverse interpretations of Fard's theology and mission. One long-term member notes that "everyone is on a different level of understanding" and that there is "diversity of understanding based on that person's learning and education."[73] Ishmael's apparent error in conversation with Imam Siraj Wahhaj may, however, have another explanation. Minister Farrakhan has made numerous efforts to gain the support of prominent African American imams and when doing so he is often played down the NOI's belief that Fard was God in person.

Ishmael's "anointing" has not yet occurred and he was not invited to deliver the subsequent Saviours' Day address in 2022. Ishmael certainly has many attributes that would lead observers to consider him his mentor's successor: he is the son of Elijah Muhammad and has worked as Minister Farrakhan's national assistant for over two decades. Moreover, he is well-known within the NOI and has personal links to high-profile African American imams and ministers. He is also the face of the NOI's executive council and often offers statements on their behalf. However, he is a relatively unknown figure nationally and much of his time is spent within the walls of Mosque Maryam. Ishmael is cognizant of the fact that he is an unknown quantity on a national scale. In a 2016 interview with the *Breakfast Club*, for example, an interviewer remarked that he "never sees" him outside Mosque Maryam to which he conceded "I do need to get out more."[74] Ishmael's profile, as noted, has been growing within his faith community for some time. The interviews and other contributions that he makes to such publications are an opportunity to introduce himself, his family, and his role in the community. Ishmael is frequently quoted and covered in the faith community's national paper. His story of faith and his lineage is also a feature of NOI magazines. In December 2021, for example, he graced the cover of the NOI's *Rise Magazine*. The interview he contributed to the magazine outlined his lineage and relationship with Minister Farrakhan. In an article entitled "A Son's Testimony: The Biological Son of the Most Honorable Elijah Muhammad Shares His Story of Faith, Findings and Prayers for the Future," author Azizah Muhammad noted:

> At the age of 7, Min. Ishmael Muhammad met his father, Elijah Muhammad. He yearned to connect with his father and become acquainted with the reality of his physical existence. "I never referred or spoke to him as a 'father' or 'daddy' … I began to study at 7 or 8 years old the Lessons and Message to the Blackman and his writings in Muhammad Speaks … Once Mother Tynetta Muhammad pledged to help Minister Farrakhan, the bond between Min. Ishmael and the Honorable Minister Louis Farrakhan began to evolve … One day, Minister Farrakhan advised Min. Ishmael Muhammad to choose a city he would like to go to. A list of possible cities, including Atlanta, GA, and Washington D.C., crossed Min. Ishmael Muhammad's mind. The list had ended once Minister Farrakhan suggested that Min. Ishmael Muhammad should settle himself in Chicago. In 1991, Min. Ishmael Muhammad relocated to Chicago and in January 1991, he started his journey in the ministry … As the biological son of the Most Honorable Elijah Muhammad and the Student National Assistant to the Honorable Minister Louis Farrakhan, Min. Ishmael Muhammad is fulfilling a role that Allah has intended for him.[75]

Ishmael's testimony in the aforementioned article provides a number of insights. First, it introduces him to readers as the biological son of Elijah Muhammad and as a devout follower and helper of Louis Farrakhan. *Rise Magazine* is aimed primarily at the NOI's faithful, many of whom know Ishmael and the story of his early life. However, the faith community's historically high turnover in membership compels its leaders to continually reintroduce themselves to members and sympathizers. Second, it indicates that like Muhammad's older children, Ishmael was not familiar with his father. His admission that he never referred to Muhammad as "father" or "daddy," for example, suggests that Tynetta, much like Clara, encouraged her children to revere and fear their father as a religious figure. Third, Ishmael's comments concerning his own readings and his love of Fard Muhammad suggest that from a young age he sought to know his father and his God via his father's published works. Last, the closing comment concerning Ishmael fulfilling the role "intended" for him suggests not so much that leadership is his birth right but that his destiny is inextricably linked with the mission of his father and Minister Farrakhan.

Minister Farrakhan's decision to deliver the 2022 address himself from Mosque Maryam may well have been made in an effort to quell any hint of discord regarding Ishmael's 2021 address. Minister Farrakhan's comments at the outset of this chapter certainly suggest that Ishmael is in fact "the face of the teachings." Moreover, the suggestion that Ishmael must "beat history" indicates that Minister Farrakhan believes that he will confront the same challenges that his brother, Imam W. D. Mohammed, encountered in 1975.[76] Farrakhan's apparent concern that his mentee will endure similar challenges to his late brother are not without qualification. The community that Wallace inherited in 1975 was theologically divided and diverse in terms of the socioeconomic background of its members. Moreover, Wallace was never publicly endorsed by his father as a successor and thus challenges to his leadership, such as that brought by Farrakhan, were possible. In short, Minister Farrakhan's continuous claim to be the rightful heir to Muhammad's throne and inheritor of his faith community would not have had any legitimacy had Muhammad publicly endorsed his son as a successor. Minister Farrakhan's refusal to offer an outright endorsement of Ishmael has thus placed him very much in a similar situation. Should Ishmael wish to present himself as Farrakhan's successor, without his mentor's outright sanctioning, he will also inherit a theologically diverse Nation composed of members who hold vastly different interpretations of Fard Muhammad's mission and teachings.

Minister Farrakhan has encouraged such diversity of belief and interpretation within his community for decades. He has continuously referred to Fard Muhammad as God in person while simultaneously endorsing and encouraging more "orthodox" or traditional Sunni teachings within the NOI. The DIA has proven instrumental in recent years in assisting NOI members to reinterpret Elijah Muhammad's teachings. DIA founder Imam Jalil Muhammad is himself a friend of Minister Farrakhan's. The DIA offers NOI members a "safe space" in which to learn more about Islam. According to the DIA, "no one is getting ridiculed" if they don't know how to make prayers. Moreover, they comment that and that it is "regrettable" that some people have in the past made "mockery" of NOI members. Imam Muhammad often invites Sunni Muslim imams to address DIA events. In doing so, however, he is cognizant of the fact that some Sunni Muslims "don't have an understanding" of the NOI and that he therefore "knows who not to ask and to ask" when it comes to assisting with the DIA's program of events. The NOI confronts "flat out racism" from immigrant Muslim communities. Moreover, there is a "slight friction" between NOI Muslims and Sunni Muslims."[77] The DIA has proven instrumental in helping the NOI and its members appear more "orthodox." It has also, however, led some NOI ministers closer to Sunni Islam. Indeed, until recently, Imam Sultan Muhammad was the only imam within the NOI. Thanks to the work of the DIA, in particular, Minister Farrakhan has recently appointed Abdul Salaam Muhammad's as the NOI's student imam. In announcing the appointed in *The Final Call*, staff writer Nisa Islam Muhammad reported:

> Student Imam Abdul Salaam Muhammad … is welcomed in Muslim communities around the country doing khutbahs at masjids, college campuses and speaking at other events. He made Umrah with Hajj Pros in 2020 and credits his journey to becoming an imam to his participation with the Ramadan Prayerline and Deen Intensive Academy. "Abdul Salaam has been preparing for this for the last 20 years with his studies, and how he handles the mosque. He's consistent in his work with the believers. He established Jumu'ah prayer for those who can make it off their job, and the five prayers," Brother Abdul Akbar Muhammad, International Representative for Minister Farrakhan and an organizer for the Ramadan Prayerline and Deen Intensive Academy, told The Final Call. "He's a blessing for our community. This assignment will have him traveling to share the abundance of knowledge that he has gained …" Khalillah Ali heard Imam Abdul Salaam at the Deen Intensive Academy when it came to Dallas in 2015. His topic was "Did the Honorable Elijah Muhammad Follow the Sunnah of Prophet Muhammad (peace be upon him)." She told The Final Call, "I was very impressed with his presentation and also to learn that he established Jumu'ah at his mosque …" Imam Abdul Salaam Muhammad was on the road to becoming an imam unbeknownst to him. In his mind, he was doing the work to serve his people under the leadership of Minister Farrakhan. Imam Abdul Salaam Muhammad recalls in the early 2000s receiving books from Minister Farrakhan that included the Muslim Prayer Book, the Religion of Islam, and others that related to the work in America as Muslims. "In

2011 during Ramadan, I established Friday prayers that the Minister had desired way back in the '80s," Imam Abdul Salaam Muhammad told The Final Call. "The Minister showed great wisdom when he introduced me to then-Sultan Rahman. The Minister said not to let air get between us. That wisdom bonded me to Imam Sultan before he received his appointment. The Minister could see our brotherhood and what we brought to the table for each other personally as well as what transformed during our travels together teaching Islamic Sciences," he continued. "When we established Jumu'ah at No. 6 (Baltimore Mosque), I asked the believers, if they wanted to continue beyond Ramadan. It was a resounding yes and we began to grow. Prior to COVID, we offered all types of programming including women's programs. It was all inspired by the Honorable Minister Louis Farrakhan, who desired back in the '80s that we institute Jumu'ah. That inspiration allows me to be a student minister and a student imam. Minister Farrakhan said I have the heart for both." Imam Abdul Salaam Muhammad credits his Islamic research with helping him see the Honorable Elijah Muhammad and the Minister much clearer in terms of the life of Prophet Muhammad, peace and blessings be upon him.[78]

Abdul's recent appointment in 2022 will be welcomed by NOI members such as Nisa and Sultan. Nisa is married to Imam Jalil Muhammad and it is perhaps therefore unsurprising that in discussing his appointment with her he chose to acknowledge the work of the DIA. Minister Farrakhan's decision to appoint another imam may be purely symbolic and a nod to that section of NOI members who identify more so with Sunni Islam. Regardless of his motive for appointing Abdul, Minister Farrakhan's faith community continue to exist in limbo between Sunni Islam and traditional NOI teachings. Such an existence leaves them vulnerable and open to criticism. It is for the NOI's national leaders and in particular the Executive Shura Council to assist members with navigating such trials.

The Executive Shura Council, or the council of thirteen, as it has been more affectionately known within the NOI, was introduced to the broader public on May 16, 2022, during a radio broadcast with Eddie Reid on the Black-owned radio show WVON.[79] Minister Farrakhan's decision to introduce the council to audiences beyond the confines of the NOI's mosques and participate in a question and answer discussion himself was significant given that by his own admission he does not "come on the radio anymore."[80] The council's appearance on WVON was reported in *The Final Call*, as "an opportunity for the world to again receive divine wisdom, insight and warning from Min. Farrakhan" and as an "occasion to present the NOI Executive Council, all appointed by Min. Farrakhan to the Black community and the world … the first time all members" would be introduced to the broader public.[81]

The NOI's council, as of May 2022, was composed of thirteen long-term NOI officials, all of whom have been personally chosen by Minister Farrakhan. The thirteen council members are Imam Sultan Muhammad, Minister Ishmael Muhammad, A'ishah Muhammad, Ahmad Muhammad, Ava Muhammad, Aminah Muhammad, Mustapha Farrakhan, Wesley Muhammad, Leonard Muhammad, Naeemah Muhammad, Abdul Arif Muhammad, Assad Muhammad, and Abdul Ra'uf. Muhammad. The council has, as noted, lost Ava Muhammad and as of yet she has not been replaced. In its current composition, the council reflects the diversity of the NOI's faithful. Sultan Muhammad is, as noted, well connected to imams and Sunni communities throughout Chicago. He is also well versed in Sunni Islam and, at least outwardly, appears to practice Sunni Islam. In relaying his role in the council, Sultan noted:

> As a student Imam or servant to the Islamic ummah or community I assist in guiding the Nation of Islam in the principles and meanings of the Islamic faith and action according to the teachings of the Honorable Elijah Muhammad and the Honorable Minister Louis Farrakhan. I lead the community in prayers and instruct the community in Arabic … as a member of the Executive Shura Council I apply my knowledge of the Holy Quran … in a deliberative capacity … The Executive Council is comprised of a group of men and women who believe in Islam as taught by the Honorable Elijah Muhammad under the leadership, guidance and direction of the Honorable Minister Louis Farrakhan. We were selected by the Honorable Minister Louis Farrakhan to govern the affairs of the Nation of Islam based on the foundation of our work … God has given us a pattern for governance that we must decide our most important affairs … The members of this council function as a community of persons who live with one common cause at our root which is to see the resurrection of our people formed into a nation under the rule and laws of God.[82]

Sultan's comments, quoted above, are telling. It is evident that he is at pains to convey to listeners that the Islam he propagates is in accordance with Elijah

Muhammad's teachings. Moreover, his closing remarks convey a sense of unity of purpose within the council in that its members consider the "resurrection" of their people and the imposition of God's rules and laws above all other concerns or priorities. Sultan has worked for the NOI since 2012 but his appointment to the council did not come until 2016.[83] Unlike Sultan, Ishmael represents the more unorthodox face of the NOI. As the biological son of Elijah Muhammad and the spiritual son of Minister Farrakhan, he is wedded to the founding theology of Fard Muhammad. Likewise, Mustapha Farrakhan represents the NOI of old. He is the sixth child of Minister Farrakhan and is tasked with overseeing the national chapters of the FOI. Mustapha was born into the NOI in 1963, two years prior to his father's appointment as the community's national minister. Mustapha appears to have never spoken publicly about his young life and especially the impact that his father's frequent absences on behalf of the NOI had on their relationship. It is, however, safe to assume that he felt his father's absence. Indeed, Minister Farrakhan has on at least a few occasions acknowledged that his children suffered as a result of his absences, which were often compelled due to the work of propagating Elijah Muhammad's teachings and his later rebuilding efforts. In 1987, for example, he told an audience that he "paid a hell of a price" to rebuild the community. That "price" was the loss of time with his children.[84] Likewise during his national address at the 2020 Saviours' Day convention, he noted that his family "suffered right along with me" when he was rebuilding the NOI.[85] Mustapha has spent much of his adult life in his father's shadow. As the national FOI captain, he is tasked with protecting his father at all times. Mustapha was appointed to the council in 2000. His own theological perspectives are largely unknown. He has never been involved with the NOI's ministry and therefore it is impossible to determine whether he is faithful to the sympathies of Sultan or Ishmael. Sultan does appear to be somewhat isolated when it comes to the NOI's theology. His co-council member, Dr. Wesley Muhammad, much like Ishmael, is a prolific advocate of the belief that Allah appeared in the person of Fard Muhammad.

Dr. Wesley Muhammad was appointed to the council in 2016. He is the author of multiple books that propagate and explicate the NOI's theology and critique of the US racial hierarchy. Such books include *Is Allah a Man? The Islam Debate* and *Understanding the Assault on the Black Man, Black Manhood and*

Black Masculinity.[86] Dr. Muhammad is a regular speaker at the NOI's national headquarters at Mosque Maryam where his lectures tend to mirror in tone and content his published work. It is important to note that Dr. Muhammad's work appears to be published largely by trade rather than academic publishers and that such work tends to have a general rather than academic audience. In many ways, Dr. Muhammad appears to simply regurgitate Minister Farrakhan's writings and lectures. His 2017 book *Understanding the Assault on the Black Man*, for example, mirrors rather closely the critique of white supremacy that Minister Farrakhan has put forth for decades. Moreover, similar critiques and comments can be found in the writings of other prominent NOI ministers:

> There is something about the Black male that even after 400 years of the best or the worst that this hostile culture (White America) has to offer, he is still a threat to be neutralized by any means necessary. What is it about the Black male in America? And also: if the white male has outlawed our Black manhood, what is the Black manhood that is actually outlawed in America? It's not machoism. He lets us have all the guns we want. In fact, he provides them to us. He lets us fight and even kill, as long as we are killing someone Black. A reason we don't really adequately appreciate this assault on Black manhood is because we really don't comprehend what Black manhood is. The white comprehends though. And he is hell-bent on no full, collective expression of Black manhood ever occurring in America. But what is really behind White Supremacy's war against the Black man? Is it racism? Well that's a part. But it's deeper than that. White supremacy is waring with the Black man, not primarily because he is Black but because he is *God*. The war against the Black Man is White Supremacy's war against God. (emphasis in original)[87]

Dr. Muhammad is a long-term member of Minister Farrakhan's ministerial team. He officially joined the NOI in 1990 and the FOI in 1992.[88] Prior to joining the NOI he had a member of the Five Percenters. Muhammad, by his own admission, was drawn to the NOI because of the FOI. In a 2015 lecture in Washington, DC, for example, he remarked that he joined the FOI in Atlanta in 1992 and longed to belong to the "righteous brotherhood" of the military training of men.[89] His rise to prominence in the community has been slow but his devotion has nonetheless paid off. As noted, he is a regular speaker at Mosque Maryam and has received growing coverage in the community's national paper. Muhammad considers Elijah Muhammad's teachings to represent what he refers to as a "body of knowledge … A teaching in which there is no conflict between what we believe and what the facts on the ground allow us to verify as true."[90] Substantiating Elijah Muhammad's theology has been something of a preoccupation for Dr. Muhammad. Indeed, his aforementioned book, *Is Allah a Man? The Islam Debate*, deals rather exclusively with outlining what he considers to be the merits of Muhammad's religious beliefs.[91] Much like Ishmael, Dr. Muhammad's ascent has come about primarily due Minister Farrakhan's failing health and growing dependency on student ministers. It is important to note that Dr. Muhammad's writings and scholarship does hold significance for NOI members and Minister Farrakhan. Indeed, Farrakhan is familiar with Dr. Muhammad's work in classical Islamic studies and points to the successful defense of his doctoral dissertation as validation of the NOI's belief that God took on flesh in the person of Fard Muhammad.

A'ishah Muhammad is one of three women on the executive council. Her role on the council as an overseer of the NOI's auditors evidences how widespread the influence of the COS and the practice of auditing has become within the NOI. NOI members appear to have embraced auditing with a great degree of zeal. As early as 2011, over 1,000 members of the community had become certified Dianetics auditors.[92] In introducing herself during the radio broadcast, A'ishah made a number of points concerning her work. First, she has been a member of the NOI for over forty-three years and as such was one of Minister Farrakhan's earliest supporters. Second, she has previously served in the NOI as the national MGT–GCC captain, a position she held for thirteen years. A'ishah has a wealth of experience in working with women and men in the community. She perceives her faith community and the mosque, in particular as "a place to come for repair." According to A'isha, the NOI's various ministries are designed to "address the needs and concerns of all of our people." Much like Minister Farrakhan, A'ishah considers auditing to be a particularly important tool for African Americans. She construed the practice as a means by which NOI members can learn to address and heal from "generational trauma." Indeed, in her introduction on WVON, she described her community as "an injured people for whom trauma is a constant companion."[93] A'ishah is a relatively well-known figure within the NOI. She is often in attendance at or a guest speaker for events that address health and women's issues. In February 2022, for example, the community's national paper noted that she had contributed a session on God's unique connection to women for a virtual conference aimed at fundraising for families in need.[94] Similarly, she has featured in and been quoted in the national paper at various events including the annual auditors graduation.

Leonard Muhammad and Abdul Arif Muhammad are also long-term members of the NOI and personal advisors to Minister Farrakhan. Leonard serves as the NOI's chief of staff and has previously overseen the NOI's efforts to acquire "historic properties" including those owned by the members and ministers of the original community. It is important to note that the NOI's property portfolio is neither as grand nor as impressive as what it was in Elijah Muhammad's community. Indeed, it is entirely unclear how many properties they own, how wealthy they are as a faith community, and which individuals are in control of the faith community's finances. Thus, it is entirely unclear what role, if any, resources may play in dictating the NOI's path post-Farrakhan. Farrakhan's children have clearly benefitted from their father's wealth. However, with the exception of Mustapha Farrakhan, Farrakhan's children no longer have a significant profile in the faith community.

Leonard joined the NOI forty years ago when Minister Farrakhan was struggling to rebuild the NOI. Leonard believes that Farrakhan is uniquely qualified and distinct from other African American leaders because of his "love and humility."[95] Abdul Arif Muhammad joined the NOI in 1979 as a college student and has often provided personal legal guidance to Minister Farrakhan. He also serves the community as the student minister.[96]

Ahmad Muhammad, also a son of Elijah Muhammad and Tynetta Muhammad, is much less known in the community than his brother Ishmael. His role on the council is nonetheless significant in that he is charged with overseeing the NOI's ministry of information. As such he is tasked with managing "talented teens" in the area of information technology.[97] The NOI's online presence and webcasts are managed by Ahmad. Online webcasts and management of NOI communication on online forums is vitally important for the NOI as a religious community. The NOI's faithful are scattered throughout the United States and in smaller regional chapters beyond the United States. As such, their members do not always have access to a local NOI mosque. Online programming has thus historically served as a vital means of keeping members in touch with one another and updated with communications from Mosque Maryam. Thus, unlike other religious communities, the NOI has long understood the importance of harnessing the internet and online platforms for both propagation and retention of members.

Naeemah Muhammad currently serves on the NOI's council in her capacity as the national MGT–GCC Captain. Naeemah joined the community in 1997 and is of Haitian descent. She is responsible for implementing and overseeing the NOI's programs for women and girls and the training of lieutenants in the MGT–GCC classes. Naeemah offered something of her testimony and story of how she came to the NOI in a recent event at Mosque Maryam. The event was organized by the executive council to commemorate the 125th anniversary of Elijah Muhammad's birth. During discussions with other panel members, Naeemah noted:

> Many nights I remember praying to God, nine years old now, begging Allah to remove the pain and suffering that not only I was going through as a child but also people who were suffering around the world. I cried myself to sleep many nights. From that point, I was seeking and searching for God. And then, here comes Minister Farrakhan … The first time I heard Minister Farrakhan's voice, a light of extreme brightness literally came on. I sensed at that time a measure of fulfillment for the first time. I was hooked, as I felt like I was introduced to the God and the Jesus that I have been searching for.[98]

Naeemah holds fast to the adage that the woman is the "very standard by which civilization is measured."[99] Her role on the executive council is an important one in that it enables women's voices, grievances, concerns, and aspirations to be heard among the hierarchy. Naeemah's task of heading the MGT and implementing NOI protocols is a difficult one. She must simultaneously advance and instill the NOI's conservative gender norms while also modernizing the MGT to ensure its remains relevant to women.

Abdul Ra'uf. Muhammad essentially works to build the NOI's network of support with other religious communities and Christian pastors, in particular.[100] His work pays dividends for the NOI. As noted, many of the NOI's high-profile marches and events in the post-1995 period depended greatly on the willingness of Christian clergy to partner with the NOI to advance shared goals. This was particularly evident in the campaign to raise awareness of and gather support for the Justice or Else March in 2015.¹⁰¹ Abdul's work with other religious communities likely means that he is cognizant of and open to diverse interpretations of the NOI's theology. He is also more likely than other council members to tolerate Christian beliefs within the NOI.

Aminah B. Muhammad is Minister Farrakhan's executive administrative assistant. The NOI's teachings have been familiar to Aminah since she was a young child. In her comments and introduction during her appearance on WVON, Aminah reiterated Minister Farrakhan's belief that African Americans are "still in a struggle for our complete freedom."¹⁰²

Ishmael was the last council member to be introduced during the WVON event. This in itself is unsurprising given his importance in the community and the fact that he introduced Minister Farrakhan in his closing remarks. For Ishmael, the executive board is a means of ensuring the NOI's life post-Farrakhan. In his remarks, for example, he noted that the "satanic forces" of the US government had historically operated to destroy Black liberation groups after the death of their leaders. For Ishmael, the council thus ensures that "the liberation struggle is not interrupted" in the event of Minister Farrakhan's exit.¹⁰³ Ishmael has worked side by side with Minister Farrakhan for over thirty years. In his comments he noted it was "an honor" to introduce his mentor. It is important to note that while Minister Farrakhan noted in his brief comments that God was "helping" him to "prepare" such "wonderful young people," the majority of council members are of an advanced age.

Minister Farrakhan's closing remarks during the WVON interview and his responses to questions exposed vulnerabilities in the NOI's leadership. For example, during questions from eager listeners, Minister Farrakhan was asked by Arthur 6X if the community "needed a universal code of conduct" that all parties could agree to. Minister Farrakhan conceded in response that the community did need such a code of conduct.¹⁰⁴ Arthur's question evidences the lack of unity that exists within the community regarding expectations and standards of behavior, dress, and conduct more generally. Minister Farrakhan does not have the same grip on his faith community as his spiritual father and thus behaviors that are tolerated in the RNOI would have likely been punishable in the ONOI. Long-term members and observers of the community are very much aware of the distinctions that exist between former and current members. Similarly, his remarks that the council members operate "as one" are wishful thinking at best. The majority of the NOI's council members hold fast, at least in public, to the belief that God appeared in the person of Fard Muhammad. However, other council members, including Sultan, appear to practice Sunni Islam. Moreover, the council is made up exclusively of African Americans. Yet, the NOI is not and has never been an exclusively African American community. The lack of diversity in the council of thirteen means that Latino and Native American members, in particular, are not represented on the board. Minister Farrakhan, as noted, takes some degree of pride in the development of his younger ministers. In his comments, quoted below, he again spoke of the "cadre of young ministers" that the community is preparing:

> I have taught you well by the Grace of God. Millions of words now are out there for us to feed on. So, I want to see now a new generation rise in that word and they are coming up fast ... Every one of these that you heard, including Brother Student Minister Ishmael. He's got a cadre of young ministers, male and female, studying now and growing in the study—and so soon you will see them. Soon you will hear them. And you will hear Elijah coming through them all or they won't speak at all. I did not live my life and offer my life for wicked, corrupt people to come to me and say they want to help me; but they really want to help themselves and use my teacher's name to deceive the people.[105]

Minister Farrakhan's faith community does indeed have several notably younger and more dynamic student ministers. Many of these ministers have published their own books and have worked to build support in their communities and beyond. Among such ministers are Nuri Muhammad, Abel Muhammad, and Demetric Muhammad. These ministers are well-known within the community not only as helpers of Minister Farrakhan but as community workers, counselors, and researchers.

Nuri Muhammad has served as the NOI's regional minister in Indianapolis since 1992. Nuri Joined the NOI in 1992 and in the same year was appointed as an assistant minister in the local study group. Two years later he relocated to Chicago to oversee the NOI's orientation and processing class for men. According to his biography on the Mosque Number 74 website, Nuri moved back to Indianapolis in 1996. In the months that followed, the study group became a chartered mosque and "has increased its membership, purchased and renovated a state of the art facility ... which houses the new Mosque,

Muhammad University of Islam, Bismillah Childcare Ministry and Learning Academy, Eat To Live Café and Studio 74 Barber and Beauty Salon."[106] Aside from building the NOI's presence in Indianapolis, Nuri has also built a reputation for his lectures and published works. He is the author of multiple books including *Before You Say I Do*, *After You Say I Do*, and *A Well Made Man*.[107] He has also featured in numerous NOI publications including *Virtue Today Magazine* and *Hurt2Healing Magazine*.[108] Nuri's speeches and lectures are often aimed at men. Indeed, even his interviews in the aforementioned publications tend to deal with the struggles of men in the community and beyond. Nuri embraces the NOI's more rigid mandates including dietary laws and gender norms with zeal. He is a fervent advocate of traditional gender norms and highly critical of men who fail to fulfil their obligations as husbands and fathers.[109] Nuri's wife, Teri, is also a devout NOI member and has worked steadily to assist with the community's ministry in Indianapolis. His profile within and beyond his faith community has grown steadily in the last decade. Nuri's devotion to the teachings of Elijah Muhammad and Minister Farrakhan are evident in his writings, activism, and lectures. He mimics Minister Farrakhan much more successfully than Ishmael or other members of the executive board. Moreover, he is a regular guest speaker at Mosque Maryam and has worked diligently to build relationships with Christian clergy and community activists. He is also more open, than perhaps other high-profile ministers, to the notion that distinctions or variations in beliefs among Christians, NOI Muslims, and Sunni Muslims are unimportant. For Nuri, belief in the oneness of God trumps theological differences. Such a position enables him, like Farrakhan, to work across religious lines.

Nuri's dynamism is shared by student minister Demetric Muhammad. Demetric joined the NOI when he was fifteen years old. He worked under James Muhammad in Mississippi as a youth minister and became a college representative of the NOI at the University of Mississippi. He then became an assistant minister at Mosque Number 55. Demetric currently serves as the NOI's "research minister." He was appointed to Minister Farrakhan's research team in 2010.[110] Demetric plays a pivotal role in the NOI's research team. He assists, for example, with research and notes for Minister Farrakhan's lectures. His published works include *But, Didn't You Kill Malcolm? Myth-Busting the*

Propaganda against the Nation of Islam and *Manhood Principles, Parables, Concepts and Characteristics from the Holy Qur'an*.[111] The former book is an admirable attempt to exonerate the NOI from charges of complicity in Malcolm's death. Indeed, Muhammad sets out in considerable detail the case to implicate the US government. His latter book developed from sermons and preparation that he was undertaking for a series of Friday Jummah services. Much like Nuri, Muhammad's effort is geared toward men. Given that the NOI has historically been a patriarchal community, their efforts are likely not to be in vain. Demetric is well versed in the literature concerning the NOI's history and the complexities of its relationship with government agencies and actors. As such, he is acutely aware of the level and intensity of interest in the NOI and its leadership. He is thus more likely than others to anticipate, rightly or wrongly, that the intelligence community will be observing current developments in the NOI.

Abel Muhammad represents the Latino membership of the NOI. He estimates that approximately 20 percent of the community's national membership is Latino.[112] Abel has been active in the NOI for decades and has worked steadily to challenge the perception that the NOI is a religion exclusively for African Americans.[113] He is a regular guest speaker at Mosque Maryam and has worked tirelessly to improve relations between Latino and African American members of the community. He credits Farrakhan with not only transforming his life but with helping him to embrace his identity as a Muslim and a Mexican:

> The Honorable Minister Louis Farrakhan has absolutely saved and transformed my life. When I was a teenager flunking out of high school, I had no clue who I was and I had no purpose for my life. It was not until I heard the Teachings of the Most Honorable Elijah Muhammad as represented by the Honorable Minister Louis Farrakhan that I began to understand who I was, who God is, and that there was a purpose for Allah (God) permitting me to be birthed into the world. Since that time as a teenager, up to the present day, the Honorable Minister Louis Farrakhan has helped me to see myself properly as a Mexican and as a Muslim. The Honorable Minister Farrakhan is showing me how to be a man, a son, a husband, a father, a brother, and a true servant of my people. I am eternally grateful for his loving guidance and beautiful example.[114]

Abel represents a small demographic of the NOI's membership but he is nonetheless a significant and high-profile figure in community's hierarchy. He will no doubt prove instrumental in efforts to prepare and assist members navigate the community and their faith post-Farrakhan.

Minister Farrakhan's leadership of the NOI in the post-1995 period has not effectively served well the interests of his followers. The tours that he construed as a means to promote the NOI and himself abroad had little in the way of any long-term benefit for the faith community. His prolonged absences hindered nation-building initiatives on US soil. The NOI, as Farrakhan notes, is active in 131 cities across the United States.[115] However, many of these cities have study groups rather than NOI mosques. The NOI's property profile has undoubtedly dwindled. Indeed, the community often host their larger events at churches rather than their own mosques. Minister Farrakhan's own theological perspectives appear to have shifted momentarily in the aftermath of his health scare in the late 1990s and again in the immediate aftermath of 9/11. His brief reconciliation with Imam W. D. Mohammed undoubtedly brought comfort to families that had been torn apart by the Nation's fall in 1975. However, in the long term, relations between NOI Muslims and their Sunni counterparts have failed to improve. Indeed, with the exception of a few African American Sunni imams who are sympathetic to the work of the NOI, the group remains peripheral in the American ummah. The work of groups like the DIA is no doubt important and the appointed of a further student Imam in 2022 indicates some growth in more traditional understandings of Islam within the community. Yet, Farrakhan and his ministers continue to propagate within their own settings belief in Fard Muhammad's divinity. The NOI's relationship with the COS has grown steadily and auditing, as noted, has become more widespread. However, the COS is not likely to have any influence in the NOI's current or future trajectory. Minister Farrakhan's work with Christian pastors and clergy has in many ways aided his community in their efforts to effect change in their respective communities. Such work on the ground has paid dividends for the NOI and aided the relatively good reputation that the community has in certain sections of the United States. Minister Farrakhan's intermittent criticisms of the Jewish community in America has done much to harm his faith community and its ability to establish new ventures and relationships. It is difficult to determine what impact the social media bans have had on the NOI's membership. Farrakhan's faith community, as noted, have been at the forefront of developing online forums for their followers for some time. Thus, they can rather easily and collectively compensate for Minister Farrakhan's absence from Twitter and other forums. For many, Minister Farrakhan is nothing more than a notorious antisemite. The lack of uproar surrounding his social media bans and the unwillingness of organizations and imams to speak in his favor suggest that he has lost much support in recent years. The NOI is no longer the force it once was. Its membership has dwindled and its leader, by and large, muted. The council of thirteen has navigated the Covid-19 pandemic and its aftermath with relative ease. The move to online services did little to interrupt the group's ability to function and commune. Yet, the faith community remains somewhat fragile and its future uncertain. Minister Farrakhan's unwillingness to effectively prepare the community and a successor for his exit will no doubt lead to some form of factionalism. In short, his failure to appoint Ishmael or any other member of his council or ministers will likely mean that history will repeat itself.

Notes

1 Michael O. West, "Like A River: The Million Man March and the Black Nationalist Tradition in the United States," *Journal of Historical Sociology*, vol. 12, no. 1 (March 1999): 81.
2 Farrakhan, "A Swan Song."
3 Muhammad, "Believers' Meeting."
4 Ishmael Muhammad, "Saviours' Day 2021 National Address." Delivered at Mosque Maryam, Chicago, February 28, 2021.
5 https://www.prisonlegalnews.org/news/2019/jul/2/federal-government-pays-nation-islam-teach-bop-prisoners/ (accessed September 20, 2020).
6 "American Mosque Survey 2020 Report 1."
7 Farrakhan, "The Unravelling of a Great Nation."
8 Ibid.
9 Vibert White, *Inside the Nation of Islam: A Historical and Personal Testimony by a Black Muslim* (Gainesville: University Press of Florida, 2001),
10 https://www.independent.co.uk/news/world/mandela-preaches-tolerance-to-farrakhan-1326419.html.

11 "Million Woman March Marked 25th Anniversary," *The Final Call*, December 6, 2022, 30.
12 De-Valera Botchway and Mustapha Abdul-Hamid, "Was It a Nine Days Wonder?: A Note on the Proselytization Efforts of the Nation of Islam in Ghana, 1980s-2010," in *New Perspectives on the Nation of Islam*, ed. Dawn-Marie Gibson and Herbert Berg (London: Routledge, 2017), 95.
13 Gibson, *A History of the Nation of Islam*, 140.
14 Dawn-Marie Gibson, "Social Activism and Interfaith Outreach in Louis Farrakhan's Nation of Islam," *Journal of Muslim Philanthropy and Civil Society*, vol. 1, no. 1 (Spring 2022): 43–4.
15 Dawn-Marie Gibson "Black Women Gather to Promote Unity at Million Woman March," *Jet Magazine*, vol. 92, no. 25, November 10, 1997 and Michael Janofsky, "At Million Woman March, Focus Is on Family," *New York Times*, October 26, 1997.
16 Dawn-Marie Gibson "Black Women Gather to Promote."
17 Abisayo Muhammad, "Reflections on the Million Family March and Its Impact," *The Final Call*, November 29, 2022, 30.
18 Muhammad, *Closing the Gap*, 261.
19 Hanna Rosin and Hamil R. Harris, "Farrakhan Has Surgery for Recurrence of Cancer: Followers 'Shaken' as His Health Worsens," *Washington Post*, April 2, 1999, AO1.
20 Sonsyrea Tate, *Do Me Twice: My Life After Islam* (New York: Strebor Books, 2007), 161.
21 Gibson, *A History of the Nation of Islam*, 146.
22 Elsayed, "After Twenty-Five Years Rift," 24.
23 Muhammad. "Believers' Meeting."
24 Kambiz GhaneaBassiri, "Islamophobia and American History: Religious Stereotyping and Out-grouping of Muslims in the United States," in *Islamophobia in America: The Anatomy of Intolerance*, ed. Carl Ernst (New York: Palgrave, 2013), 53.
25 Ibid., 54.
26 Curtis, *The Black Muslim Scare of the Twentieth-Century*, 76.
27 https://noi.org/nation-of-islam-responds-911-attacks-on-america/ (accessed October 10, 2012).
28 Interview with NOI member, July 7, 2022.
29 Louis Farrakhan. "Message to the University of the West Indies." Speech delivered at the University of the West Indies, March 21, 2002.
30 Margaret Ramirez, "Farrakhan Now Opens Arms with Millions More March," *Chicago Tribune*, October 11, 2005, 22.
31 Gibson, *A History of the Nation of Islam*, 154.

32 Ibid., 176.
33 Ibid., 177.
34 Ibid., 179.
35 Louis Farrakhan, "Saviours' Day 2008 Keynote Address: The Gods at War: The Future Is All about Y.O.U.th." Speech delivered at McCormick Place Convention Centre, Chicago, February 24, 2008.
36 Mary Mitchell, "Why Obama 'Denounced' Farrakhan: It Wasn't Candidate's Best Move—But Most Blacks Understand," *Chicago Sun-Times*, March 2, 2008, 13.
37 https://www.newyorker.com/culture/annals-of-appearances/the-politics-of-race-and-the-photo-that-might-have-derailed-obama.
38 Louis Farrakhan, Speech delivered at the 2018 SD convention, January 28, 2018.
39 Louis Farrakhan, "We Are Farrakhan Community Rally."
40 Gibson, *A History of the Nation of Islam*, 172.
41 Algernon Austin, *America Is Not Post-Racial: Xenophobia, Islamophobia, Racism and the 44th President* (Santa Barbara: Praeger, 2015), X.
42 https://new.finalc all.com/2011/11/01/u-s-role-in-libya-s-fall-overseas-meddlingleading-to-fall-of-nation-warns-min-farrakhan/ (accessed April 2, 2013).
43 https://new.finalcall.com/2011/11/01/u-s-role-in-libya-s-fall-overseas-meddling-leading-to-fall-of-nation-warns-min-farrakhan/ (accessed April 2, 2013).
44 Gibson, *The Nation of Islam, Louis Farrakhan*, 177.
45 http://www.rollingstone.com/music/news/kanye-west-talks-mikebrown-beck-new-album-status-in-surprise-interview-20150220 (accessed December 8, 2015).
46 Gibson, *The Nation of Islam, Louis Farrakhan*, 163.
47 King, "Clearing the Planet," 219.
48 Ibid., 220.
49 Gibson, *A History of the Nation of Islam*, 172.
50 Louis Farrakhan, Keynote speech delivered at the Saviours' Day convention, February 25, 2018.
51 T. Muhammad, "If We Don't Help Ourselves, Who Will? *The Final Call*, 16 March 2021, 6; "A Labor of Love and Service to Humanity: Nation of Islam Distributes Thousands of Face Masks Nationwide," *The Final Call*, December 8, 2020, 6.
52 https://new.finalcall.com/2020/07/14/the-criterion/ (accessed September 10, 2022).
53 Farrakhan, "A Swan Song."
54 "Covid-19 and the U.S. Policy of Depopulation," *The Final Call*, November 29, 2022, 7.

55 Michael Z. Muhammad and Anisha Muhammad, "The Reopening: NOI Mosques, Study Groups to Return to Regular Meetings," *The Final Call*, November 16, 2021, 3, 34.
56 Muhammad, *Closing the Gap*, 261.
57 Taking on the mission: Interview with Min. Ishmael Muhammad (finalcall.com) (accessed October 19, 2022).
58 Ibid.
59 Louis Farrakhan, "Make Straight in the Desert a Highway for Our God." Speech delivered at the Annual Saviours' Day convention, February, 25 2001.
60 "Letter from the Honorable Minister Louis Farrakhan," *Final Call News* (accessed October 19, 2022).
61 Gibson, *A History of the Nation of Islam*, 184.
62 Louis Farrakhan, "Saviours' Day 2008 Key Note Address: The Gods at War: The Future Is All about Y.O.U.th," *Final Call*, February 27, 2008.
63 Farrakhan, "A Swan Song."
64 "Mother Tynnetta Muhammad—A Heartfelt and Fitting Tribute to a Perfect Example" (finalcall.com) (accessed October 22, 2022).
65 "28 Years after the Death of Malcolm X …The Hon. Elijah Muhammad Cleared of All False Charges: Wives Of Muhammad Testify at Historic Saviour's Day event," *The Final Call*, March 15, 1993, 2.
66 "Dreams, Delusions and Slander." *Final Call News* (accessed October 22, 2022).
67 https://media.noi.org/watch/NOI-wvon-May-16-2022 (accessed September 20, 2022).
68 https://anchor.fm/muhammad-mosque-32/episodes/Separation-The-Creative-Process---Sis--Dr--Ava-Muhammad-e2tad9 (accessed October 22, 2023).
69 Gibson, *The Nation of Islam, Louis Farrakhan*, 163.
70 "Saviours' Day 2021: Nation of Islam Hosts Its First Virtual Convention," *The Final Call*, February 23, 2021, 3.
71 Interview with NOI member, July 7, 2022.
72 Student Minister Ishmael SD2021 correction—Bing video.
73 Interview with NOI member, July 7, 2022.
74 Ishmael Muhammad Breakfast Club Interview, October 27, 2016.
75 Muhammad, "A Son's Testimony."
76 Farrakhan, "A Swan Song."
77 Interview with DIA representative, November 17, 2021.
78 Nisa Islam Muhammad, "Nation Welcomes New Student Imam," *The Final Call*, November 15, 2022, 31.
79 NOI—Video Platform | WVON: Hon. Minister Louis Farrakhan & Executive Council (accessed September 20, 2022).
80 Ibid.

81 Starla Muhammad, "Min. Farrakhan and the NOI Executive Counsel Appear on WVON AM Radio," *The Final Call*, May 31, 2022, 2.
82 NOI—Video Platform | WVON: Hon. Minister Louis Farrakhan & Executive Council (accessed September 20, 2022).
83 Ibid.
84 Farrakhan, "Satan and the Mastery."
85 Farrakhan, "The Unravelling of a Great Nation."
86 Wesley Muhammad, Is Allah a Man? The Islam Debate (Atlanta: A-Team Publishing, 2016) and Wesley Muhammad, *Understanding the Assault on the Black Man, Black Manhood and Black Masculinity* (Atlanta: A-Team Publishing, 2017).
87 Muhammad, *Understanding the Assault*, 5–6.
88 Wesley Muhammad, "A Message to the FOI: Brothers, Soldiers, and Black God Protocol." Speech delivered at Muhammad Mosque Number 4, Washington, DC, April 6, 2015.
89 Ibid.
90 NOI—Video Platform | WVON: Hon. Minister Louis Farrakhan & Executive Council (accessed September 20, 2022).
91 Muhammad, *Is Allah a Man?*.
92 https://new.finalcall.com/2012/07/05/a-weekend-of-healing-at-mosque-maryam/ (accessed November 22, 2022).
93 NOI—Video Platform | WVON: Hon. Minister Louis Farrakhan & Executive Council (accessed September 20, 2022).
94 https://new.finalcall.com/2022/02/16/virtual-womens-conference-shines-light-on-healing-and-health/ (accessed November 24, 2022).
95 NOI—Video Platform | WVON: Hon. Minister Louis Farrakhan & Executive Council (accessed September 20, 2022).
96 A Witness of Saviours' Day 1981: Nation of Islam Student General Counsel of Abdul Arif Muhammad: Commemoration of the 125th birth anniversary of The Most Honorable Elijah Muhammad, Mosque Maryam, October 7, 2022.
97 NOI—Video Platform | WVON: Hon. Minister Louis Farrakhan & Executive Council (accessed September 20, 2022).
98 https://new.finalcall.com/2022/10/11/he-lives-commemoration-of-the-125th-birth-anniversary-of-the-most-honorable-elijah-muhammad/.
99 NOI—Video Platform | WVON: Hon. Minister Louis Farrakhan & Executive Council (accessed September 20, 2022).
100 Ibid.
101 Gibson, *The Nation of Islam, Louis Farrakhan*.
102 NOI—Video Platform | WVON: Hon. Minister Louis Farrakhan & Executive Council (accessed September 20, 2022).

103 Ibid.
104 Ibid.
105 https://new.finalcall.com/2022/05/24/a-new-generation-rising-in-the-word-min-farrakhan-and-noi-executive-council-appear-on-wvon-am-radio/ (accessed November 25, 2022).
106 http://mosque74.org/student-minister/.
107 Nuri Muhammad, *Before You Say I Do* (Phoenix: Bashirah House Publishing, 2016) and Nuri Muhammad, *After You Say I Do* (Phoenix: Bashirah House Publishing, 2018); Nuri Muhammad, *A Well Made Man* (Phoenix: Bashirah House Publishing, 2022).
108 Nuri Muhammad, "The Value of Faith and Family," *Virtue Today Magazine*, Fall 2012, 10; Audrey Muhammad, "Striking the Right Balance In Life w/ Nuri Muhammad," *Hurt2Healing Magazine*, March 23, 2021.
109 Gibson, *The Nation of Islam, Louis Farrakhan*, 105.
110 Muhammad, 'The Plot to Outlaw the Nation of Islam."
111 Demetric Muhammad, *"But, Didn't You Kill Malcolm?"* and Demetric Muhammad, *Manhood Principles, Parables, Concepts and Characteristics from the Holy Qur'an* (Memphis: Nation of Islam, 2019).
112 Gibson, *A History of the Nation of Islam*, 162.
113 Ibid.
114 "Latin American Representative of the Honorable Minister Louis Farrakhan and the Nation of Islam: Abel Muhammad," *Rise Magazine*, September 2020, 17.
115 Farrakhan, "The Unravelling of a Great Nation."

Conclusion

In a recent address published in *The Final Call* newspaper, Minister Farrakhan discussed the origins, nature, and implications of rapper Kanye West's fallout with Jewish Americans. In his address he noted: "Don't try to buckle us under, because of all your power … For nearly 40 years, I have withstood you. Everything you've said and done to hurt me and those with me, I am here! I've withstood the action, and the effect, and I remain undamaged."[1] As noted in Chapter 4, West has long nurtured a love for Minister Farrakhan. West (also known as Ye) tweeted an antisemitic outburst in late 2022 and subsequently lost lucrative business deals with Adidas and other business partners.[2] Observers have rightly questioned the origins of West's antisemitism. Indeed, a recent opinion piece in the *Wall Street Journal* pointed to Minister Louis Farrakhan as the likely source behind Ye's antisemitism.[3] Former ADL director Abraham Foxman has endorsed the opinion piece, noting that Farrakhan "preached black pride and anti-Semitism … But whenever we condemned it, we were told by black and white leaders to ignore him, as he was fringe, without influence. They wouldn't condemn him, of course, arguing that his message of black pride was more important. Today, we are witnessing this policy's poisoned fruit."[4] It is beyond doubt that West has been influenced to a considerable extent by Minister Farrakhan and that he sympathizes with his critiques of male–female relationships and structural racism in the United States. Indeed, he referred to Minister Farrakhan as his "sensei" in his music.[5] West is not, however, the only individual to be influenced by Minister Farrakhan. Hundreds of thousands of men and women both within and beyond America's borders have heard him speak and consumed his writings for decades. Such individuals are not all "poisoned fruit." Minister Farrakhan's efforts to uplift African American people and deliver effective outreach ministries have transformed lives.

Minister Farrakhan is, as noted, almost ninety years old. In the final chapter of his life, he is considered beyond his own community, to be, first and foremost, America's most notorious antisemite. Minister Farrakhan has retained some degree of support within African American communities. However, his record of antisemitism has cost him dearly. His various social media bans have effectively "muted" his voice."[6] His words are, however, retweeted and promoted by his so-called "Twitter Army."[7] Minister Farrakhan is no longer the giant that he once was in Black religious and Nationalist circles. Moreover, his own faith community is divided by faith and without a clear successor. Minister Farrakhan has left his community fragmented and unprepared for his exit. For his thousands of faithful followers, he remains a symbol of defiance and a "defender" of Black Americans.[8]

The teachings of Elijah Muhammad have consumed Minister Farrakhan's life. His love for Muhammad and his efforts to rescue his name from the dustbins of history have ensured that generations born since 1975 have some awareness of Muhammad's life and contribution to Islam in the US context. Minister Farrakhan has long considered Muhammad to be a spiritual father. His closeness to Muhammad may well explain the fact that he has never searched for or sought out his biological father. Minister Farrakhan's son, Mustapha, spoke of his father's love for Elijah Muhammad in a recent interview with the council of thirteen. He remarked that his father "was made by God for that man. I have never seen a man so in love with another man in the spiritual aspect like that until I saw how my father is in the presence of the Most Honorable Elijah Muhammad."[9] Minister Farrakhan's journey into the fold of the NOI is often understood to have occurred in 1955 when Elijah Muhammad addressed him directly at the annual Saviours' Day convention. However, as noted in Chapter 1, Minister Farrakhan was first introduced to Black Nationalism as a child. His mother's influence was profound. Indeed, his journey began not in 1955 but in his maternal home. Manning instilled in her son an understanding of and critique of the US racial hierarchy. She was a formidable woman who taught her son to embrace and love his heritage. Manning shaped, more than anyone else, Farrakhan's life and career. Indeed, it is to his mother that he owes his life's work.

Minister Farrakhan's career in the NOI in the 1950s and early 1960s was overshadowed by the magnitude of Malcolm X. Farrakhan's plays and music certainly contributed to the NOI's propaganda war. However, he was very much Malcolm's subordinate. Minister Farrakhan's devotion to Elijah Muhammad was tested when he was asked to give up his music. His willingness to surrender his love of music for Muhammad earned him Muhammad's good graces. Minister Farrakhan utilized the power struggles that gripped his faith community to prove his devotion to Muhammad. Indeed, Muhammad prized loyalty more dearly than anything else. As noted in Chapter 3, Minister Farrakhan has publicly acknowledged his role in creating an atmosphere in which Malcolm's death could occur. He is not without blame for Malcolm's isolation from the NOI and the historical record evidences that he did indeed feed into the hatred that surrounded Malcolm in his faith community. Farrakhan's elevation in the NOI post-1965 could not have occurred while Malcolm was still a national assistant. Minister Farrakhan relocated to New York with his young family in 1965. In Harlem, he walked the streets brandishing the words of Elijah Muhammad at a time when many blamed the community for Malcolm's death. His task in rebuilding the trust of Harlemites was not an easy one. Yet, he had considerable success as a national minister. The community did not experience a mass exodus of members and Farrakhan ensured that the NOI's voice was heard on television, on radio, and in universities and colleges where he was invited and permitted to speak.

The Nation's fall, as discussed in Chapter 2, devastated Minister Farrakhan and thousands of NOI members. As noted, many such individuals were confused by the rapid introduction of Sunni Islam and appalled by Wallace's efforts to disband structures that had ultimately given purpose and positions to the community's members. Minister Farrakhan's time in service to Wallace was by no means time wasted. As noted earlier, his work in CRAID and introduction to Sunni Islam served him well in both the short and long term. Minister Farrakhan found favor with Black Christians and it is to Black Christians and Black churches that he owes much of his subsequent success. His decision to leave the WCIW in 1979 and rebuild the work of Elijah Muhammad caused serious financial difficulties and burdened his family. Yet, his steadfast work and willingness to revise and reinterpret Muhammad's teachings paid off.

Minister Farrakhan reintroduced Muhammad's theology, words, and work when he sought out to rebuild the original NOI. His community, as noted in Chapter 3, was distinct from the original Nation. Moreover, its theological positions were markedly different. Minister Farrakhan's theological positions were distinct from those of his spiritual father. As noted in Chapter 3, Farrakhan presents himself as a Christian and Elijah Muhammad as the prophesied Christ figure in the Bible. His belief in Muhammad's immortality served to further isolate him from Muhammad's family. For Farrakhan, however, Muhammad's immortality was confirmed in 1985 when he encountered his spiritual father in a vision while in Mexico. The intricacies of the NOI's theology were largely unknown to those outside the community. It is thus unlikely that Jesse Jackson fully comprehended Farrakhan's religious beliefs when he befriended him in the 1980s. The alliance between both men gave birth to Minister Farrakhan's reputation as an antisemite. Indeed, it is worth noting that Jackson's career in the long term has been largely unaffected by his own antisemitic remarks.

Minister Farrakhan's antisemitism and message of racial uplift were given a platform by countless journalists and media outlets in the late 1980s and 1990s. His success at securing funding for the NOI and ability to draw sizeable crowds further aided his ascent. Minister Farrakhan's rise to national prominence, as noted in Chapter 3, would not have been possible without the broader context of mass incarceration and regression in race relations. The MMM brought Minister Farrakhan to the apex of his career. It was not, however, a one-man show. The march was made possible by the work of several organizations including the NAACP and secular groups. Moreover, support among Christians and Black Churches was vital. Minister Farrakhan's subsequent tours in the post-1995 period cost him a significant amount of support, as noted in Chapter 4. Subsequent marches and interventions were less successful in terms of attendance. Indeed, not even the more inclusive message of the Millions More Movement rivaled the success of the 1995 march.

Minister Farrakhan's personal health struggles moved him closer to Sunni Islam. Indeed, as noted in Chapter 4, he sought the support of the ISNA as early as the 1990s. His subsequent departure from the NOI's foundational theology created a measure of panic in the NOI and compelled him to spend the remaining decade oscillating between Sunni Islam and more traditional NOI teachings. The frequent changes in the NOI's professed line of faith evidence the extent to which Minister Farrakhan is beholden to his followers. He is not, as noted, the master of his faith community. Indeed, his statements are often a reflection of the temperament of his followers. Minister Farrakhan has suffered considerable reputational damage in the United States. Indeed, as noted in Chapter 4, it can be damaging both personally and professionally for individuals to be associated with or photographed with him. The uproar surrounding his support for Obama, for example, testified to his souring reputation. Minister Farrakhan's willingness to voice his support for Obama while also refusing to criticize him for much of his presidency evidenced a personal desire for Obama's success. Obama's presidency failed to usher in a post-racial America. The creation of the Black Lives Matter Movement and the Justice or Else campaign in 2015 revealed that little had changed in the United States for African Americans, particularly as it relates to their experiences with police and the judicial system.

Minister Farrakhan's ongoing health problems and advanced age compelled him to reorganize the NOI's leadership structures. As noted in Chapter 4, the NOI has had some form of executive board since the early 2000s. The current council of thirteen is comprised of Minister Farrakhan's most senior advisors and ministers. However, council members are themselves much older than the community's body of student ministers. There can be no doubt that the council has a wealth of knowledge about the faith community's administration and management. Moreover, there appears to be some agreement in the council that Ishmael should be "the face" of the teachings.[10] Minister Farrakhan's inability or unwillingness to publicly endorse Ishmael as a successor has, as noted, left him and the community vulnerable. Minister Farrakhan's faith community continue to exist in no-man's land. They exist and move fluently between Christianity, Sunni Islam, and the world of the Black Church. As such, the community currently lacks a consistent theological position. This predicament is both a strength and a weakness. On the one hand, it enables Christians who love the Black Nationalist ideals of the NOI to join the community without ever fully abandoning their faith. Likewise, it enables NOI members to practice Sunni Islam while never having to leave the NOI. On the other hand, it has the potential to confuse members about the future theological trajectory of the community. This, of course, mirrors to some extent the unfortunate position that Elijah Muhammad placed his own followers in. The test for the NOI post-Farrakhan will be how they can navigate the community's divisions while also affording space for the many beliefs that exist within the faith community.

Notes

1. "The Honorable Minister Louis Farrakhan Addresses the Ye (formerly 'Kanye West') and Kyrie Irving Controversy," *The Final Call*, November 22, 2022, 23.
2. https://edition.cnn.com/2022/10/25/business/adidas-ye-ends-partnership/index.html (accessed December 2, 2022).
3. https://www.wsj.com/articles/kanye-west-louis-farrakhan-jews-anti-semitism-lost-tribes-planned-parenthood-nation-of-islam-white-black-supremacy-crown-heights-israel-11667419455 (accessed December 2, 2022).
4. https://www.wsj.com/articles/kanye-west-ye-kyrie-irving-black-anti-semitism-jewish-louis-farrakhan-11668034077 (accessed November 10, 2022).
5. https://www.wsj.com/articles/kanye-west-louis-farrakhan-jews-anti-semitism-lost-tribes-planned-parenthood-nation-of-islam-white-black-supremacy-crown-heights-israel-11667419455 (accessed December 2, 2022).
6. https://media.noi.org/watch/NOI-wvon-May-16-2022 (accessed September 20, 2022).
7. "Behind the #FTA100 Awards Ceremony: How It All Began—The Exclusive with Brother Jesse Muhammad & Mosque Flow," *Hurt2Healing Magazine* (accessed December 2, 2022).
8. Muhammad, "The Plot to Outlaw the Nation of Islam."
9. https://new.finalcall.com/2022/10/11/he-lives-commemoration-of-the-125th-birth-anniversary-of-the-most-honorable-elijah-muhammad/ (accessed November 2, 2022).
10. Farrakhan, "A Swan Song."

Bibliography

Ahmad, Yusuf. "Voice of the People—What Courier Readers Think: Thoughts on 'Muhammad Pro and Con: Is Mr. Muhammad a 'Fake'," *Pittsburgh Courier*, August 18, 1956, 10.

Alexander, Michelle. *The New Jim Crow: Mass Incarceration in the Age of Colorblindness*, New York: New Press, 2011.

Anderson, Javonte. "Minister Farrakhan Invited to St. Sabina after Facebook Ban," *Chicago Tribune*, May 7, 2019, 2.

Austin, Algernon. *America Is Not Post-Racial: Xenophobia, Islamophobia, Racism and the 44th President*, Santa Barbara: Praeger, 2015.

Bagby, Ihsan. "The American Mosque Survey 2020: Growing and Evolving." Institute for Social Policy and Understanding.

"Behind the #FTA100 Awards Ceremony: How It All Began—The Exclusive with Brother Jesse Muhammad & Mosque Flow," *Hurt2Healing Magazine* (https://hurt2healingmag.com/behind-the-fta100-ceremony-how-it-all-began-the-exclusive-with-brother-jesse-muhammad-mosque-flow/) (accessed December 2, 2022).

Berg, Herbert. *Elijah Muhammad and Islam*, New York: New York University Press, 2009.

Beynon, Erdmann. "The Voodoo Cult among Negro Migrants in Detroit," *American Journal of Sociology*, vol. 43, no. 6 (May 1938): 894–907.

"Black Women Gather to Promote Unity at Million Woman March," *Jet Magazine*, vol. 92, no. 25, November 10, 1997.

Booker, James. "Why I Quit and What I Plan Next," *New York Amsterdam News*, March 14, 1964, 51.

Bowen, Patrick. *A History of Conversion to Islam in the United States, Volume 2: The African American Islamic Renaissance, 1920–1975*, Boston: Brill, 2017.

Bowen, Patrick. "Propaganda in the Early NOI," in Dawn-Marie Gibson and Herbert Berg (eds.), *New Perspectives on the Nation of Islam*, 135–53. London: Routledge, 2017.

Cheers, Michael. "Untold Story of How Jesse Jackson Won Navy Flyer's Freedom," *Jet*, January 1984, 14.

"Chicago Muslim Oral History Project: Muhammad, Sultan—Oral History Collection (Chicago History Museum)—CARLI Digital Collections" (illinois.edu) (accessed November 15, 2021).

Clarke, John. "Marcus Garvey: The Harlem Years," *Transition*, no. 46 (1974): 17–23.

Clegg, Claude. "Rebuilding the Nation: The Life and Work of Elijah Muhammad, 1946–1954," *The Black Scholar*, vol. 26, no. 3/4 (Fall/Winter 1996): 49–59.

Cleotha, X. "Has Not Seen Messenger, Yet," *The Final Call*, May 1982, 16.

"Community Outraged; D.C. Police Assault 'Dopebusters,'" *The Final Call*, October 3, 1988, 3.

"Covid-19 and the U.S. Policy of Depopulation," *The Final Call*, November 29, 2022, 7.

Curtis, Edward. "The Black Muslim Scare in the Twentieth Century: The History of State Islamophobia and Its Post 9/11 Variations," in Carl W. Ernst (ed.), *Islamophobia in America*, 75–106. New York: Palgrave Macmillan, 2013.

Curtis, Edward. *Islam in Black America: Identity, Liberation and Difference in African-American Religious Thought*, New York: State University of New York Press, 2002.

Delaney, Paul. "Shift of Malcolm X's Successor Stirs Black Muslim Speculation," *New York Times*, June 12, 1975, 20.

Earmon, Keith. "Thanks for Minister," *The Final Call*, April 22, 1991, 16.

Editor. "Intended Voodoo Victims' Number Still Mounting," *Detroit Free Press*, November 23, 1932.

Editorials. "Now Is Not the Time to be Silent," *The Crisis*, January 1942, 7.

Ellis, Mark. "J. Edgar Hoover and the 'Red Summer' of 1919," *Journal of American Studies*, vol. 28, no. 1 (1994): 39–59.

Elsayed, Sheikh. "After Twenty-Five Years Rift, Farrakhan Joins Warith Deen Muhammad," *American Muslim*, vol. 1, no. 2 (April 2000): 24.

Ernst, Carl. *Islamophobia in America: The Anatomy of Intolerance*, New York: Palgrave, 2013.

Essien-Udom, E.-U. *Black Nationalism: A Search for An Identity in America*, Chicago: University of Chicago Press, 1962.

Fanusie, Fatima, and Beboppers Ahmadi. "Veterans and Migrants: African American Islam in Boston, 1948–1963," in Theodore Trost (ed.), *The African Diaspora and the Study of Religion*, New York: Palgrave, 2008.

"Farrakhan in the Caribbean," *Muhammad Speaks*, January 24, 1975, 29.

Farrakhan, Louis. "The Black Man Must Do for Self or Suffer the Consequences," *The Final Call*, October 28, 1991, 21.

Farrakhan, Louis. "Closing Remarks at the 2021 Saviours' Day Address." Speech delivered in Chicago, February 27, 2021.

Farrakhan, Louis. "The Criterion: Worldwide Address." Speech delivered in Michigan, July 4, 2020.

Farrakhan, Louis. "Have No Fear for the Future: The Future Is Ours: Part 1." Speech delivered in Detroit, February 19, 2017.

Farrakhan, Louis. "Final Call," *Chicago Defender*, September 29, 1979, 6.

Farrakhan, Louis. "Final Call," *Chicago Defender*, November 10, 1979, 12.

Farrakhan, Louis. "Final Call: Institutional Destruction," *Chicago Defender*, June 23, 1979, 6.

Farrakhan, Louis. "The Immeasurable, Limitless Value and Beauty of a Woman." Speech delivered in Chicago, May 10, 2009.

Farrakhan, Louis. "Insight," *Chicago Defender*, April 14, 1979, 10.

Farrakhan, Louis. "Insight," *Chicago Defender*, June 9, 1979, 6.

Farrakhan, Louis. Interview with Jamaica Radio RJR, Kingston, June 17, 1996.

Farrakhan, Louis. Interview on the Rock Newman Show, April 27, 2013.

Farrakhan, Louis. "Justice or Else! The Twentieth Anniversary of the Million Man March: Main Address." Speech delivered in Washington, DC, October 10, 2015.

Farrakhan, Louis. "Let Us Make Man." Speech delivered in New York, January 24, 1994.

Farrakhan, Louis. "Memorandum to the Black Nation," *The Final Call*, vol. 2, no. 5, May 1982, 10–11.

Farrakhan, Louis. "Message to the University of the West Indies." Speech delivered at University of the West Indies, March 21, 2002.

Farrakhan, Louis. "The Murder of Malcolm X: The Effect on Black America." Speech delivered in Chicago, February 21, 1990.

Farrakhan, Louis. "Preparation of the Mind and the Qualifications to Act for Christ," *The Final Call*, March 15, 2011, 21.

Farrakhan, Louis. *The Meaning of F.O.I.*, Chicago: Elijah Muhammad Education Foundation, 1983.

Farrakhan, Louis. "Satan and the Mastery of Sexual Urges." Speech delivered in Chicago, April 8, 1987.

Farrakhan, Louis. "Saviours' Day Keynote Address." Speech delivered in Chicago, February 25, 2018.

Farrakhan, Louis. "Saviours' Day 2008 Key Note Address: The Gods at War: The Future Is All about Y.O.U.th." Speech delivered in Chicago, February 27, 2008.

Farrakhan, Louis. "A Saviour Is Born for the Whole of Humanity. No One Need Perish." Speech delivered in Chicago, February 17, 2019.

Farrakhan, Louis. "The Sentence of Death on America—The Reality of Genocide." Speech delivered in Wisconsin, February 1, 1980.

Farrakhan, Louis. "A Swan Song." Speech delivered in Chicago, February 27, 2022.
Farrakhan, Louis. *A Torchlight for America*, Chicago: Final Call, 1993.
Farrakhan, Louis. "A Tribute to the Honorable Elijah Muhammad," *The Final Call*, vol. 1, no. 3 (1979): 2–3.
Farrakhan, Louis. "The Ultimate Challenge: The Survival of the Black Nation," *The Final Call*, May 1979, 12.
Farrakhan, Louis. "The Unravelling of a Great Nation." Speech delivered at the 2020 Saviours' Day convention in Detroit, February 23, 2020.
Farrakhan, Louis. "We Are Farrakhan: Community Rally in Support of the Honorable Minister Louis Farrakhan." Speech delivered in Chicago, May 9, 2019.
Federal Bureau of Investigation File: Elijah Muhammad.
Federal Bureau of Investigation File: Muslim Cult of Islam.
Felber, Garrett. *Those Who Know Don't Say: The Nation of Islam, the Black Freedom Movement, and the Carceral State*, Chapel Hill: University of North Carolina Press, 2020.
"The Final Call Is Now Weekly," *The Final Call*, June 4, 1996, 29.
Finley, Stephen. "The Meaning of 'Mother' in Louis Farrakhan's 'Mother Wheel': Race, Gender, and Sexuality in the Cosmology of the Nation of Islam's UFO," *Journal of the American Academy of Religion*, vol. 80, no. 2 (June 2012): 434–65.
"First Official Interview with the Supreme Minister of the Nation of Islam, The Honorable Wallace D. Muhammad," *Muhammad Speaks*, March 21, 1975, 3.
Foner, Nancy. "West Indian Identity in the Diaspora: Comparative and Historical Perspectives," *Latin American Perspectives*, vol. 25, no. 3 (May 1988): 173–88.
Gardell, Mattias. *Countdown to Armageddon: Louis Farrakhan and the Nation of Islam*, Durham, NC: Duke University Press, 1996.
"Garvey Preaches Faith in Black God: Negro Leader Makes Plea for Free African Republic with a New Religion. Cheered by Big Audience Says White Man Can Have America and Europe, But 'We Are Going to Have Africa,'" *New York Times*, August 4, 1924, 7.
Gates, Henry. "Farrakhan Speaks," *Transition*, no. 70 (1996): 140–67.
GhaneaBassiri, Kambiz. *A History of Islam in America*, New York: Cambridge University Press, 2010.
Gibson, Dawn-Marie. *A History of the Nation of Islam: Race, Islam and the Quest for Freedom*, Santa Barbara: Praeger, 2012.
Gibson, Dawn-Marie. "Making Original Men: Elijah Muhammad, the Nation of Islam and the Fruit of Islam," *Journal of Religious History*, vol. 44, no. 3 (September 2020): 1–19.

Gibson, Dawn-Marie. *The Nation of Islam, Louis Farrakhan and the Men Who Follow Him*, New York: Palgrave, 2016.

Gibson, Dawn-Marie. "Nation Women's Engagement and Resistance in the Muhammad Speaks Newspaper," *Journal of American Studies*, vol. 49, no. 1 (2015): 1–18.

Gibson, Dawn-Marie, and Herbert Berg. *New Perspectives on the Nation of Islam*, London: Routledge, 2017.

Gibson, Dawn-Marie, and Jamillah Karim. *Women of the Nation: Between Black Protest and Sunni Islam*, New York: New York University Press, 2014.

Glanton, Dahleen. "Some African Americans Look Past Farrakhan's Bigoted Words and Hear a Message of Love," *Chicago Tribune*, May 6, 2019, 2.

Gomez, Michael. *Black Crescent: The Experience and Legacy of African Muslims in the Americas*, New York: Cambridge University Press, 2005.

Hakim, Malik. "Serving the Community," *Bilalian News*, February 11, 1977, 13.

Hakim, Nasir. *The True History of Elijah Muhammad: Messenger of Allah*, Atlanta: M.E.M.P.S., 1997.

Harrison, Wanda. "Islam Addresses Questions Church Cannot Answer," *The Final Call*, May 1982, 16.

Haywood, D'Weston. *Let Us Make Men: The Twentieth-Century Black Press and a Manly Vision for Racial Advancement*, Chapel Hill: University of North Carolina Press, 2018.

Herbert, Bob. "In America, Endless Posion," *New York Times*, August 29, 1999.

Herman, 2X. "Farrakhan Tells Wayne State Students of the Right Leader," *Muhammad Speaks*, June 4, 1971, 15.

Historical Research Department of the NOI. *The Secret Relationship between Blacks and Jews*, Chicago: NOI, 1991. https://www.adl.org/news/op-ed/louis-farrakhan-again (accessed October 18, 2021).

"The Honorable Minister Louis Farrakhan Addresses the Ye (formerly 'Kanye West') and Kyrie Irving Controversy," *The Final Call*, November 22, 2022, 23.

https://podcasters.spotify.com/pod/show/muhammad-mosque-32/episodes/Separation-The-Creative-Process---Sis--Dr--Ava-Muhammad-e2tad9 (accessed October 22, 2023).

https://edition.cnn.com/2022/10/25/business/adidas-ye-ends-partnership/index.html (accessed December 2, 2022).

https://www.pewresearch.org/fact-tank/2019/01/17/black-muslims-account-for-a-fifth-of-all-u-s-muslims-and-about-half-are-converts-to-islam/ (accessed November 15, 2021).

http://mosque74.org/student-minister/ (accessed June 10, 2022).

https://noi.org/nation-of-islam-responds-911-attacks-on-america/ (accessed October 10, 2012).

https://www.nytimes.com/2005/02/24/obituaries/nathan-wright-jr-black-power-advocate-dies-at-81.html (accessed June 10, 2019).

https://new.finalcall.com/2022/05/24/a-new-generation-rising-in-the-word-min-farrakhan-and-noi-executive-council-appear-on-wvon-am-radio/ (accessed November 25, 2022).

https://new.finalcall.com/2022/10/11/he-lives-commemoration-of-the-125th-birth-anniversary-of-the-most-honorable-elijah-muhammad/ (accessed December 1, 2022).

https://new.finalcall.com/2011/11/01/u-s-role-in-libya-s-fall-overseas-meddling-leading-to-fall-of-nation-warns-min-farrakhan/ (accessed April 2, 2013).

https://new.finalcall.com/2022/02/16/virtual-womens-conference-shines-light-on-healing-and-health/ (accessed November 24, 2022).

https://www.prisonlegalnews.org/news/2019/jul/2/federal-government-pays-nation-islam-teach-bop-prisoners/ (accessed September 20, 2020).

https://www.nytimes.com/2021/11/17/nyregion/malcolm-x-killing-exonerated.html (accessed March 22, 2022).

https://www.ispu.org/report-1-mosque-survey-2020/ (accessed November 15, 2021).

https://www.rollingstone.com/music/music-news/kanye-west-talks-mike-brown-beck-new-album-status-in-surprise-interview-172161/ (accessed December 8, 2015).

https://www.washingtonexaminer.com/news/congress/keith-ellison-pans-louis-farrakhans-nation-of-islam-nobody-listens-to-them (accessed October 18, 2021).

https://www.washingtonexaminer.com/politics/nation-of-islam-defends-federal-funding-for-prison-lectures-as-a-blessing-to-prisoners (accessed February 1, 2020).

https://www.wsj.com/articles/kanye-west-louis-farrakhan-jews-anti-semitism-lost-tribes-planned-parenthood-nation-of-islam-white-black-supremacy-crown-heights-israel-11667419455 (accessed December 2, 2022).

https://www.wsj.com/articles/kanye-west-ye-kyrie-irving-black-anti-semitism-jewish-louis-farrakhan-11668034077 (accessed November 10, 2022).

Kasinitz, Phillip. *Caribbean New York: Black Immigrants and the Politics of Race*, Ithaca: Cornell University Press, 1992.

Khadijah, X. "Family Saved By Islam," *The Final Call*, July 1985, 27.

King, Jacob. "Clearing the Planet: Dianetics Auditing and the Eschatology of the Nation of Islam," in Herbert Berg and Dawn-Marie Gibson (eds.), *New Perspectives on the Nation of Islam*, 218–35. New York: Routledge, 2017.

Klarman, Michael. *From Jim Crow to Civil Rights: The Supreme Court and the Struggle for Racial Equality*, New York: Oxford University Press, 2004.

"A Labor of Love and Service to Humanity: Nation of Islam Distributes Thousands of Face Masks Nationwide," *The Final Call*, December 8, 2020, 6.

"Latin American Representative of the Honorable Minister Louis Farrakhan and the Nation of Islam: Abel Muhammad," *Rise Magazine*, September 2020, 17.

"Letter from the Honorable Minister Louis Farrakhan—Final Call News" (https://new.finalcall.com/2006/09/22/letter-from-the-honorable-minister-louis-farrakhan/) (accessed October 19, 2022).

Larry, X. "To Serve His Own: Thumbnail Sketch of Minister Louis Farrakhan," *Saviour's Day 1981 Historic Souvenir Journal*, February 21–22, 1981.

Lawrence, X, and James Hoard Smith. "Farrakhan Warns Blacks 'Stay Vigilant,'" *Muhammad Speaks*, February 14, 1975, 7.

Lawrence, X, and James Hoard Smith. "The Honorable Elijah Muhammad Day: Oakland and Berkeley Deliver Simultaneous Proclamations," *Muhammad Speaks*, February 14, 1975, 7.

Lincoln, Eric. *The Black Muslims in America*, Boston: Beacon, 1961.

Lokke, Geoffrey. "The Muslims Present Orenga," *The Drama Review*, vol. 62, no. 2 (2018): 78–96.

Louis, X. "Malcolm-Hypocrite," *Muhammad Speaks*, December 4, 1964, 15.

Magida, Arthur. *Prophet of Rage: A Life of Louis Farrakhan and His Nation*, New York: HarperCollins, 1996.

Majied, Kamal. "FBI Fear Tactics Wasted on Muslims," *Muhammad Speaks*, June 15, 1973, 4.

Malcolm, X. *The Autobiography of Malcolm X*, New York: Penguin, 1965.

Malcolm, X. "Telegram to Muhammad," *New York Amsterdam News*, March 14, 1964, 151.

"Malcolm X Tells of Death Threat," *Amsterdam News*, March 21, 1964, 50.

"Malcolm's Murder: His Widow Says 'Of Course' Farrakhan Was Involved," *Philadelphia Daily News*, March 14, 1994, 7.

Mary, X. "Two Great Families Unite," *Muhammad Speaks*, February 14, 1975, 4.

Marable, Manning. "Black Fundamentalism: Farrakhan and Conservative Black Nationalism," *Race and Class*, vol. 39, no. 4 (1998): 1–22.

Marable, Manning. *Malcolm X: A Life of Reinvention*, New York: Viking, 2011.

Marable, Manning. "Recovering Malcolm's Life: A Historian's Adventures in Living History," *Souls: A Critical Journal of Black Politics, Culture and Society*, vol. 7, no. 1 (2005): 20–35.

Margolis, Jon. "Jackson Denounces Farrakhan Remarks," *Chicago Tribune*, June 29, 1984, 1.

McCloud, Aminah. *African American Islam*, New York and London: Routledge, 1995.

"Million Woman March Marked 25th Anniversary," *The Final Call*, December 6, 2022, 30.

Mitchell, Mary. "Why Obama 'Denounced' Farrakhan: It Wasn't Candidate's Best Move—But Most Blacks Understand," *Chicago Sun-Times*, March 2, 2008, 13.

Morgan, Iwan, and Mark White. *The Presidential Image: A History from Theodore Roosevelt to Donald Trump*, London: I.B. Tauris, 2020.

"Mother Tynnetta Muhammad—A Heartfelt and Fitting Tribute to a Perfect Example" (finalcall.com) (accessed October 22, 2022).

Muhammad, Abdul. "Arab World Welcomes Farrakhan," *The Final Call*, vol. 5, no. 2 (May 1985): 4.

Muhammad, Abdul. "Jamaican Welcomes Native Son," *The Final Call*, January 13, 1986, 3.

Muhammad, Abdul. "Nation Reflects on Death of Minister's Mother," *The Final Call*, December 30, 1988, 6.

Muhammad, Abdul. "$5 Million Loan Announced in D.C.; Col Qathafi Helps Launch P.O.W.E.R.," *The Final Call*, vol. 5, no. 2 (July 1985): 3–4.

Muhammad, Abdul. *A Soldier in the Movement of Christ*, Atlanta: Independently Published, 2020.

Muhammad, Abiyso. "Reflections on the Million Family March and Its Impact," *The Final Call*, November 29, 2022, 30.

Muhammad, Anisha. "The Mission Comes First: Faith, Hope and Healing as Black Families Search for Missing Loved Ones," *The Final Call*, November 9, 2021, 4.

Muhammad, Askia. "Memories of the Honorable Elijah Muhammad," *The Final Call*, October 19, 2021, 17.

Muhammad, Azizah. "A Son's Testimony: The Biological Son of the Most Honorable Elijah Muhammad Shares His Story of Faith, Findings, and Prayers for the Future," *Rise Magazine*, December 2021.

Muhammad, Betty. "Ode to the Honorable Minister Louis Farrakhan," *Virtue Today Magazine*, February 2022, 3.

Muhammad, Demetric. *"But, Didn't You Kill Malcolm?" Myth-Busting the Propaganda against the Nation of Islam*, Chicago: Nation of Islam, 2020.

Muhammad, Demetric. *Manhood Principles, Parables, Concepts and Characteristics from the Holy Qur'an*, Memphis: Nation of Islam, 2019.

Muhammad, Demetric. "The Plot to Outlaw the Nation of Islam." Speech delivered in Chicago, June 24, 2018.

Muhammad, Elijah. *Message to the Blackman in America*, Chicago: MEMPS Press, 1965.

Muhammad, Elijah. "Mr. Muhammad Speaks," *Pittsburgh Courier*, July 4, 1959, 14.

Muhammad, Elijah. "'Mr. Muhammad Speaks': Jesus' History Misunderstood by the Christians," *Pittsburgh Courier*, November 9, 1957, 10.

Muhammad, Ishmael. "Believers' Meeting." Speech delivered in Chicago, March 3, 2021.

Muhammad, Ishmael. Opening Remarks at the 2018 Keynote Address for the Annual Saviours' Day Convention, Chicago, February 25, 2018.

Muhammad, Jabril. *Closing the Gap: Inner Views of the Heart, Mind & Soul of the Honorable Minister Louis Farrakhan*, Chicago: FCN, 2006.

Muhammad, Jabril. *Is It Possible that the Honorable Elijah Muhammad Is Still Physically Alive?* Phoenix: Nuevo Books, 2007.

Muhammad, Jackie. "Facebook's Ban on Farrakhan," *The Final Call*, June 2019.

Muhammad, Michael, and Anisha Muhammad. "The Reopening: NOI Mosques, Study Groups to Return to Regular Meetings," *The Final Call*, November 16, 2021, 3, 34.

Muhammad, Naba'a. "A Step toward Justice, But Much More Is Required," *The Final Call*, November 30, 2021, 16.

Muhammad, Nisa. "Nation Welcomes New Student Imam," *The Final Call*, November 15, 2022, 31.

Muhammad, Nisa, and Askia Muhammad. "A Legacy of Brotherhood and Unity: Reverend Willie Wilson Celebrates 37 Years of Faith in Action," *The Final Call*, May 11, 2010, 2.

Muhammad, Nuri. *After You Say I Do*, Phoenix: Bashirah House Publishing, 2018.

Muhammad, Nuri. *Before You Say I Do*, Phoenix: Bashirah House Publishing, 2016.

Muhammad, Nuri. Breakfast Club Interview, 18 December 2019: Brother Nuri Muhammad Speaks On Malcolm X, Valuable Relationships, Economic Empowerment + More—YouTube (accessed November 3, 2021).

Muhammad, Nuri. "Striking the Right Balance in Life w/ Nuri Muhammad," *Hurt2Healing Magazine*, March 23, 2021.

Muhammad, Nuri. "The Value of Faith and Family," *Virtue Today Magazine*, Fall 2012, 10.

Muhammad, Nuri. *A Well Made Man*, Phoenix: Bashirah House Publishing, 2022.

Muhammad, Philbert. "Malcolm Exposed by His Brother," *Muhammad Speaks*, January 15, 1965, 15.

Muhammad, Richard, and Donald Muhammad. "A Step toward Healing," *The Final Call*, May 24, 1995, 3.

Muhammad, Starla. "Min. Farrakhan and the NOI Executive Counsel Appear on WVON AM Radio," *The Final Call*, May 31, 2022, 2.

Muhammad, Toure. "If We Don't Help Ourselves, Who Will?," *The Final Call*, March 16, 2021, 6.

Muhammad, Tynetta. "Revisiting Minister Farrakhan's Vision-Like Experience on September, 17 1985—The Magnificent Wheel Within a Wheel-The Mother's Wheel," *The Final Call*, vol. 32, no. 51.

Muhammad, Wesley. *Is Allah A Man? The Islam Debate*, Atlanta: A-Team Publishing, 2016.

Muhammad, Wesley. "A Message to the FOI: Brothers, Soldiers, and Black God Protocol." Speech delivered in Washington, DC, April 6, 2015.

Muhammad, Wesley. *Understanding the Assault on the Black Man, Black Manhood and Black Masculinity*, Atlanta: A-Team Publishing, 2017.

"The Mustafa Family, 'Islam Works,'" *The Final Call*, July 1985, 27.

Najiy, James. *The Nation of Islam's Temple #7 Harlem, USA: My Years with Louis Farrakhan and Malcolm X*, Atlanta: Rathsi Publishing, LLC, 2012.

"A New Imam and a New Day of Unity, Cooperation" (finalcall.com) (accessed November 15, 2021).

"N.O.I. Prison Ministry Helps Settle Differences," *The Final Call*, July 20, 1994, 17.

"NOI—Video Platform | WVON: Hon. Minister Louis Farrakhan & Executive Council" (https://www.youtube.com/watch?v=bqwC2MS3EZ8) (accessed September 20, 2022).

O'Donnell, Maureen. "Farrakhan to Muslims: Honor Elijah Muhammad," *Chicago Sun-Times*, February 22, 1993, 10.

Ogbar, Jeffrey. *Black Power: Radical Politics and African American Identity*, Baltimore: Johns Hopkins University Press, 2019.

"Orenga Tells True History of Afro-Americans," *Muhammad Speaks*, December 1960, 7.

Patsides, Nicholas. "Allies, Constituents or Myopic Investors: Marcus Garvey and Black Americans," *Journal of American Studies*, vol. 41, no. 2 (2007): 279–305.

Perry, Ernest. "It's Time to Force a Change: The African American Press' Campaign for a True Democracy during World War 11," *Journalism History*, vol. 28, no. 2 (Summer 2002): 85–95.

Rahman, Ajile. "She Stood by His Side and at Times in His Stead: The Life and Legacy of Sister Clara Muhammad: First Lady of the Nation of Islam," Doctoral Dissertation, Clark-Atlanta University, 2000.

Ramirez, Margaret. "Farrakhan Now Opens Arms with Millions More March," *Chicago Tribune*, October 11, 2005, 22.

"Remembering the Million Man March: Testimonies from People Who Attended," *Virtue Today Magazine*, October 2021, 11.

Ruth 4X. "Elijah," *Muhammad Speaks*, October 7, 1966, 7.

Satter, Beryl. "Marcus Garvey, Father Divine and the Gender Politics of Race Difference and Race Neutrality," *American Quarterly*, vol. 48, no. 1 (March 1996): 43–76.

"Saviours' Day Convention on the Continent of Africa," *The Final Call*, July 20, 1994, 15.

"Saviours' Day 2021: Nation of Islam Hosts Its First Virtual Convention," *The Final Call*, February 23, 2021, 3.

Shabazz, John. "Open Letter: Muslim Minister Writes to Malcolm," *Muhammad Speaks*, July 3, 1964, 9.

Shabazz, Lance. *Blood, Sweat & Tears: The Nation of Islam and Me*, Morrisville, NC: Lulu Publishing Services, 2015.

Sitkoff, Harvard. "Racial Militancy and Interracial Violence in the Second World War," *Journal of American History*, vol. 58, no. 3 (December 1971): 661–81.

Smith, James. "'Muhammad Week' Proclaimed in Gary, Ind.," *Muhammad Speaks*, December 27, 1974.

"Study of Al-Islam Wins New Convert," *Bilalian News*, September 9, 1977, 12.

Reel, William. "Call Muslims the Richest Black Group," *Daily News*, April 16, 1972, 60.

Rosin, Hanna, and Hamil R. Harris. "Farrakhan Has Surgery for Recurrence of Cancer: Followers 'Shaken' as His Health Worsens," *Washington Post*, April 2, 1999, A01.

Sahib, Hatim. "The Nation of Islam." *Contributions in Black Studies*, vol. 13, no. 3 (1995): 1–113.

Singh, Robert. *The Farrakhan Phenomenon: Race, Reaction, and the Paranoid Style in American Politics*, Washington, DC: Georgetown University Press, 1997.

Smith, James. "Delegates Get Disturbed Over Snub to Farrakhan," *Muhammad Speaks*, April 5, 1974, 10.

"Taking on the Mission: Interview with Min. Ishmael Muhammad" (finalcall.com) (accessed October 19, 2022).

Tate, Sonsyrea. *Do Me Twice: My Life after Islam*, New York: Strebor Books, 2007.

Tawwab, Fatima. "Doing for Self: The Nation of Islam's Temple No. 11 and Its Impact on Social and Economic Development of Boston's African American Community, 1948–1968," Master of Arts Thesis, Temple University, 2001.

The Nation of Islam Rebirth Series. Produced by Never Fall Again Studios, 2019.

Tonlay, Stewart. "The African American 'Great Migration' and Beyond," *Annual Review of Sociology*, vol. 29 (August 2003): 209–32.

Topping, Simon. "'Supporting Our Friends and Defeating Our Enemies': Militancy and Nonpartisanship in the NAACP, 1936–1948," *Journal of African American History*, vol. 89, no. 1 (Winter 2004): 17–35.

"'The Trial' Becomes Broadway Smash Hit," *Muhammad Speaks*, December 1960, 10.

Tripp, Luke. "The Political Views of Black Students during the Reagan Era," *The Black Scholar*, vol. 22, no. 3 (Summer 1992): 45–52.

Trotter, Joe. *The African American Experience*, Boston and New York: Houghton Mifflin Company, 2001.

Tuck, Stephen. *We Ain't What We Ought to Be: The Black Freedom Struggle from Emancipation to Obama*, Cambridge, MA: Harvard University Press, 2011.

"28 Years after the Death of Malcolm X … The Hon. Elijah Muhammad Cleared of All False Charges: Wives of Muhammad Testify at Historic Saviour's Day Event," *The Final Call*, March 15, 1993, 2.

"Unity, Stronger Than Ever," *Bilialian News*, March 19, 1976, 15.

Vincent, Ted. "The Garveyite Parents of Malcolm X," *The Black Scholar*, vol. 20, no. 2 (March/April 1989): 10–13.

Voogd, Jan. *Race Riots and Resistance: The Red Summer of 1919*, New York: Peter Lang, 2008.

Washburn, Patrick. *The African American Newspaper: Voice of Freedom*, Evanston, IL: Northwestern University Press, 2006.

Walker, Joe. "College Students, Professionals Coming to Nation of Islam," *Muhammad Speaks*, February 3, 1974, 3.

Walker, Joe. "Farrakhan Addresses Conference," *Muhammad Speaks*, May 11, 1973, 3.

Walker, Joe. "Media Attempt to Undermine Muslim Progress Exposed," *Muhammad Speaks*, February 1, 1974, 3.

Walter, John. "West Indian Immigrants: Those Arrogant Bastards," *Contributions in Black*, vol. 5, no. 3 (September 2008): 17–27.

Watson, Ted. "Activity Plentiful at Muslim Convention in Chicago," *Pittsburgh Courier*, March 16, 1957, 20.

Watson, Ted. "The Rise of Muhammad Temple of Islam: Hard-Working, Thrifty and Dedicated Moslems in Chicago Are Showing a New Side of This Movement in America," *Pittsburgh Courier*, April 7, 1956, 3.

White, Vibert. *Inside the Nation of Islam: A Historical and Personal Testimony by a Black Muslim*, Gainesville: University Press of Florida, 2001.

Wilson, Jamie. "Come Down Off the Cross and Get Under the Crescent," *Biography*, vol. 30, no. 3 (Summer 2013): 494–506.

Wooten, Melissa, and Enobong Branch. "Defining Appropriate Labor: Race, Gender, and the Idealization of Black Women in Domestic Service," *Race, Gender and Class Journal*, vol. 19, nos. 3–4 (2012): 292–308.

Wright, Nathan. *Black Power and Urban Unrest: Creative Possibilities*, New York: Hawthorn Books, Inc, 1967.

"Young Gallowshaw's Mother Strengthened by New York Minister's Womanhood Talk," *Muhammad Speaks*, October 21, 1966, 8.

Index

abortion 29, 34, 36
Accra 109, 120
Ahmadiyya Movement 4–5, 54
Ali, Noble Drew 3, 44–5
American Muslim Mission 123
Anti-Defamation League 2, 12, 98, 100, 104, 107, 128, 163
antisemitism 12, 97–102, 112, 118, 163–4, 166
The Autobiography of Malcolm X 107

Black Power 38, 39
Bilalian News 19, 76, 78
Black Lives Matter 131, 167

Church of Scientology (COS) 17, 117–18, 131–2, 156
Civil Rights Movement 22, 39, 57, 67, 70, 71–2
Clark, Percival 29, 33, 35
Clinton, Hillary 100, 129, 132, 138
Clinton, Bill 105, 118, 132
Coleman, Milton 12, 98–9
Committee for the Removal of All Images of the Divine 78–9, 89, 165
Council on American-Islamic Relations 10, 15
Covid-19 Pandemic 132–3, 138, 145, 157

Deen Intensive Academy 10, 16, 143–5, 156
Dianetics Auditing 17, 24, 131–2, 149

Ellison, Keith 2
Executive Shura Council 1, 3, 117–18, 134, 138–9, 141, 145–57, 164, 167

Facebook ban 1–2, 157, 164
Faith Community of Saint Sabina 1, 129
Farrakhan, Khadijah (*see also* Ross, Betsy) speech at MWM 121

Farrakhan, Louis
  conversion to NOI 46–8
  criticism of Jewish Americans 1, 12, 98–100, 107, 128–9, 156, 163
  criticism of Malcolm X 66–7, 108
  early life 21, 30, 35, 36, 37, 39–42
  early writings 12, 86–8
  embrace of Christianity and clergy 17, 22, 23, 30, 38, 43, 46–7, 78, 88–9, 112, 117, 119, 130, 131, 151, 154, 156, 165, 166
  health problems 14, 122, 127, 134, 135
  music career 11, 42, 43, 60, 165
  plays 22, 53, 58–60
  reconciliation with Dr. Betty Shabazz 108–9
  relationship with Elijah Muhammad 11, 23, 85, 164, 165, 166
  relationship with Malcolm X 9, 64–5, 66
  relationship with Imam W. D Mohammed 14, 24, 78, 94, 118, 122–3
  relationship with the Church of Scientology 17, 117, 118, 131
  "Twitter Army" 164
Farrakhan, Mustapha 138, 146, 147, 150, 164
Federal Bureau of Investigation
  FBI and Wallace's succession 74, 90–1
  interest in and surveillance of the NOI 60, 61
  Malcolm X's assassination 10, 67, 108
  power struggles in ONOI 22
  surveillance files 62
  surveillance of RNOI 21, 71
The Final Call newspaper 20
The Final Call to Islam 88
Foxman, Abraham 163
Fruit of Islam 5, 11, 13, 23, 37, 46, 58, 68, 72–3, 77, 91, 103, 104, 121, 138, 147, 148

Garvey, Marcus 3, 21, 29–30, 33–5, 36, 39, 47, 102
Great Migration 4, 31–2

hajj 126, 144
The Hate that Hate Produced 8, 57–8

Inner-city Muslim Action Network 16
Islamophobia 15, 43, 126
Islamic Society of North America 123, 166

Jackson, Jesse
  alliance with Louis Farrakhan 98–100
  Operation Breadbasket 97
Jamaica 22, 29, 33, 35, 73, 101–2
Justice or Else March 100, 120, 130–2, 138, 152, 167

Kennedy, John F. 9, 64, 65
King, Martin Luther 7, 72, 87, 97
Ku Klux Klan 8

Lee, Spike 12, 13, 23, 107–8
Libya 101, 119–20
Little, Earl 8
Little, Louise 8
Lomax, Louis 57

Malcolmology 107
Mandela, Nelson 120
Mandela, Winnie 120
Manning, Sarah
  conversion to NOI 30
  early life 29, 33
  interest in Garveyism 35, 38, 47
  parenting 30, 37–8
  pregnancy with Louis 29, 35–6
  racism 32, 40–1
  relationship with Louis Walcott 35–6
  relationship with Percival Clarke 33, 35
Million Man March 2, 21, 23, 24, 86, 100
  impact on Farrakhan's career and its aftermath 166–7
  lack of support after the March 127, 129–30
  NOI members recollections of the March 117–19
  organization and pledge 109–11
Millions More Movement 120, 127, 166

Million Woman March 120–1
Moorish Science Temple of America 3, 45
Muhammad, Abel 153, 155–6
Muhammad, A'isha 149
Muhammad, Abdul 150–2
Muhammad, Ahmad 146, 150
Muhammad, Akbar 40, 93–4, 101, 109, 144
Muhammad, Aminah 146, 152
Muhammad, Assad 146
Muhammad Ava 137–8, 146
Muhammad, Clara 6–7, 45, 90, 142
Muhammad, Demetric 13–14, 134, 153, 154–5
Muhammad, Elijah
  death 74
  early engagement with the African American press 55
  early life and introduction to the NOI 6
  early relationship with Louis X 11, 46
  efforts to engage Muslims beyond the NOI 56–7
  Elijah's ministers 8–9
  extramarital relationships 62–4
  incarceration and leadership of the early NOI 7–8, 45
  recognition in the post 1965-period 70–1
  request that Louis give up his career as a musician 59
  silencing of Malcolm X 64
  succession 6–7
Muhammad, Fard
  disappearance 6
  identity and theology 3–6
  positioning in Elijah Muhammad's and Louis Farrakhan's community 6, 128, 141, 143
Muhammad, Ishmael 14, 16, 21, 24, 117, 124, 133, 135, 138–43, 146, 147, 149, 150, 152, 153, 154, 157, 167
Muhammad, Jalil 16, 143, 145
Muhammad, Leonard 146, 150
Muhammad, Naeemah 146, 151
Muhammad, Nuri 1, 17, 153–4
Muhammad, Wallace
  departure from NOI 67
  early life and relationship with Elijah Muhammad 7

reconciliation with Farrakhan 14–15, 24, 122, 123
relationship with Malcolm X 63
succession 53, 73–6, 91, 143
structural reforms 23, 77, 165
tension with Louis Farrakhan 79, 91–2
tension with RNOI members 94
Muhammad, Wesley 146–7
Muhammad Speaks newspaper
　censure of Malcolm X 66–7
　criticism of Christianity 87
　founding of 8, 19, 58
Muhammad, Sultan 15, 16, 144–7, 153
Muhammad, Tynetta 14, 96, 121, 136–7, 142, 150
Muslim Girls Training and General Civilization Class 5, 11, 23, 77, 91, 121, 149, 151

National Association for the Advancement of Colored People 31, 39, 41, 57, 72, 110, 131, 166

Obama, Barack 118, 128–32, 167
Operation Breadbasket 97
Operation PUSH 78, 97
Orgena 22, 53, 58–9

polygamy
　Elijah Muhammad's relationships with secretaries 62–3
　Louis X's response to Elijah Muhammad's relationships 64
　Louis Farrakhan's polygamous wives 103–4
　See also Muhammad, Tynetta
Prison Ministry 104–7, 118

Ross, Betsy
　conversion to NOI 46
　early relationship with Louis and pregnancy 42

Shabazz, Betty 108–9
Shabazz, Lance 90
Shabazz, Qubilah 108–9
The Secret Relationship between Blacks and Jews 107
The Secret Relationship between Blacks and Jews Volume 2 128
Southern Christian Leadership Conference 97, 131
St. Cyprian's Episcopalian Church 22, 30, 38–9
　see also Wright, Nathan

The Trial 22, 53, 58–60
Trinity United Church of Christ 127, 129

Umra 44
Universal Negro Improvement Association (*see also* Garvey, Marcus) 3, 5, 8, 29, 30, 33–4, 35, 38, 39

Wahhaj, Siraj 16, 126, 141
Wallace, Mike 57
West, Kanye 130, 163
Wright, Jeremiah 127, 129, 131
Wright, Nathan 30, 38–9, 43

X, Malcolm
　assassination 9, 10, 13, 14, 21, 23, 67, 107–8, 136–7, 154–5
　campaign to discredit 9, 66–7, 165
　commercialization 107
　departure from NOI 53, 65, 108
　early life 8
　and Elijah Muhammad's domestic life 9, 64–5, 137
　relationship with Elijah Muhammad and Louis Farrakhan 43, 46, 64, 165
　work in NOI 9, 22, 164

Zimbabwe 119, 126

www.ingramcontent.com/pod-product-compliance
Lightning Source LLC
Chambersburg PA
CBHW052121300426
44116CB00010B/1759